The
Wake
of the
Unseen
Object

The
Wake
of the
Unseen
Object

AMONG THE NATIVE CULTURES

OF BUSH ALASKA

TOM KIZZIA

HENRY HOLT AND COMPANY   NEW YORK

Copyright © 1991 by Tom Kizzia
All rights reserved, including the right to reproduce
this book or portions thereof in any form.
Published by Henry Holt and Company, Inc.,
115 West 18th Street, New York, New York 10011.
Published in Canada by Fitzhenry & Whiteside Limited,
195 Allstate Parkway, Markham, Ontario L3R 4T8.

Library of Congress Cataloging-in-Publication Data
Kizzia, Tom.
The wake of the unseen object : among the native cultures of bush
Alaska / Tom Kizzia. — 1st ed.
p.   cm.
1. Eskimos — Alaska — Social life and customs.   2. Indians of North
America — Alaska — Social life and customs.   3. Alaska — Description
and travel — 1981–   .   I. Title.
E99.E7K444   1991   91-41150
979.8′004971 — dc20   CIP
ISBN 0-8050-1471-3
ISBN 0-8050-1860-3 (An Owl Book: pbk.)

Henry Holt books are available at special discounts
for bulk purchases for sales promotions, premiums,
fund-raising, or educational use. Special editions
or book excerpts can also be created to specification.
For details contact:
Special Sales Director, Henry Holt and Company, Inc.,
115 West 18th Street, New York, New York 10011

First published in hardcover by Henry Holt
and Company, Inc., in 1991.

First Owl Book Edition — 1992

Book design by Claire Naylon Vaccaro
Map by Claudia Carlson
Printed in the United States of America
Recognizing the importance of preserving the written word,
Henry Holt and Company, Inc., by policy, prints all
of its first editions on acid-free paper. ∞

1   3   5   7   9   10   8   6   4   2

1   3   5   7   9   10   8   6   4   2
pbk.

Contents

For Sally
and for the elders

His speech to man comes not through ordinary words, but through storms, snowfall, rain showers, the tempests of the sea, through all the forces that man fears, or through sunshine, calm seas or small, innocent, playing children who understand nothing. When times are good, Sila has nothing to say to mankind. He has disappeared into his infinite nothingness and remains away as long as people do not abuse life but have respect for their daily food.

—Inupiat shaman Najagneq, to Knud Rasmussen

Alaska

Barrow

CHUKCHI SEA

U.S.S.R.

CAPE PRINCE OF WALES

Shishmaref

Kotzebue

Wales

Teller

Nome

Golovin

BERING SEA

Koyukuk R.

Yukon R.

Fairbanks

Yukon R.

MT. McKINLEY

Tanana R.

Tok

Lower Kalskag

Scammon Bay

Kuskokwim R.

Tetlin

Red Devil

Akiachak

Bethel

Sleetmute

Anchorage

Valdez

Copper R.

Tuluksak

Koliganek

Togiak

New Stuyahok

Homer

Dillingham

Seward

Prince William Sound

ROUND ISLAND

English Bay

see below

Bristol Bay

Kodiak

GULF OF ALASKA

ALEUTIAN ISLANDS

KEY

Highway ——————

National borders —··—··—

Pipeline ——————

Road ——————

mi. 40 80 120 160 200 240
km.40 80   160 240 320 400

CANADA

SOUTHEAST ALASKA

GULF OF ALASKA

Juneau

1. Forest Primeval

A storm had been gathering in the Gulf of Alaska. Dark snowy clouds from the outer coast reared up over the peaks. I was new to the country, new to air taxis, and the six-seat Cessna seemed an insubstantial bird: the plastic windows scratched, the door latch thin aluminum. Everything about the plane seemed fragile except the cold metal seat-belt clasp in my lap.

The only other passenger was a small dark elderly man strapped into the copilot's seat. I was full of wild excitement, bound for a place remote from civilization, but I remember that the old man's presence confused me, and for a moment I wondered how it would feel instead to be going home.

I tucked my boots under the bare metal legs of the old man's seat and the pilot clapped the door shut.

We rattled and squeaked down the runway and then shouldered up into the wind. Across the bay we turned west to skirt the dark summits. The plane swerved and dipped like a fish nosing upstream. For nearly an hour we flew above surging coves and rocks awash in surf until a cleft opened in the mountains. There on a rise between beach and lagoon were a few small homes clustered around the cupola and cross of a whitewashed Russian Orthodox church.

Suddenly we were plummeting at the trees. Forested slopes blocked the approach to the lagoon, where the airstrip was wedged on a short spit. As I began to make out individual spruce needles, the Cessna banked, touched one wheel to gravel, spun and set down the second wheel. We rolled to a halt just short of the weather-stripped fuselage of an airplane wreck.

The old man climbed silently on back of a three-wheeled ATV and rode off behind a heavy woman up the hill. I waited under a wing, out of the wind. After a few moments a bashful young Sumo wrestler came down the hill on foot. Bobby Kvasnikoff had dark Russian-Aleut eyes and the smile of a slightly deranged cherub. As the only villager among eighty to have gone away to high school, he had been put in charge of day-to-day affairs, including the still-in-those-days-unheard-of visit of a reporter from the local weekly paper.

Deep snow had buried the village. While the afternoon grew dark, we followed a footpath between small peeling plywood houses. Maybe it was the prominence of the Orthodox church, or the alpine blanket of winter, but my first impression was not of an Indian reservation but of some preindustrial, Old World peasant village, where the main social pastime was still visiting your neighbors. The evening blurred into a succession of smears of window light, living-room walls painted cobalt blue, cups of coffee, and sour-smelling kitchens full of friendly chatter where stove heat made my cheeks glow.

Two small children stood by a sink and screamed with laughter at each of my sheepish questions.

"You be quiet." Their mother waved a fleshy arm at them. "Or maybe Bigfoot's going to come get you."

The old man across the table said he'd seen a Bigfoot one time, near the lagoon. There's a strong smell of wet rope, he said, when it's hiding in the bushes close by you.

The next morning, wind off the Gulf of Alaska hammered crossways at the spit. No planes could fly. I was not sorry to be weathered in. Bobby led me at low tide onto a reef they called *atanenguaq*, their word for the backbone removed from a salmon when it is filleted for drying, and counted off the wild animals on which the village still depends for food: salmon in the river, tomcod in the lagoon, snails on the rocks, the occasional seal. A warmly dressed family was beyond us on the reef, rummaging through wet matted kelp like shoppers at a vegetable bin.

The village's name was English Bay, a name applied to the area after a British officer following Captain James Cook in 1786 stopped by to trade for dried salmon. Russian fur traders had called the lagoon and spit Alexandrovsk when they arrived several years earlier to set up a post, the first settlement by whites on the mainland of Alaska. The local people, Pacific Eskimos whose language is known as Sugcestun, may well have called the place *atanenguaq*. The British left and the Russians stayed, and for years the local Natives were put to work hunting sea otters and mining coal out of the bluffs. Now of course the Russians were gone as well, leaving behind their church and long surnames like Kvasnikoff. Lately it was American designs on their land that had the Natives worried: the U.S. Department of the Interior had sold permits allowing oil companies to drill exploratory wells off English Bay. Villagers feared an oil spill.

On the gray horizon, past where the oil rigs would go, the summit of an island volcano was wrapped in steam. Long ago the island had erupted, and a thirty-foot wave had crashed into the beach where the old village was. Recently the volcano erupted again, and villagers stayed up all night retelling the old stories over CB radios and watching the sea.

Bobby pried the black pyramidal shell of a chiton off a boulder with his sheath knife. A bidarki, he called it, cutting out two pieces of flesh from inside the shell and offering one to me.

"That's what we're worried about losing," he said.

The meat was tough and flavorless. We both laughed at how long I chewed.

Then Bobby brought me home to look through his record collection—the albums in one dusty stack, their covers filed separately, like a card catalog. His wife and two small children hung back in the bedroom while Bobby got out his electric guitar. The living room was kept clear of furniture to leave space for amplifiers and drums. He said the village rock-and-roll band's name was The Electric Wires. No, I'd heard wrong—The Electric Warriors. I told Bobby that back in high school I had played a small Farfisa organ in a garage band. The one thing English Bay lacked, Bobby said, was a keyboard player.

"This has *got* to be the saddest day of my life," Bobby crooned that night in earnest imitation of Motown melancholy. He had convened the village for a dance in my honor—an honor I understood to be modest, since Bobby's readiness to perform exceeded even the eagerness of his neighbors for midwinter diversions. In the bright light of the community hall, a potluck supper was spread on a table: salmon pies, Shake 'n Bake tomcod, bidarki salads, Jell-O. Bobby leaned into the microphone, his electric guitar surfing out beyond his broad midsection, the neck a delicate piece of kindling in his hammy fist. His technique was sharp. Two brothers and a cousin had been pressed into service on bass, rhythm guitar, drums. I filled in chords on a borrowed home organ, watching Bobby for cues, while village elders danced with little girls in party dresses.

Only late in the night, when I looked up into the black wedge between mountains and saw stars and realized the storm had cleared, did I remember how far from the familiar world I had come.

I am a native of nowhere, spawn of a modern American suburb. Where I grew up, in New Jersey, the original landscape was long since covered over with highways and shopping-center parking lots. The original people were not there even in memory. When I finished college in New England I headed west. Wild places had always touched and lifted me. Now I would see if they could also sustain me.

I stopped when I got to Alaska. I built a cabin along the coast, in a country of hilly meadows and spruce. The cabin was barely half a mile from the nearest gravel road—hardly the outback of the continent. But it was fresh and wild and beautiful, and I suppose that for a while I felt that dubious pioneer pride of knowing a place first and best. Beyond a meadow of pink fireweed blossoms, across an inlet of the sea, mountain

peaks floated up from a mantle of ice. The view of that gleaming untouched glacial world was unobstructed. The illusion was nearly perfect.
There seemed to be nothing at all between that untouched world and
the place I lived. After a few years I no longer felt like I was hiding out
from the world. I felt like I was getting to know it for the first time.

I kept my improvements simple and my stake modest—in keeping
with my abilities, true, but also with my notion of propriety. I did not
want to intervene too much in that place. I held my breath when moose
passed close by the door. When fall storms from the Gulf of Alaska
blasted across the glaciers, my cabin walls trembled. I came to expect
these things, and found their indifference to my presence comforting,
though I did try to chink the log foundation and keep the cabin from
shaking so.

Later, after I had moved away to Anchorage, forsaking the fireweed
meadow for the police beat at a daily paper and a morning commute
and lunches at fast-food taco restaurants, my life in the woods came to
seem a boy's dream, simpleminded as one of those Aurora Borealis
paintings sold to tourists on gold pans. Since the pipeline boom of the
1970s, the fast pace of change on the Last Frontier had become a
cliché. Anchorage was a satellite of the world "outside," a full-blown
city with half Alaska's 500,000 residents. Multinational corporations
prowled through the map's last blank spaces. The wilderness was being
quarantined in new national parks under the watchful eye of civil
servants. State legislators were selling off remote lake and riverfront
lots to their constituents, turning primal landscapes into recreational
neighborhoods where weekend trappers caught each other's dogs.

I would get homesick and return to my cabin, only to find things
changing there too. The road had been widened and paved. The
country of hilly meadows and spruce was filling in with houses, power
lines, even a rural elementary school. I wrote sulky letters to the school
principal, asking her to turn off the parking lot's butterscotch lights
when she went home at night. I told myself I needed something less
perishable than the purity of nature to nourish my sense of the sacred.

At the same time, I found myself remembering the sense of timelessness I'd felt at English Bay. Life had obviously changed there, but something powerful endured. I remembered the cursive script left by snowmachines on the white lagoon, old women on the ice dropping lines for tomcod, the trail to the lake past the waterfall where salmon leap in summer. The valley had been home for centuries, yet the forest was still wild enough for an occasional whiff of a Bigfoot. It was, I see now, a picture from an old storybook: the forest primeval, and in the foreground the figure of the Native American, in harmony with his natural surroundings, moving lightly in his moccasins—or were they running shoes?

To a native of nowhere, that vision of an aboriginal landscape somehow surviving into the age of *USA Today* had a powerful appeal. Probably I should have been more suspicious of any notion so timely to the end of the twentieth century as harmony with nature. Our images of the Indian—primitive, savage, mystic, saint, ghost—have generally said more about changing American attitudes toward the continent than about the changing realities of Native American life. I knew that life in bush Alaska was changing fast, especially since a 1971 congressional settlement of aboriginal land claims left the state's 80,000 Eskimos and Indians and Aleuts title to their traditional hunting grounds only as shareholders in landholding corporations. Bankruptcy, sale of stock, and a kind of self-immolating capitalism all threatened to dispel traditional relationships to the land forever. Reports from the bush that reached the newsroom where I worked were usually depressing: drunken family men shooting up their fish camps with hunting rifles or plunging through the ice on snowmachines, teenagers getting high on gasoline fumes or killing themselves in games of Russian roulette. I'd heard it said that the rural villages, subsidized, purposeless, were dying—that Alaska's Natives today were more in tune with satellite television schedules than with the seasonal rounds of hunting and gathering.

But wasn't it true that, unlike the Indians to the south, Alaska's Indians and Eskimos and Aleuts had never been pushed out of their ancestral landscapes by white settlers? Except in a few isolated cases, the hunter-gatherers of the North were never defeated in battle, never uprooted and herded onto reservations. The wild animals they hunted were never wiped out. They were the last people to live in the wilderness.

I did not imagine a traveler to the bush would find Nanook of the North eking out his subsistence with kayak and harpoon, but it seemed possible that, somewhere between James Fenimore Cooper and Chuck Berry, Alaska's indigenous people remembered something about the world the rest of us have forgotten.

My chance to see those last ancestral landscapes came with an assignment from my newspaper, the *Anchorage Daily News.* The editors agreed to try something they'd never done before: send somebody off to travel through the bush and write about what he finds. For two years my only rule—even that one self-imposed—would be to go places I couldn't drive to from Anchorage.

Four-fifths of Alaska still cannot be reached by road, and so it is seldom visited at all, even by most Alaskans. A handful of people live scattered across an area half the size of the western United States. There are a few regional centers, towns like Nome and Bethel, each home to a couple thousand hardy whites and Natives (with an uppercase *N*, a typographical clue used by newspapers in Alaska to distinguish indigenous people from the sons and daughters of pioneers). Beyond those hubs, the bush consists of tiny, isolated villages, Eskimo, Indian, and Aleut, whose names can evoke surrealist landscapes: Sleetmute, Nightmute, Mary's Igloo. It is not a country used to receiving curious visitors.

Even in the continent's last wilderness, I knew, there might be nothing to see of the earlier world except its vanishing wake. All I had to go on was an image of a snowy coastal village, burnished by the years, a memory clutched like an icon whisked from a Russian Orthodox church: two-dimensional, naive, and holy.

I booked on a plane for Nome and flew northwest to the Bering land bridge.

2. Spirit World

*T*he few dozen gable roofs of the village were strung along dunes behind the beach. The tundra in back was lumpy with the mounds of prehistoric settlement. Farther still, long shadows of a summer night climbed down a burial ridge.

I stood alone on the sand and looked around at the sky and sea. I could see myself spinning through the heavens at a precise spot on the globe, so familiar from maps was the promontory where I stood. Siberia was just over the horizon. Cape Prince of Wales is the knuckle on a fist of Alaska that punches to within fifty miles of the Soviet Union. "The western extremity of all America hitherto known," Captain Cook called it when he passed by on his final voyage, in search of a Northwest Passage. The sun, close to midnight, rolled north along the rim of sea. Red light filled the Bering Strait.

From the long view—say, of time immemorial—Cape Prince of Wales is a remnant buttress of the Bering land bridge, that broad, windy steppe across which the first human beings migrated into North America. Ten thousand years ago, melting ice caps flooded the strait and cut off the new world, covering the continental shelf with a shallow sea. Those who were the last aboard—the most Asian, genetically and linguistically, of all Native Americans—hung back along the northern coast. Some settled here, beneath a rocky headland, where, to judge from the broad beach and gentle progress of the breakers, the water ran shallow a long way out, as if it might still be possible to wade back into the world from which they came.

The village of Wales was quiet. It had been late when the skiff from Tin City dropped me on the sand. On my first night in a northern Eskimo village, I walked out to the water's edge, skirting the houses, uncertain how to approach. I looked up and down the beach, like a pedestrian in a dangerous street. The previous winter, when north winds shoved the ice pack on shore, I'd heard there was a problem at Wales with polar bears getting into the garbage.

A reason for the beachfront alignment of the village became apparent as I walked. Families used the sand as an extension of their yards. The dunes beyond the reach of storms were neatly parceled into stacks of driftwood (valuable in a land without trees), outboard motors, fishnets, snowmachines, firepits, heavy knives and washpans, and bright bubble-gum-pink buoys, the chattel of an outdoor life. Wooden skeletons of retired walrus-hide skinboats, the *umiaks,* were elevated reverently on bony driftwood biers. Aluminum skiffs with their outboards cocked had been pulled up beyond the tide. Sifted through the soft gray sand at my feet were white bits of shell and bone, traces of a thousand years of Inupiat Eskimo subsistence.

In the middle of the village rose a satellite dish, a wind generator, and a geodesic dome. But I let it go—why not, I thought, on the coast of the Bering Strait: a three-story plywood igloo.

The "high bluff" that gave Cape Prince of Wales its original Inupiaq name of Kingikin was an amphitheater stubbled with rocks. What would they say if I climbed up there? In pre-Christian times, the dead of Kingikin's several villages were carried to the bluff and laid out with weapons and other goods among the rocks to help the spirits in the afterlife. The bluff blocked off the rest of North America. Out on the rim of the continent, the people of Wales were alone with their ancestors. If I wanted to look for a place where ancient spirits still walked the land, Cape Prince of Wales seemed a good place to start.

Smoke of burning driftwood was in the air. Two young men stood over an open fire in the dunes, watching something boil in a galvanized pan. Tips of tusks protruded from the top. I wondered how they had come by ivory at this time of year, when walrus had moved north with the ice pack. Had they eaten the meat? Or taken the tusks, as I'd heard cynical young hunters sometimes do today, and left the rest? The two men watched me pass. They probably had questions, too: Who was this white man washed up on their beach, walking through their front yard? They nodded in greeting when I lifted my hand a little.

Two large brown heads, defanged, sat like medicine balls near the tide line, waiting for a storm to roll them away. I stepped across a small stream and my boot came down on a bloated walrus carcass half buried by sand. It shimmied underfoot like a waterbed.

My pack lay at the end of the village where I'd dropped it after the skiff ride. Above the beach rose a slope of a squeaky green plant that I'd heard them call stinkweed. The slope was pockmarked by foundation holes from prehistoric sod-and-driftwood huts. I climbed skittishly, thinking there might be villagers who would resent my trespassing.

A curious white monument caught my attention and drew me down the bluff, away from the village. A granite obelisk, waist high, stood alone above a sea cliff. An epitaph on the monument read, "A good soldier of Christ Jesus."

The first spirit I encountered at Cape Prince of Wales belonged to a white man who'd come to banish the other spirits forever.

In the early winter of 1889, Harrison R. Thornton answered a missionary society advertisement "for volunteer teachers to go to the barbarous Eskimo of Arctic Alaska" and thereby became the first white man ever to live among the Inupiat at the cape. Also the first to die there.

Looking back, it's easy to say that an unbending Virginian, son of an officer who died at Antietam, a young man unable to hold a teaching job because of recurring depression, might not want to choose the Bering Strait as the place to begin life anew. It made Thornton's prospects no better that the Eskimo village he was sent to civilize already had a reputation as the most aggrieved and hostile in northern Alaska.

The Inupiat of Kingikin were a seafaring people, even if the sea was frequently frozen when they fared upon it. Strategic location was everything. The cape was a spectacular perch from which to intercept sea mammals migrating through the strait. They dominated the iron and copper trade from Siberia. Kingikin had once been a capital of northwest Inupiat culture. As many as seven hundred people had lived along the exposed beach at Cape Prince of Wales—a huge population to support with hunting expeditions.

But when Thornton arrived to establish a Congregationalist mission school, he found the population shrinking, the people hungry and in despair. He wasn't the first white man in the region after all.

By the middle of the nineteenth century, the commercial whaling fleet of Europe and America had penetrated the Bering Strait and found the last untouched whaling grounds on the globe. The ships hunted the Arctic bowhead nearly to extinction, then fell upon the walrus, whose fat, like whale blubber, could be rendered into lubricating and lighting oil. The Eskimos of northwest Alaska were whalers, but to them the walrus were like buffalo to the Plains Indians. Walrus provided oil for heat and light, tough skins for tents and boats and rope, ivory and bone for tools, and meat for people and dogs. Half-digested clams from the walrus stomach were eaten as delicacies. The walrus also played an important role in Eskimo spiritual life. Tusks were carved into amulets meant to intercede with the *inua*, the spirits of animals and men that hovered around the Inupiat world. Each walrus in turn had to be treated with respect, honored in ritual, to ensure that its *inua* would return in another walrus to provide for the human beings.

Now the *inua* had stopped coming back. For a while, commercial hunters retrieved ten to twenty thousand walrus a year, with many more wounded and lost. Ivory added to the profits. It was a far bloodier business than whaling. Hunters off the ships used large-caliber buffalo rifles to shoot into masses of walrus where they rested on ice floes, "like cattle lying in a barnyard," as a horrified John Muir put it after returning from a trip to Alaska. There were times when the heat of the blood spilling from butchered walrus ate through the ice floes, dumping an entire catch into the sea. In the year Thornton reached northwest Alaska, a government census enumerator for Alaska declared the Pacific walrus "almost extinct." Hunters from Cape Prince of Wales sometimes paddled for days without finding meat, and other villages fared even worse. A decade earlier, during a particularly harsh winter on St. Lawrence Island 150 miles southwest from the Bering Strait, six villages had died off or been abandoned. Two-thirds of the island's 1,500 Eskimos were reported to have starved. Some villages cut up their skinboats to make soup. At Ukivok, on King Island, villagers caught only two walrus the year Thornton passed by. They made it through the winter by butchering their sled dogs and eating seaweed.

Harrison Thornton went among the Eskimo, then, with some anxiety. The Inupiat knew the white men's ships were taking their food, and as whalers en route warned Thornton, the Natives of Cape Prince of Wales had additional reason for resentment. A decade earlier, in a shipboard fight with a trader over rum, a Kingikin chief had been killed, his men had fatally knifed a Hawaiian deckhand, and before it was over, a dozen other villagers were killed in retaliation—some of them dragged out from hiding with gaff hooks, shot, and thrown overboard. Since the massacre, Kingikin had given up the marauding that had given it a reputation, in the words of one ship captain, for "brazen effrontery." But trading ships still avoided the cape where the navy cutter dropped Thornton.

The people of Wales kept a respectful distance that first summer, while the navy stood by and carpenters nailed up amid the sod huts a white frame schoolhouse for Thornton and a partner, William T. Lopp. Though they were missionary teachers, they were also official government agents in charge of "educating and civilizing the natives," as Thornton noted in his memoir of that first year. Then the navy cutter sailed south ahead of the ice, and, Thornton wrote, the Eskimos closed in, banging on doors, peering in windows, "determined to try at all events to browbeat and bully the two foreigners, just for the fun of seeing how they would take it." The teachers opened a school, and villagers came to stay warm, but classes had to be suspended for several days in early winter because children and adults were sliding off the roof into snowdrifts.

It was there on the Seward Peninsula, some thirty years later, that the ethnographer Knud Rasmussen came upon an old shaman who told of the spirit Sila, "upholder of the universe," who speaks to men through the weather and punishes them when they abuse life. To Thornton, the people were fearful animists. Hunters depended for success on faithful observance of ceremonies and taboos, on personal hunting songs sung under their breath, and on amulets punched through their lips or hung from boats to charm the *inua*. Thornton's interest in these animist beliefs perked up when several dozen villagers died of a sudden illness that fall and there was passing talk of expelling the two white men. Thornton said it was the grippe, attributable to an early winter storm that caught many villagers out hunting. An *unutkoot,* a village shaman, blamed the sickness on the practice of writing and drawing pictures on slate in the schoolhouse. He also claimed that the bell on the school was frightening away seals. An *unutkoot* was a powerful figure said to be in touch with the spirit world. Thornton was dismissive: "Some of these sorcerers affect long hair and a peculiar wild look, which are doubtless intended to instill into the vulgar a high opinion of their preternatural power and superhuman knowledge."

Some Eskimo practices made Thornton squeamish. Up on the high bluffs, rough-hewn driftwood planks were weighted with stone atop dead bodies to keep out wolves, not always with success. One day Thornton found a raven and a sea gull feeding on a corpse just outside the village. A dog had dragged the body down from the burial ridge.

Another time Thornton saw a puppy playing with a frozen human foot. He wrote that Eskimo children found the sight amusing, and his horror even funnier. They could even tell him the name of the old woman whose foot it was. However, with permafrost several feet down year-round and ice in the topsoil even in summer, the case for proper Christian burials was hard to make. It was two years before someone at Cape Prince of Wales would be buried underground: Thornton himself.

I had read Thornton's account of his short-lived mission to the cape hoping to learn something of Wales before the coming of white civilization. I thought I might get a clue of what to look for beneath the village's Westernized surface, though a missionary can be the worst kind of guide in such matters if he spends all his time writing about what the people ought to become. Fortunately Thornton showed some appreciation for the culture he persisted in calling "savage." He came to admire the people's stoicism and honesty, their "peaceable genius," and especially their good humor. He had not known it was custom for an Eskimo never to speak his own name. When the teachers first arrived in the village and asked people their names, they were told, "*Wunga*" ("I") or "*Neluga*" ("I don't know"). Only much later did they come to comprehend the merriment caused those first weeks as they went about the village greeting the many Wungas and Nelugas.

The teachers loaned tools, dispensed medicines, shared picture books. They persevered. Only two or three times did they have to use muscle or revolvers to run troublemakers out of school. The splendid arrival of thousands of eider and old squaw ducks in spring gave Thornton a chance to hunt with the Eskimos and show off his shotgun. Eventually, he wrote, the teachers "succeeded in 'breaking the people in,' so to speak." No one converted to Christianity, but it was too early for that; the teachers' purpose, as they saw it, was to win respect for "the religion and country we represented."

Over the second winter, Thornton went back to the States for several months. When he returned in spring he brought a wife, a young social worker he'd met through the New York City Mission and Tract Society. He also brought a second young female teacher whom he introduced to Lopp. In a short time, there were two married couples at the cape. Thornton's memoir devotes several chapters to Eskimo family relationships, but regrettably offers no details of courtship practices among the missionaries.

By this time conditions in the village were growing more desperate. Back east Thornton had lobbied without success for the government to halt commercial hunting of walrus and the sale of liquor to Natives. Now drinking and distilling were on the increase. The presence of the two ladies added to his anxieties. Thornton wrote that some of his neighbors drank only to become "blind, howling, disgustingly drunk." Friendly Eskimos turned belligerent under the influence, and Thornton took to carrying a revolver with him at all times. When villagers gathered by the windows of his house to stare in at the white man's belongings, he chased them away. Once he dismissed school for a week because matches were stolen from the schoolhouse and no one confessed. An old chief whose sons had been killed in the trading ship massacre took a drunken shot at Thornton. By August of 1893, with Mrs. Thornton five months pregnant and the Lopps moved on to another village, Thornton had resolved to leave for good.

Late one night, several weeks before the navy cutter was to come retrieve them, Thornton answered a knock at his door. Three boys he'd expelled from school were outside. One pulled the trigger on a whaling gun, blowing a hole in the door the size of a fist. Thornton died in his wife's arms.

She paced the house until daylight, then called to an old man who lived nearby. He helped her move the body, told her now there was going to be shooting, and ran off. The sound of shots came from the beach. The bodies of two of the teenage boys were dragged to her doorstep. The third boy ran up the burial ridge and escaped into the mountains, but after several days he returned and was shot in his knees.

The swift response of the village may have come from fear of outside retribution as much as from a code of tribal justice. When the navy cutter finally came to see to Thornton's burial and carry off his wife, the entire village had gone into hiding.

"It is true that the number of the *Kinik-Mete* is comparatively small," Thornton had said of the Kingikin people at the conclusion of his memoir, "but he alone can rightly estimate the importance of the work who shall be able to appraise the value of more than five hundred immortal souls and, looking into the long vista of future ages, prophesy what benefits may accrue to the world from their civilized and Christianized descendants."

As I stood at his grave on the bluff, I felt myself looking back across that vista from the future Thornton had wondered about. Spread along the beach below was the old Kingikin site, where one hundred twenty Inupiat live on today in the wake of history.

What benefits had accrued to the people of Kingikin?

Twenty-five years after Thornton's death, in the autumn of 1918, the worldwide epidemic of Spanish influenza reached Nome and swept across the Seward Peninsula. In two weeks half the population of Wales died. The survivors were too weak to carry bodies to the ridge, so the victims were buried in a mass grave in the dunes. The grave was marked by a tall wooden cross, for Thornton's vineyard had finally borne fruit: a local boy had been sent to church boarding school in the Aleutians, and he returned to baptize the people of the strait. Christianity had reached Cape Prince of Wales, dispelling the *inua* with a biblical view of Nature that separated light from darkness and man from the beasts. The young Inupiat missionary was carried off in the epidemic with the rest, as was an old man named Kuzshuktuk, one of the last well-known *unutkoots* of the Bering Strait region. He had just returned from the States, where he had been sent by the whites to a mental institution.

I walked back down to the beach and erected my nylon tent. After I had crawled in, a young man with a thin mustache appeared in the dusk. I crawled back out, ready at last for an encounter with the people of Kingikin.

"You want to buy ivory?" he said.

It was very old ivory, he said. Fossilized ivory, dug up from one of the prehistoric sites.

I told him no thanks. He persisted. He bragged of his skill as a carver. He said he could carve well even when he was drinking. There was a smell of alcohol in the air. He wanted to know what I was doing in the village if I didn't want ivory.

Too many white people were coming to Wales, he said.

The young carver pointed along the bluff toward the granite monument.

"See that? A white guy is buried there. One night somebody blew his head off with a whaling gun."

I said I hadn't come to convert anybody. I just wanted to see the village. I heard myself arguing that it was in the village's interest to be receptive to outsiders. Visitors would learn to respect the Inupiat culture, I said.

I tried to stay calm. Finally he smiled and said he hoped I had a good visit to Wales. Apparently he'd decided that if I wasn't a customer, at least I wasn't a competitor. The problem, he explained, was artifact hunters. Grave robbers. Some called themselves scientists. They dug for prehistoric ivory in the bluff, in the collapsed foundations of old sod houses. What they took from the ancient villages, he said, they stole from the people of Wales.

It was theft by outsiders that upset him, however, not the pillaging of the past. There were village people who took care of that themselves.

"These are my ivory beds," he said, gesturing at the mounds of stinkweed. "I thought you were going to dig in them."

It was just the sort of disheartening reception that might have been predicted for me during the several days it took to work my way out the Seward Peninsula to Wales. Among the whites I visited on the way, the view of the Eskimos was often strikingly unsympathetic. I took it in stride—their lack of sentimentalism about the local Native Americans seemed an absolutely authentic frontier trait. As for me, what I'd glimpsed of the Natives on my way to Wales had intrigued me more than ever.

A commercial jet had lofted me north from Anchorage over the Alaska Range and a broad pelt of clouds to the open water of Norton Sound. We found the coast again at Nome, the government center of the Seward Peninsula. Nome's several thousand residents today include many transplanted Natives, not to mention a handful of Vietnamese refugees working on the local gold dredges. But the waterfront town dated only from the beginning of the white man's century. In 1900 twelve thousand would-be gold miners jammed the beach. They were not the spirits I was looking for.

My plan had been to fly directly from Nome to the far cape at Wales, then work back along the coast, stopping at the few villages along the way. There was a lot of country to cover. The Seward Peninsula extends roughly two hundred miles from the Buckland and Koyuk rivers west to Cape Prince of Wales, and from Cape Espenberg south to Nome the peninsula is one hundred fifty miles wide. Deducting for bays and inlets, I figured the Seward Peninsula to be nearly the size of the state of Maine, which is 33,215 square miles. Writers swept up by the size of Alaska frequently resort to comparing its geographical fragments to entire other states. The lower forty-eight states do offer a handy standard of measurement—more useful, say, than the United Arab Emirates, which is also about the size of the Seward Peninsula— though too-frequent comparisons to Rhode Island can cheapen the effect. In any event, I was planning to drop in at the three tiny villages between Boston and Brunswick until an old-timer at a bush plane service convinced me to add a stop at Tin City.

"Worst weather in America out there," the old-timer told me while I waited for a mail plane to carry me the final hundred miles. It had been blowing at the cape for three days. Mail plane hadn't been able to get in, he said. The man had big ears and a pleasant chatty manner. He was born and raised in Nome—his parents met working the beaches—and knew people all around the peninsula. Now that he was retired, he liked to spend mornings at the airport picking up gossip from the outlying villages.

A pilot came in from a flight to Teller and said the wind was letting up. The mail plane to Wales might fly today.

"When it's not fogged in, it's blowing sideways rain," the old-timer said. He helped himself to more coffee, which was cooking darker as the morning wore on, and settled back on a plastic turquoise couch. If I was going all the way to the cape, he said, I should stop off at Tin City and visit Dick Lee.

"He runs a trading post. Stays there by himself all winter."

I'd seen Tin City marked on the map, a few miles short of Cape Prince of Wales. The name conjured ramshackle tenements of corrugated sheet metal rattling in a gusty downpour. I had taken it to be another of the abandoned mining camps that speckled the Seward Peninsula. It did not look like a prudent location for a convenience store.

"What does he do for customers?" I asked.

"The Eskimos travel cross-country to get to *him*. They come from, I don't know, Shishmaref, Diomede, Wales . . ."

He hesitated, as if he wasn't sure he should mention it, then added a hint of mysterious wealth, the inducement of frontier dreams: "I hear he's got a fortune in ivory."

The ride to Tin City in the small single-engine plane left me jerky with motor vibration and excitement. We'd flown over bare, flinty mountains, the last spruce trees having given out more than a hundred miles back down the coast. The plane hit the gravel airstrip with a jolting squeak and rolled to a stop. I stepped out on a bluff above the shining sea. The sun burned down on a bright country of rock and bowing ribs of grassland. A gumdrop mountain blocked the view of the Bering Strait.

Dirt flew up behind a pickup truck racing to the airstrip. I waited in the shadow of the plane's wing for the truck to arrive. The driver wore aviator glasses and a heavy wool shirt. I told him I was looking for a place to spend the night before I walked the last few miles to Wales. When I had helped load several boxes into his truck, Dick Lee told me to get in.

The seat in the cab erupted with dust under my blue jeans.

"So. How long have you lived out here?" I chirped as the truck rattled away from the strip.

"Twenty-four years," he said, and drove on silently.

"I don't imagine you get many visitors coming through?"

No, probably not.

His gleaming, sun-reddened dome was fringed by raffish silver hair. He looked fit and strong, though his age—he was in his seventies—showed in the puffy blue of his hands and the deltas of tiny purple veins coloring his cheeks.

"Once in a while," he said finally, "somebody comes through planning to cross the sea ice and visit the Russians. They don't usually get too far."

We were driving into a dusty historical tableau: a mining camp, a fort, and a trading post for the Natives. Lonesome wanderers would fit right in.

We crossed a gravel benchland covered in thin grass and tiny yellow flowers. The landscape had a messy, morning-after look. Shards of lumber and concrete littered the ground. Strange rusting contraptions sat out in the open like machine-age sculpture.

The sights of Tin City did not take Dick Lee long to enumerate. A road disappeared into a ravine being stripped by bulldozers. The tin deposit had been worked off and on since prospectors spilled out this way after Nome—it was the only working tin mine in North America.

There'd been another boom just down the coast at York, Lee added, but that strike hadn't amounted to much. Yes, I said—I'd read that an Eskimo shaman at Wales took credit for making the gold in York Creek disappear to be rid of the white men who'd been burning up the region's driftwood.

Toward the cape, a shining white radar dome was teed up on top of the gumdrop mountain. From Tin City the air force kept an eye on the Soviet coast across the water. The strait was a back alley across which modern superpowers glare. Some sort of cable car or chair lift tied the Cold War watchtower to the blocky architecture of a base camp. Did air force enlistees ski the slopes in winter? Giddy questions bubbled up. What iron would a giant use to reach Siberia with a chip shot? How long did you say it takes to walk across the strait?

I cast around for a more sober topic and hit upon the weather. It seemed an unusually compelling conversational gambit in Tin City. Did winter ever get to be too much?

"Heckfire, no. We don't have to go out of the building here for anything we need. We have enough fuel in the tank for almost a year." We had turned toward a rambling plywood shack that sat alone on a bluff. "This country is rocky, mountainous, barren, windy, and cold, but it doesn't weigh on me at all. When it's nice weather, I think the scenery is beautiful. When it's bad, you can't see anything anyway."

No sign identified the charmless shed as Tin City's central business district, no throng of customers waited outside. But Lee unlocked the door and flicked on lights to reveal room after room richly packed with goods: canned foods, frozen pizzas, pork rinds, ammunition, candy bars and Pepsis, hand tools, sweatshirts, electric skillets.

"There's no store on the peninsula outside of Nome that's better stocked," he said proudly. "None of the village stores can come close to it."

Dick Lee first moved to Tin City to work the tin claim, but from the start, Eskimos came looking to purchase any extra supplies. In time he and his wife, Phyllis, sold the mine—with the price of tin, they were just "trading dollars"—and went full time into storekeeping. The current mine owners shipped in all their supplies by barge during the brief summer, and the air force used C-130s, so the Lees' business came almost exclusively from Eskimos in a sixty-mile range. Customers came by skiff in summer, by snowmachine in winter. Only big storms slowed the traffic.

"It's not in the nature of the Eskimo to look ahead and prepare," Lee said matter-of-factly.

"Makes a serious trip to the store for a dozen eggs," I joked. The joke lodged in my throat when Lee said he'd lost a customer that summer. Several young men from Little Diomede had been on their way home from Tin City and stopped at Fairway Rock in the strait to collect murre eggs. Murre nest on cliffs, and their eggs are lopsided, pear shaped, so the eggs roll in semicircles and cling to narrow ledges. The young men became completely engrossed climbing for seabird eggs, and their boat drifted away. A member of the party, the Diomede postmaster, dove into the frigid water to retrieve the boat and disappeared beneath the waves. A day later searchers rescued the others. Lee added that he'd written off the postmaster's unpaid balance at the store.

Lee led me back through a narrow hallway stacked with tins of corned beef that had come to Tin City from Brazil. The warren housed trading post, living quarters, workshop, and warehouse space. Lee had puzzled its pieces together from barracks and sheds salvaged from the base. He'd had to badger the air force to get them; regulations said surplus buildings were to be destroyed, even out here where materials had to be flown in by C-130. Shaking his head over such foolishness, he left me at a spare room with two cots and walked off to tinker with his generator. On a wall was a yellowing 1956 *National Geographic* map of the federal territory of Alaska. It was Dick Lee's country.

I walked into the living room and discovered the fortune in ivory.

The room looked like the storeroom of a Native arts museum. Shelves were crammed with Eskimo handicrafts: sealskin fur dolls, greenish fossilized ivory bracelets, scrimshaw tusks and ivory birds and polar bears. Boxes of the stuff were stacked on the floor.

"Quite a collection, isn't it?" said Nicole, the young cook who was helping around the trading post with her husband. "A lot of the customers pay for their groceries this way."

Walrus ivory was now the Bering Strait's cash crop. Trading in raw tusks had been outlawed to prevent wholesale commercial slaughter, but under a federal law that barred all other hunting, Alaska Natives could still take walrus—for meat, and for ivory to make traditional art forms.

I looked through the booty. Some of the work was lovely, but on the whole it seemed designed to charm a cruise ship passenger rather than the *inua* of a bowhead. Many of the carvings were of small, Buddha-like figures with bare feet, pudgy grins, and pointed heads: "billikens" sold in Anchorage as Eskimo charms, though in fact the design was patented in 1908 by a Kansas City art teacher who marketed it with the slogan "The God of Things as They Ought to Be." The billiken found its way north after the 1909 Alaska-Yukon Pacific Exposition in Seattle. In-upiat carvers learned they could sell billikens by the hundreds to miners in Nome. A new Eskimo tradition was born.

The god of things as they ought to be. Maybe the billiken was an appropriate product for the modern age. Still, I couldn't help feeling disappointed by what seemed diminished in the art. I told myself that probably Dick Lee's art collection said no more about the spiritual life of the local Eskimos than did their grocery orders. But I recalled that only a generation before the billikens arrived, the first surveyors to reach the Seward Peninsula had been unable to persuade any Eskimo to sell spiritual amulets or carve copies.

I asked Nicole if she ever saw any walrus around Tin City.

"I've seen a few on the beach this summer," she said. "Until yesterday, never one with its head on."

The day before, she'd seen a sick walrus on the beach. A young man from Wales came along on a balloon-tired three-wheeler and dispatched the animal with a rifle. He drove off with the head, big as a motorcycle helmet, on the rack behind his seat.

Later in the afternoon I asked Lee about the ivory and the people who carved it. We were standing in a glassed-in porch off the living room. Though we were near the Arctic Circle, the atmosphere was almost tropical. The crown of a pineapple was beginning to emerge from a planter; a green Mexican parrot watched nearby, perched on a disconnected television antenna. The sun's reflection off the water filled the glass enclosure with a shimmery warmth.

"If it's really crude work, I won't take it. I couldn't sell it if I did," he said. "I've got way too much already."

He helped the Natives by giving them a market for their work, he said. He matched the price of itinerant wholesalers—and offered more than bar owners in Nome, some of whom took ivory for drinks. But if Lee profited from the federal law allowing Native hunting of marine mammals, he didn't like the law. He said it wasn't fair that Natives in the bush could "slaughter" marine mammals like walrus and polar bear when whites couldn't.

"Another thing that galls me is that only Natives can own reindeer," he said.

Reindeer, once numerous on the Seward Peninsula, were making a comeback. The village of Wales had a herd of reindeer running loose around the cape. Once a year villagers rounded up the animals for a harvest, Lee said. Caught between two worlds, the reindeer were not exactly wild, not exactly domesticated. They were first introduced by the government and missionaries at the end of the last century to combat starvation among the Eskimos. Beyond charity, the reindeer scheme had a component of moral instruction, intended as it was to teach the virtues of husbandry to hunters and gatherers. The restriction against non-Native ownership was imposed in 1937 after white-owned shipping and trading companies took control of the biggest herds to develop a market in the States. The early herds expanded, overran the tundra, and after a few decades their numbers crashed. Lee had been a young man then, and he remembered "silver thaws" when a cold snap turned spring melt on the tundra to a slippery glaze, and starving reindeer tried to crack through it with bleeding hooves.

Lee considered himself as much a part of the Seward Peninsula as the Eskimos. His parents met in Nome during the gold rush, and he had been living in his family's mining camp at Solomon when Phyllis answered an ad for a cook at the mine and moved up from Seattle. Now Phyllis was in the hospital in Nome with emphysema. The doctors had said they weren't sure she would ever be well enough to move back out to Tin City.

Lee was looking out at the water. They set up housekeeping down by the beach when they first moved to Tin City, he said. A storm flooded them out; washed the dry-goods store clear up the creek.

"My wife liked it better living by the beach," Lee said. "She could hear the surf and see the birds. Watch the seals pop up."

Lee's sentimental bubble burst when I asked if he had any friends in Wales I might drop in on. Aside from being able to associate faces with the long Inupiaq names in his account books and distinguish good credit risks from bad, he professed to know little about the local Natives. In twenty-four years he'd rarely traveled to the villages and said he had no close friends there. Too much socializing was bad for business, he said.

"We're friendly with all, but we don't carry our friendship to the social standpoint," he said. "They'll try to work their way into your goodwill and run their credit as far as they can."

Nicole had set out a supper of fried chicken. At the table, the green parrot hovered like a spoiled pet and landed in my hair. "He's looking for Phyllis," Lee said. "He won't land on my head. He's afraid of sliding off."

As soon as Lee reached for the mashed potatoes, the bell at the store rang for the first time that afternoon. He sighed.

"It's always that way. Not a customer all day . . ."

I followed him through the halls. He opened the door to a small elderly couple dressed in quilted jackets, followed by a teenage boy in a light windbreaker.

Roland and Edna Angnaboogok and their grandson Tony had waited all afternoon in Wales for the fog to lift so they could go shopping. Finally the fog backed off far enough for their small open skiff to slip around the rocky headland to Tin City.

The couple stacked a flour sack and breakfast cereal and a can of plums on the counter. Tony set down three boxes of .22 cartridges. He told me they were getting ready to go out to camp on the Mint River. The camp was in the grassy lagoons north of Wales, an area rich with fish and birds and the camps of other families going out to live off the land. It sounded like a paradise for a young village boy.

"Don't get too many," his grandma said. "You're going to high school soon."

She had a timid, downcast look, but she traded gossip with Lee in a friendly fashion and asked after Phyllis.

"You hear about that family that drowned?" she asked, clucking her tongue at the news from Savoonga. An entire family, babies and all, had been lost when a skiff loaded with furniture and a three-wheeler capsized off St. Lawrence Island. The family had been on its way to summer fish camp. The news was broadcast statewide on satellite television. "Their kids were so young," she said.

Their shopping done, the Angnaboogoks carried a box of groceries down to the beach. I walked out to the bluff and watched their figures, tiny with distance, shove off for their own brave skiff ride home.

The next morning I rode with Dick Lee up to the air force base, whose satellite phone he used periodically to call the Nome hospital.

The countryside looked overexposed in the morning sun, even

forbidding—especially after being shut inside Lee's space station. Except for the radar dome, shining white on the ridge like a chapel on a treeless Greek isle, there was nothing imperious about the military citadel as we approached. The base camp was hunkered down in a little corner of the landscape between mountain and beach, where it might evade bombardment or the full wrack of winter. I squinted at the concrete, battered as if war-scarred. Above, a line of rocky gargoyles guarded a far ridge. They were natural outcroppings, but looked like the man-sized cairns that early Eskimos on the cape built to scare away war parties paddling across from Siberia.

A weathered sign warned it was illegal to enter without permission of the installation commander, citing a section of the Internal Security Act of 1950. Apparently the warning was as out of date as my notion of a top-secret radar installation. The main office building was done up in the drab green of faded military fatigue, with red arrows pointing down dark concrete hallways to "Shelter," but air force uniforms were long gone from Tin City. If Soviet troops ever invade North America, they will find the first line of defense staffed by a handful of civilian contractors holding down the Western front for $22 an hour.

While Dick Lee got in line—the normal detachment had been reinforced by building crews from Anchorage, so the phone was in demand—I went off to see if I could get to the summit and peer down on Wales. Tom Hull, the base supervisor, gave me a lift up a winding service road in his power wagon. A stocky, bearded engineer who'd worked the Cold War picket line for twenty-five years, Hull was proud of the adversity he faced every day. In winter, he said, there was no edge between land and sea: the sky was often a whiteout, the mountain was windblown and icy, and the road to top camp drifted shut. The only access to the radome then was on the cable car tram, which was now closed down for repairs. When winter winds reached forty knots, they couldn't use the tram either. Forty-knot winds were not uncommon on the Bering Strait. Hull said radar technicians have been trapped on the summit for a week after their shift.

"This country's not for everyone," Hull said. "I've seen people turn around when they get to the airport. They take one look and say, 'Oh, no, I ain't staying here no six months.'"

On the summit a shed of galvanized steel was tied to the shale by cables. The white radome bubbled out of the roof. The Tin City base, one of eighteen posts tacked across western Alaska, was built in 1952 to watch for bomber attacks. Two radar technicians live inside the shed at all times, sitting in front of screens that flash data to Elmendorf Air Force base in Anchorage. Everyone else stays below.

The radar techs, accustomed to a priestly solitude, withdrew into the top-secret dome at the sight of visitors. Hull admitted me to the living quarters: dark, windowless bedrooms below, and upstairs a fluorescent kitchen area with a television screen, a phone line to bottom camp, and a poster of a Los Angeles Rams cheerleader on the refrigerator. Two tiny windows admitted shafts of daylight into the mountaintop perch, like the slotted windows of a medieval fortress. This is no occupying army, I thought. This is an outpost under siege.

I went back outside and breathed in the view from two thousand feet. To the early Eskimo, mountains had *inua*, as did ice packs and offshore breezes. Everything in the land was shifting, migrating, becoming something new. From the summit, there was undeniable power in the geography of this sub-Arctic Gibraltar, where two oceans and two continents came together. Fog off the sea to the South reached the coast and extended fingers into the mountains. The strait itself was clear and blue, ice-free. Cape Dezhnev in Siberia looked close enough to build a bridge to. If human beings today tried to follow the route of the first people across the strait, they'd show up on the radar at Elmendorf.

Between us and the Soviet Union lay the Diomede Islands—one ours, one theirs. The Soviet Diomede is larger, but we have the satisfaction of knowing ours is still inhabited; the Soviets drove away their Eskimos after World War II and replaced them with gun turrets.

Alaska villagers are supposed to observe the international line when they hunt on the ice in spring, but I'd been told that on their first trip to Nome after hunting season, some Diomeders liked to share the harvest by passing out Russian cigarettes.

Hull said it was rare for them at Tin City ever to see villagers from Wales. One time, however, the Eskimo National Guard unit from the village had come to Tin City on maneuvers.

The Eskimo Scouts are well-known in Alaska. The coastal people who once fought wars against Siberians still have a role to play in the high-tech defense of the Arctic. Hardened to cold, equipped with the patience of seal hunters waiting beside a blowhole, the Eskimo Scouts will be our Vietcong in the event of an invasion. They travel cross-country in a cavalry of snowmachines, their M-16s wiped dry of lubricant so they won't freeze. They sleep on caribou skins instead of government-issue pads and fight the cold by supplementing C-rations with high-octane seal oil and whale fat. Every two years, when the army holds winter war games in Alaska for troops from the Lower Forty-eight, the Eskimo Scouts like to count coup against soldiers in the enemy camps by sneaking past their sentries and turning heating oil drums upside down. The tent stoves suck freezing air and die.

Hull said the Eskimo Scouts from Wales wore white uniforms when they came to Tin City and set up white tents in the blowing snow. The wind chill had been eighty-five below. "We watched them through the windows. We could barely see them."

I looked down toward the village of the winter warriors. Wales was still shielded by a ridge, but it looked like I'd be able to sling on my pack at the trading post and walk there from Tin City in a day. The Chukchi Sea to the north was peaceful and blue. Over all arched a bright dome of high summer. It was hard to picture the winter as Hull described it, when all the elements were indistinguishable shades of white—land, sea, sky, and Eskimo. Gazing toward the few high clouds above Siberia, winter was as alien a prospect as war.

Nicole had said something about a picnic on the beach that night. One of those Alaska picnics, anyway, where people dress in wool and dance away from the smoke of a driftwood fire while the sun lazes orange toward midnight.

At supper, however, the store bell rang, and suddenly my plans changed.

Dick Lee admitted an Eskimo couple to the store. The woman wore a scarf over her head and had a warm pleased-to-see-you smile that flashed on like neon and off just as suddenly, giving way to a look of cringing uncertainty. While her husband set groceries in a box, she unfolded a cloth and revealed a nine-inch doll more elegant than anything I'd seen in the living room. The doll wore a parka of sealskin trimmed with beaver, and an Arctic ground-squirrel ruff enveloped a placid thumb-sized face of carved ivory.

Lee had assumed his customary position behind the counter by the adding machine, in front of the rack of rifles. He wrote her name in his ledger: Betty Oxereak, sixty dollars credit for the doll and ten dollars each for two pairs of sealskin slippers.

I lurched forward and asked Betty's husband if I could have a ride home with them to Wales. I spoke softly, as if my normal voice might startle them. I offered money for outboard gas, and mentioned that I had called ahead to clear my visit with the mayor of the village. Ernest Oxereak blinked up at me and thought for a moment. He cautioned that the boat would be full.

My conversation with the mayor of Wales had actually been rather brief. I'd never said when I would show up or clarified what would happen when I got there. It seemed important to have called, just the same. The literature of early Alaska is full of stories of white explorers who owed their success, and often their lives, to Natives along the way. Most villages still graciously allow white explorers to presume upon their hospitality, but a traditional Native village in Alaska, whether Indian or Eskimo, remains a private reserve. One visits as a guest; seldom are there public accommodations where a tourist can buy temporary purchase. Now that more government workers and contractors and opportunists are traveling to the bush, some villages have grown cool toward strangers who show up unannounced at their airstrips, grinning helplessly.

With a tent in my pack and no one expecting me, I felt a delirious anxiety setting off that evening toward the rocky cliffs of Cape Prince of Wales.

The skiff was pulled up on sand near the mouth of a ravine, where the water was milky from the strip mining. Three Oxereak sons were waiting. The eldest, in his early twenties, turned out to be Gilbert Oxereak, the mayor of Wales. He didn't seem to remember my call. He nodded but had even less to say here than on the telephone. It was the last I'd see of him.

We pushed the boat into the ripples, and the elder Oxereak gestured for me to climb in. The boat was so loaded I had to sit on my pack. I thought about the family from St. Lawrence Island who capsized and drowned. As I pulled on my rain slicker to guard against sea spray, the Oxereak men shoved us into the shallows with a well-rehearsed dance of hip waders and oars.

I looked up and saw the reindeer. The herd from Wales, maybe one hundred strong, was galloping across a grassy slope beneath the concrete blocks of the radar base. The animals had evidently crossed the roads of Tin City into a cul-de-sac where they were now hemmed in by ocean and cliffs. They ran around and around the slope in a panic. A dog was chasing them. The reindeer lunged before the dog in unison, like a school of fish, as if they shared a common brain. Ernest Oxereak shook his head sadly. They could not seem to find their way back past the trucks and buildings to the open country beyond.

No one spoke over the ring of the outboard and the slap of the skiff on the waves. The boat was made of sturdy aluminum for pushing through ice, with a second outboard hung ready on the stern in case the first died: a family boat.

Long-necked cormorants watched from shadows as we rounded the cape into rich late-evening sunlight. We approached a broad beach across an indigo chop.

The Oxereak home was one of the first houses. A muddy path led up the bluff. "All down this way," Ernest Oxereak said, pointing north into the sun, "this is the village." He turned to the bluff where the small houses left off. "This was the old village, long time ago," he said. "You can put your tent down here on the sand."

He pointed to an object near the water. "If the wind comes from over that way, you might have to move."

Oxereak followed his family up the bluff and left me alone on the beach. I walked over to the water's edge where he'd pointed. The white ribs of a gray whale leered up from melting flaps of flesh.

I slept late the next morning, curled in my sleeping bag on the sand. About nine, the cape breeze shifted onshore. A foul stink of death and rotted flesh filled my tent. A wake-up call from the gray whale. Gasping for oxygen, I pulled on my pants and staggered toward the village.

A sandy lane led between two rows of houses. Most were newer houses of the prefab sort now common in Arctic development, disconcerting to the traveler at first, so characterless and unrevealing. The whitewashed chapel and older houses with steep Cape Cod roofs gave the village a more particular flavor, a touch of New England primness. The satellite dish for village phones was tilted at the equator—these days you can always tell south in an Eskimo village. In the midst of all this, the new-age geodesic dome still didn't fit the pattern. Or perhaps I had yet to comprehend the real pattern.

I thought I might call on the Angnaboogoks and their Huck Finn grandson, whom I'd met at the store in Tin City, but a young man with long black hair said they had already gone off to their camp in the lagoons. When I said I'd come to write about Wales, he shunted me off to the oldest woman in the village.

Katie Tokeinna had grown up in a sod house and now lived in a new modular home. She was sitting in the sun on her doorstep. She was eighty-one and said flatly she didn't know anything. When I hung on to talk about the nice weather, she nodded in resignation and heaved herself indoors to her living room, where she turned on "The Price Is Right" with the sound very loud.

For several years the State of Alaska had been sending a specially selected channel of commercial television programming by satellite to every bush village, where it was picked up on state-provided telephone dishes. The Alaska legislature had deemed it important for rural villagers to join the global village. I had tried to be as enlightened about this as the legislators. I'd told myself the important stories today are not the paleolithic myths surviving in quaint isolation, but rather tales that make us conscious of common planetary bonds. It was no use. I kept thinking of the meeting I'd attended in Anchorage of the committee of rural delegates, one from every region of Alaska, who chose the bush television programming. They showed almost no interest in Alaskan or Native shows. I'd written down the names of some of the shows they added—"Hot Pursuit," "Glitter," "Paper Dolls." The delegates had traded votes with the fierceness of senators carving up a public works budget. The delegate from Kodiak Island openly gave away her votes on other shows to fend off an assault by "Donahue" backers on the time slot of "The Price Is Right." However, they did manage to fend off pressure from Anchorage churches to broadcast the Billy Graham Crusade. "I worship the whale," the young delegate from Barrow had said, drolly insisting on whale worship programs if Christian shows went over the state satellite.

Now Bob Barker was let loose on the Bering Strait and I couldn't concentrate. The excited jabber about washer-driers drew my attention away from questions about Eskimo life. Katie Tokeinna was better able to keep her thoughts focused. She stared at the screen while I stared at the intent creases in her face, and just when I thought I was forgotten in the array of prizes, she would turn.

"It's not always storming up here like people say," she said, addressing herself to some slander on her mind. "Those people must be out of their head who say those things. And every time I go to their place, it's storming, storming."

And the actual retail price is . . .

Her father came from Siberia, her mother from Alaska. They met on the ice at hunting camp in spring. Katie tossed out story fragments as they came to her, as evidently she had trotted them out, not long before, to a university researcher. There was a woman, one time, who suffocated from too many mosquitoes.

The linoleum floor of her living room was bare and what furniture she had was back against the walls. A bookshelf was crammed with golden spines of *National Geographic*s. Grandchildren or great-grandchildren ran through the house and out the back door, which opened onto white beach and blue ocean.

"Old Eskimo houses were warm," Katie said. It was another strike against the modern world. It is an old joke in Eskimo country that people used to live belowground and bury their dead aboveground, and after the white man came they had to live aboveground where it was cold and bury their dead in the permafrost. However, the old underground houses of driftwood and sod had also been damp and smoky. When archeologists uncovered a prehistoric house in Barrow that had been buried by *ivu,* a sudden surge of shelf ice over the coastal bluff, they found well-preserved bodies with lungs full of black soot from the smoke of burning seal oil. Sod houses had been abandoned when the first nails and dressed lumber became available. Those earliest wooden houses were now handed down to young people starting out in life; as an elder, Katie had been at the top of the list for new modular housing. But she complained of drafts in her boxy new home: the doors didn't fit right and in winter a cold wind raced under the foundation. In fact, many of the bush housing projects turned out to be design disasters requiring expensive additions.

"I've been cold ever since I moved into a white man's house," she said.

Katie Tokeinna! Come on down!

Katie sent me off to another elder's house. The porch at Winton Weyapok's home was dark and cool and had a smell faintly reminiscent of the gray whale. Tall sealskin boots hung from nails above a freezer. A woman in the house, a relative visiting from Anchorage, apologized for the odor. "It smells like Eskimo food," she said.

Winton Weyapok was the village's oldest man. He smiled and offered me tea and short answers in broken English. Most people still eat Eskimo food, he said. Including walrus, yes, but sometimes they catch more walrus than they can eat. I asked about the whale ribs I'd seen rising out of the cotton grass in back of the village. He said that was where they buried the whaling captains killed fighting against the white man's ship.

Winton Weyapok said he didn't know anything about what happened in that fight. He wasn't that old! He was only eleven when the flu epidemic hit. The village of Shishmaref, next up the coast, sealed entry even to relatives from Wales and saved itself. In Wales, though, both Weyapok's parents died, and he moved into the schoolhouse with the other orphans. Many children left the village to go to foster homes.

He said he was sorry he didn't have more stories about the old days.

"Maybe so many old people died, I don't know," he said. "The people who knew the stories died. Young people never got to hear 'em."

As I left Winton Weyapok's, I was beginning to sense a futility in walking around a village knocking on doors and asking for old stories. As if some door might swing open and the spirit world stand suddenly revealed. Was it the abiding presence of the aboriginal past, in the landscape if not in the living rooms, that was drawing my attention away from the present? Or was it simply that the past seemed more exotic, more . . . Native? I knew I should leave the sifting of folklore to graduate students. But if I wasn't looking for ghost stories, what *was* I looking for?

Coming to the Oxereaks' door, I knocked and stood there, grinning helplessly.

Ernest Oxereak invited me into the living room and offered me coffee from a Thermos. Betty Oxereak was sitting on the linoleum floor, sorting through furs for her ivory-faced dolls. She flashed her smile and said nothing while her husband spoke with me.

I was excited to find he knew of the 1877 battle on the trading ship. He said the fight started when villagers were accused of cheating a trader. It was a case of mistaken identity, he said: the real culprits were from another village. There was a great Eskimo fighter in the battle who, though unarmed, leaped back and forth over the heads of the whaling crew, kicking them from behind. This Inupiat kung-fu warrior came close to winning the battle single-handed, according to Oxereak, but when he paused to help a friend he was shot and thrown overboard with the rest.

Historical texts tell only the sailors' side of the fight. It was the first version I'd heard from the other.

I asked about their work, hoping to draw Betty Oxereak into the conversation. She just smiled. As in the traditional division of labor, Betty sewed and Ernest carved the ivory. It was clear from his animated description of their work that it was a source of pleasure and pride. He went to a bedroom and returned with a small seal carved of brown, aging ivory. The carving had a smooth hole and was probably some kind of toggle. The seal was an heirloom, made by his great-grandfather. The son of the man who made the seal, Oxereak's grand-father, was a famous hunter who had kept a diary on an ivory tusk, etching a record of every animal he caught.

The smooth little seal in my palm made me wonder about the man who carved it. I would have liked to know what kind of thoughts went through his mind—not as a receptacle for an age-old consciousness, but as an artist making something useful and beautiful. Being in the presence of the carver's great-grandson, who was busy showing me his own vise and iron files, made me more curious about the particular story of this seal than about general theories of Eskimo art.

Oxereak told me a story about his grandfather. Three times while hunting on the ice in the strait, Oxereak said, his grandfather had been trapped by leads of open water. In spring the ice is dangerous, and hunters must watch for changes in the wind that can open a sudden lead along the shore. Once cut off, a hunter was likely to freeze or starve; Harrison Thornton, in his memoir, wrote of four hunters from Wales who survived by chewing on sealskin thongs for six days. But Oxereak's grandfather could always catch enough food to survive. The first time he was trapped, he floated north with the ice and reached the coast near the village of Point Hope, as far from Wales as Boston is from Washington, D.C. He spent so much time among the people of Point Hope that he married a second wife there. He was caught out two more times, and those times too he survived and reached Point Hope.

"The first time he went, it was by accident," Oxereak said. He laughed, and the lines on his face shattered. "Maybe second time he went on purpose."

A man about my age was sawing lumber by his house near the Congregational chapel later that afternoon. Herb Anungazuk agreed that there wasn't likely to be a storm anytime soon. Then when I explained my visit, he said I should come back during whaling time if I wanted to know about Eskimo life. He was a member of a whaling crew—he told me this proudly. At one time, he said, whaling had died out in Wales. Kingikin had been one of the southernmost villages in Alaska to hunt bowhead whales. The bowheads came in early summer with the receding ice, drawn by the abundant sealife bloom of the long Arctic days. Mounting a hunt for the sixty-ton bowheads required greater communal effort than anything else in northern Eskimo culture, and as a consequence the bowhead communities tended to be larger and more organized. Hunting such huge animals with hand tools did seem a daunting task, but the Eskimo method was ingenious:

detachable harpoon blades were fixed to lines and floats, so that a whale, once struck, could be followed until it tired. Even with the coming of rifles, harpoons and floats were still used to keep track of or tire the prey. As the one responsible for organizing the hunt, whaling captains were the great men of the bowhead villages. Their greatness was made known in the community distribution of meat and blubber.

In Wales, Herb Anungazuk said, they had stopped whaling after the flu epidemic killed most of the hunters. The hunt was revived in 1969 at the urging of a white schoolteacher. Now the time of the hunt each spring was again a ceremonial occasion, a celebration of the survival of the *inua* of the whale and of the survival of a seafaring people.

Herb led me to a house with walrus tusks drying in the sun on the roof. It occurred to me that however the relation of the Inupiat to walrus and bowhead had changed, it was more of a relationship than the Plains Indians had with the buffalo. Herb knocked and, hearing no answer, pushed open the door. The living room was dark. Three long-haired teenagers sat on a couch beneath a curtain and looked on sullenly as Herb dug through a pile of boxes. The mood in the room was less Iron Age than Heavy Metal. Herb pulled out his harpoon and we left.

The long steel harpoon was heavy and awkward. I tried to hurl it and it fell like a tree. Herb said he got into shape in spring by throwing the harpoon into sand dunes. I imagined the whole village getting into shape for the hunt, out doing jumping jacks in sweat suits.

We talked about the village, and I asked about digging up artifacts to sell to collectors. Wasn't that considered disrespectful? Herb waved his arm in an arc, as if to say there's so much history here, or there are so many reasons here. These weren't graves where people dug, he said. Mostly they were old homes.

But he knew what I was asking. There is one old village where nobody digs, he said: the mounds in the marsh called Kurigitavik, a word that means "to run aground going upriver." In prehistoric times there were always several villages at Kingikin, with their own chiefs and clans. The people of Kurigitavik had disappeared mysteriously, the old people said. The story he'd heard was that somebody from Kurigitavik killed a person in another village. The people of Kurigitavik feared the lower village would seek revenge against them all, so an *unutkoot* summoned a thick fog and the whole village slipped away overnight. Eventually they resettled near Point Hope, the story went. Now the Kurigitavik site was on the National Register of Historic Places—there was a plaque on the church.

Herb pointed to the rocky ridge where the villages used to bury their dead. He said you could still find personal possessions left with the bodies. No one went there to take things, he said.

"They always told us never to touch anything up there when we were growing up. You'd have a curse on you if you robbed a grave."

I noticed a white spot on the slope. It did not appear to be snow. I asked Herb if it was another granite monument, like the one at Thornton's grave. The ridge was, after all, a cemetery.

"That's a rock somebody painted," he said. "They call it The Door."

An Eskimo shaman had been buried there long ago. Old people told of a strange man someone saw once dragging a seal up the mountain. Other times the *unutkoot* appeared as a flash of light, a comet flying out to sea on hunting trips. The rock on the burial ridge was a door into the spirit world. Behind the rock, Herb said, spirit people lived. They had sharp fangs in mouths that stretched from ear to ear.

"Do people ever see lights up on the ridge these days?" I asked, at last reaching the heart of my inquiry.

"My wife and I saw it once," said a middle-aged neighbor who had walked over to join our conversation.

"I believe in ghosts," the neighbor said. "I never seen one, but I sure read about them all the time in the *Enquirer*."

"Too many Christian radio stations these days," Herb Anungazuk said. "They can't fly through all that gospel."

The next day I learned the secret of the giant igloo.

Danial Richard was working inside the plywood dome when I peeked in. He was a big, slabby white man in his thirties with a curly beard. He had a carpenter's tool belt around his girth and a sweaty bandanna around his forehead. Dan Richard was the city manager of Wales. It was his idea to build a geodesic dome on the site of an ancient *qalgi*, the village's ceremonial meeting place. Someday it would be the new meeting place: everything a remote Eskimo village needed in one three-story igloo.

He gave me a tour. The interior was being framed into rooms that the imagination had to finish. Here on the ground floor was the post office, always a busy place in a village. This space was a theater for movies and plays. They would sell popcorn here at the snack bar. The city manager hoped the theater would draw people away from their televisions and restore some of the old community feeling. He moved up the winding stairs. Next he had space for a small library and a museum for historical artifacts. The museum exhibits were being assembled by his wife, an Inupiat who grew up in Wales. A teen center and pool hall were situated—strategically?—next to the village public safety office. The health clinic over here would have a hot tub for hypothermic walrus hunters. A small apartment would provide lodging for official visitors, and under skylights on the top floor were the city offices.

We stopped in the city council alcove. A picture window gave onto the village's most commanding view of the Bering Strait. A skiff was being pushed into the surf—bound for Little Diomede, Dan said. There was no airstrip on the island, so Diomeders returning from Nome made the last leg by boat. In the foreground, three-wheelers raced by on hard-packed sand.

Dan said he got the idea for the geodesic dome from reading Buckminster Fuller. It struck him as an ingenious marriage of Inupiat tradition and modern, energy-efficient techniques. He'd been worried about the way things were developing in Wales. With Alaska's sudden oil wealth, government construction money had poured into the bush without enough consideration of heating and maintenance costs. Dan knew Wales could never run the new school and water system without regular government handouts. What if the new health clinic, museum, and city office were scattered throughout the village as well? Nobody was looking to the future.

Dan was soft-spoken and reflective. He seemed more than a little embarrassed to be a white man running the affairs of a Native village. In the bush the role was all too familiar, especially in villages where traditional leadership had broken down. Personal power had never been his aim, he said, but after he married into the village and kept making helpful suggestions, his neighbors pushed him to run for city council.

"I still believe they should be doing this without me," he said.

He'd always been impressed by the clever carving and artwork of the Wales people, so when the new community center was designed, he proposed building it with local labor. Jobs being scarce, everyone liked that idea. "I thought with the artistry of people here, it would be easy for them to build it themselves."

But the multitude of strange angles and intersecting planes proved perplexing. The dome had taken five years so far. The original budget had already doubled. They had to tear down the old community hall to build the dome, and people complained of going without a center too long. But when Dan tried to bring in professional carpenters to finish the job quickly, a petition was circulated to fire him as city manager.

"I was carrying the feeling that I was the white man who was going to come out and clean up what the other white men had messed up," he said. "That was the theory, but a heart attack is where it led me."

That evening as I crouched in my tent with a snack of crackers and an orange, I wondered what it was about the village of Wales that made missionary zeal hazardous to your health. It didn't seem to matter that what Dan Richard thought people ought to be was more or less what Harrison Thornton thought they should change. All of us arrived with our own amulet, the billiken, God of Things as They Ought to Be.

I opened a tin of duck liver pâté I'd found in a gourmet section in Anchorage—a camping experiment, meat that wouldn't spoil. Not exactly Eskimo food, I admonished myself. But dining alone, I had to admit, was a pleasant escape. The tent was a low-slung mountain design in which I could sit up, write in my journal, and otherwise curtain myself off after a second frustrating day of knocking on doors. As I ate, I imagined Thornton at the end of *his* day: retreating to his white frame house, like Dick Lee and the technicians of Tin City, drawing the shades. However much he'd cut himself off, Thornton had an access to the Inupiat past I couldn't help envying. Gloomily I reflected that I could probably learn more about ancient Eskimo ways reading between the lines of his memoir than hiking around the village of today.

I hurled myself out of the tent and away from the squeals of offshore birds. The beach had the same casually littered feel as the land around Tin City, only instead of iron and concrete this was a culture of wood and bone and plastic. The shadows of the houses were lengthening, and the sandy lane through the village was deserted, ghostly. I had a sense of something stirring behind those doors, between the lines, beyond my reach.

Dan Richard had invited me to come by. I hoped to meet his Inupiat wife, but she was out visiting a relative. Dan sat with his year-old son in his lap, watching a cartoon version of *The Lord of the Rings* on video-cassette. It came as no surprise that the designer of the community hobbit hole was a fan of Tolkien as well as Buckminster Fuller.

When the movie ended, I asked Dan how he'd ended up in Wales. He talked about Vietnam, where he'd served in a flight crew on missions over Cambodia. His best friend died in his arms, and Dan had wanted to withdraw from the world. He asked the air force for a radar job to get out of combat, and they sent him to Las Vegas. More madness. So he asked to be sent to the loneliest radar station he could find on the map. He got the transfer and shipped out to Tin City.

"As soon as I was flying out of Nome, I knew I was headed in the right direction."

He liked being at the edge of the world. When he wasn't staring at a radar screen in the dark, he took long hikes down the beach and across the rolling tundra. No one else at the base was interested, so he went alone. He walked seven miles around the mountain to Wales and got to know the Eskimos there. After a number of visits, he fell in love with the sister of an Eskimo buddy. The love affair got him in trouble on the base. Dan said Tin City's commanding officer at the time was a strict old-school southerner who didn't believe in mixing socially with the Natives. Dan found himself confined to base. When his leave time came, he had to fly 100 miles to Nome, then get on another plane and fly 107 miles back to Wales. In 1977 he left the air force and married Ellen Oxereok.

Relations between the village and Tin City had mellowed since then, he said. There was a problem for a while with the base selling booze. Then two young men disappeared making a New Year's Eve booze run around the cape on sea ice. One of their snowmachines washed up on the beach the following summer. For Dan, who was living in the village by then, the successful campaign to close off liquor sales at the base was the beginning of a life in local politics. Now most of the drinking problem that had so troubled Thornton was exported to Nome.

"This is the most peaceful place I've ever been," he said. "My parents own a Christmas tree farm in California. Ellen would just as soon live in California or wherever, but I really enjoy it here. I bitch and complain sometimes, but these are the best people I've ever met in my life."

Ellen returned, and Dan excused himself to go get some groceries. He set out on a three-wheeler on the bouncy overland route to Tin City.

Ellen, a slender woman who wore designer jeans and blue eye

shadow to work at the office, was city clerk in Wales. She had lived away from the village, and did not seem the kind of traditionalist who would be content picking wild greens for salads and tending the fire at hunting camp. She spoke of her culture with the ardor of one who had come back to it from a great distance.

These were difficult years for Wales, she said. The old people in the village didn't approve of young hunters taking walrus heads and wasting the meat—though they might not express this disapproval to outsiders. However, I shouldn't be disappointed at not seeing much of the traditional life. I'd come to Wales at the wrong time of year. In midsummer families are out at their camps in the marshes, hunting and fishing.

On the question of digging relics from archeological sites, her husband had stood back, saying it wasn't for him as an outsider to judge what use the Eskimos made of their own ancestors' work. Ellen was blunt in her disapproval of the practice. How could any culture survive that treated its past as a resource for sale?

"They're selling our heritage," she said. "If we don't start preserving, the younger generation won't know anything about Wales. I don't know that much myself."

Ellen got the idea for a museum when village workers were tearing down the old community hall to make way for the geodesic dome. In the attic they'd found a box of artifacts: ivory drum handles, dolls, carved handles for nets used to catch seals through the ice. Some of the old items were just toys and there was nothing sacred about them—though she had seen an ivory doll with its head snapped off, which was how her ancestors buried the toys of a dead child.

Ellen thought a museum might give tourists a reason to come to Wales and provide a source of income. These days, all Wales got were a few birdwatchers looking for Asian birds blown off course and Americans who wanted to defect. Recently, she said, the city had received a letter from a man introducing himself quite bluntly as a paranoid-schizophrenic who had just been released from a mental institution. He had seen Wales on a map and thought it looked like just the place for him to recuperate. He wanted hotel and restaurant information.

I asked if she knew any stories about Harrison Thornton. She shook her head. Wales always seemed to attract these missionaries, she said. A few years ago they had another odd preacher. This one's mission wasn't to the Eskimos, however, but to the barbarous Soviets. Ellen said he planned to cross the strait and start working his way west toward Moscow, converting Russians as he went. The preacher had walked up and down the beach at Wales, muttering to himself, until state troopers flew out from Nome to retrieve him. He was having coffee with her husband when the troopers arrived.

D an and Ellen Richard lived in the last house in the village. The sandy road led farther down the beach to a cluster of white-washed buildings belonging to the United States Navy. The navy said it was a weather station but villagers were under the impression that the navy was in their midst to listen for submarines passing through the strait. A pale, balding man stood in a doorway and watched me walk by. In order to expand the weather station the navy had recently asked the village to lease them more land.

The road stopped and a three-wheeler trail continued into tall dunes tufted with grass. A white wooden cross as tall as a man stood on top of a dune, presumably marking the mass grave from the flu epidemic. There were smaller crosses as well. The old practice of carrying bodies to the open ridge continued in Christian times, but during World War II, when an Army Signal Corps detachment sent to the strait to watch for Japanese warships took up souvenir hunting in their off-hours, Wales began to bury its dead in the dunes.

Several of the graves in the sand were surrounded by white picket fences, adding to the tidy Congregationalist air of the village. But the new graveyard was a shifting and impermanent place. Some crosses were tipped sideways and rotting. A picket fence protruded three feet down a grassy bank; the coffin beneath was thrust clear at one end where wind had clawed away the sand. Corners of other wooden boxes protruded nearby. Maybe this was not alarming to a people accustomed to open burials. Maybe the wind knew what it was doing.

There was still time that evening to hike up to the burial ridge. Ellen Richard had said it was all right to go if I didn't touch anything. When she was a little girl she'd been afraid to pick berries up there. She and her friends went anyway, of course, and when darkness fell they ran back to the village screaming.

I set out with a similar mix of anticipation and anxiety, but the mood was promptly dispelled by the sight of someone jogging on the dirt road ahead of me. The runner seemed weirdly out of place, though there was something almost noble about the figure he cut: a picture of private determination in the midst of the landscape's immense calling toward selflessness. I recognized him as the plumber who had flown in that afternoon to work on the village water system. We'd met among the laundry machines in the pumphouse, which was something of a community hall in the temporary absence of a *qalgi*. We sat together there and flipped through a recent issue of *Soviet Life* magazine; somebody sent this village on North America's back alley a free subscription.

Following the jogging plumber at a more self-consciously respectful pace, I walked out the road across the marsh toward the hillside of the dead. Whale ribs like gray tree stubs poked up from a rise, marking the burial of those who died fighting the sailors in 1877. Where the overland trail to Tin City climbed toward a notch, road and jogger turned left toward the village water tanks. I began to work my way up through the grassy ledges to the right. I had decided to climb up and knock at one last door. I would see for myself if any sharp-fanged spirits were still around.

In the time before Thornton, the Kingikin people had never come to the ridge except during funerals. When they carried up the dead, their processions hummed with precautionary songs, while mourners swung their arms to ward off the *koklomuluks*, the bad spirits. If the departed soul had been an evil man, they cut the sinews of his legs to keep him from walking at night. Only an *unutkoot*, with an open channel to the unseen world, would dare climb the ridge alone as I was doing now.

I picked my way along ledges of grass and lichen and around boulders, watching for the white rock above. From this distance, the houses below looked small and temporary, the larger landscape undiminished. Where the south coast around Tin City was rocky and bare, Wales opened onto a rich coastline I could now see stretching north, emerald-green marshes and barrier islands swept up by currents in the strait, a glistening lagoon. The dome of high pressure held fast over the Bering Sea, though I could not believe it would hold much longer. There was an air of expectancy about the weather, as there was about everything in this landscape.

I came upon a few weathered boards among the rocks—pieces of a coffin? Delicate curves of driftwood lay nearby. I stopped and looked more closely. The driftwood fragments were gray deteriorating animal bones—whale bones, caribou antlers—left to mark the grave of a hunter. I descended to a ledge below. More boards were scattered about. Wedged between two small rocks was the top of a human skull.

Whether it was because I had come upon a central burial zone, or because I adjusted my vision knowing what to look for, I found the remains of other graves on nearby ledges. Objects were dispersed over a wide area, as if the old cairn graves had flown up mystically and scattered themselves. Sometimes I would come across a human bone or two, but mostly there were remains of animals and personal belongings: the rusted barrel of a rifle, a chipped enamel coffee cup.

I touched nothing but felt like a voyeur. Even pulling out a notebook to write down what I saw seemed a defilement, a damaging exposure that might arrest these things in time, inhibit their return to wind and dust. The *unutkoot* who tried to stop the writing on slates in Thornton's schoolhouse would surely disapprove.

At one grave a windup alarm clock with a cracked plastic face sat ready for the Book of Revelation. Some of these, I supposed, were

Christian burials. It made the hillside less spooky, thinking the spirits might be lounging this minute in a familiar heaven of clouds and angels. Was it so tragic, really, that missionaries had dispelled the *inua*? For every *unutkoot* in the old stories who helped his people, there was one who terrorized with evil spells. Was the *unutkoot* a wise man, as the romantic view would have it? A spiritual leader in touch with the forces of nature, or a tyrant? The fact is that once the missionary teachers had "broken the people in," as Thornton put it, Christianity took hold in the Bering Strait. The promise of personal salvation through Christ must have had ready appeal to a people hemmed in by starvation and taboo. They were told they had the power to separate themselves from nature, to rise above the fallen world. Imagination split from consciousness. Medicine, art, hunting—everything started to change.

But the sight of the rusting gun barrel held me. The introduction of the breech-loading rifle in the last century must have had as much to do with dispelling the spirit world as the coming of the Bible. How much easier hunting suddenly was! Enough perhaps to make redundant the amulets and charms—though I'd heard of one hunter from Point Hope who still sang the old songs for hunting luck as he snowmachined onto the ice with his rifle. It amazed him that his ancestors had survived without guns; he figured those old songs must have been pretty powerful medicine.

Powerful enough to prevail over radar beams and TV signals and all those years of gospel? It had only taken a few days at Cape Prince of Wales to make me wonder. Time had brought this isolated world closer to my own. On top of the mountain, beyond the sight of this sacred ridge, a white radar dome was poised for World War III—even the people of Kingikin will be in the line of fire when the cracked alarm clock rings.

I looked around and saw that I was lost. I could no longer see the white rock. I made a guess and kept climbing. Then I looked up and the megalith was right there.

Sure enough, someone had smeared white paint over the face that looked toward the village. I approached slowly and peered around The Door.

There was only daylight and more rocks.

For a sacred site, it seemed a sloppy job. White streams of paint ran down the rock. I wondered if the slab had been painted as a joke. With the skulls of their ancestors looking on, I doubted it. I didn't know what to think about the paint, except that it held the attention of the living on this land of the dead.

A one-gallon paint can had been tossed into the rocks below, where it was rusting away like the rifle barrel and the alarm clock.

I suppressed a sacrilegious rock climber's urge to finger the few moves up to the top of the whitewashed boulder. I sat instead on a rock nearby, waving at the mosquitoes around my head and considering the centuries at my feet.

The beach was a mile below. Except for houses and a geodesic dome, the bluff and dunes and shining sea looked as they must have when *inua* controlled every movement along the strait. Across the water I could finally see the line of Cape Dezhnev in Siberia. I sat there a long time in the slow-setting sun. The land and water grew brighter, like stained glass filling with light. After a while I could chase away the specter of Soviet missiles and see the opposite coast, still faintly ominous, as it looked to the stone cairn sentries, the guardians of Kingikin. I could flush away the water in the strait and see rock-hard bone beneath skin.

It was evening. Two oceans mingled. I waited uneasily beside The Door, listening to the wind as the sun disappeared on the far side of Asia.

3. People of Kauwerak

1 flew back to Nome and rented a dirty station wagon from a bar owner who sold carved ivory out the back of the bar.

Despite the trackless distance between Nome and the frayed ends of the North American highway system, the town is restless with automobiles and trucks shipped north by barge each summer. Roads have been pushed into the hills in three directions. I headed west along the coast on a seventy-mile gravel stub leading to an old mining town. "Bob Blodgett's driveway," people called it, after a white storekeeper at the road's end who held a seat on the state senate finance committee at the time funds were found for the road's construction.

I had his driveway to myself that day. The road curved and lifted over a treeless flower-strewn landscape that could have been alpine tundra but for the blue sea to my left. Near Cape Woolley, a dirt track led to a beach where I'd heard King Island Eskimos go in summer to fish. A pickup truck, the first vehicle I'd seen, was lurching down that way. I stopped the car in the middle of the road and looked out to sea, but King Island lay beyond the horizon.

In photographs, King Island is an imposing fortress of basalt. Knud

Rasmussen described King Island in 1924 as the most inhospitable place he had ever seen. This was saying something, considering that the Dane had just spent three years crossing the Arctic from Baffin Island. For centuries the people of King Island clung fiercely to the rocky walls. They carved sod homes into the slopes and later, after the whalers came, suspended wooden houses above cliffs on stilts, mooring them to windy rocks with plaited thongs of walrus hide. They used handlines to pull themselves up from the water. They were hardy, skillful hunters—Rasmussen also observed that their skin boats and harpoons had the best workmanship he'd seen in Alaska. Eventually, however, the island's advantageous location as a hunting blind fifty miles out to sea came to be outweighed by its drawbacks as a site for a modern village. There was no flat ground for an airstrip and no protected water for an anchorage. The island is locked in by ice for nine months. In the 1960s King Island was abandoned and the villagers moved to Nome. Now the stilts on the island are rotting away. Houses pitch into the sea, and part of the old school building had been taken out by a rockslide.

Summer at Cape Woolley is the one link to the past. The King Islanders used to paddle fearlessly across the horizon to the mainland each summer, in small ships of walrus skin that could hold thirty passengers. They fished for salmon near the cape, turning their boats upside down on the beach for shelter, then returned to spend the winter hunting on the sea ice from their offshore perch. Now when the fish are running the Islanders drive out to the cape from Nome and bring their children along for a few months of camp life on the beach. They pitch their tents looking out at the empty horizon.

I left the King Islanders to their memories and drove on in the station wagon toward the mining town of Teller, through empty mountains that had been depopulated, like King Island, in the past century. A few mining operations grind away in the interior of the Seward Peninsula, but the indigenous population is largely gone. Native life was transformed early in this part of Alaska. With the Nome gold strike in 1898 and the smaller strikes that followed, Eskimo families were drawn to the flour and tea of the trading posts, to the lights and schools of the white men's towns. For all its sad history, Wales is one of the few ancient sites still inhabited. Other small settlements were abandoned, especially as commercial hunters cleared out the game, and epidemics spread, and missionaries buried the dead.

I wondered what the Inupiat of this grassy mountain country had been like and what had become of them. I didn't know they were still here, the caribou people, people of Kauwerak.

I was expected. Once again I had called ahead to the village mayor— only this time the mayor was one of the two main reasons for wanting to visit the village. Joe Garnie, the mayor of Teller, was one of the top young Eskimo dog racers in Alaska. My other reason was his girlfriend, Libby Riddles, the first woman to win the Iditarod sled dog race and probably the first woman from the bush to have a feature spread in *Vogue* magazine devoted to her.

The gravel road flew over a ridge into an open, clean landscape full of the bright blue water of Port Clarence. Here was the finest harbor on the Seward Peninsula, and until the boom at Nome it was the region's principal trading center. By the mid-1880s the Victorian veneration of the feminine hourglass had given new life to the Arctic whaling fleet, and as the steamships pushed farther north into the Beaufort Sea hunting whalebone for corsets, they developed Port Clarence as a way station. One problem with the newly valuable cargo was that baleen could be nibbled away on the voyage home, and often a ship's first chore on reaching Port Clarence was to seal the cracks in the holds, light charcoal fires, and then sit up on deck for a day while the rats below were asphyxiated.

Again I parked in the middle of the road and stepped out. The small town of Teller was at the base of a long sand spit thrust into the bay. Distant low mountains lifted like ashen waves from the soggy green of thawed tundra. Not a ship in sight, nor a tree, nor any sign of habitation beyond the road's end on the spit. A brisk wind blew up from the water. A cloud of mosquitoes gathered in my lee. I retreated to the car.

I drove slowly the length of town on a waterfront street, then back on the second street. Several three-wheelers shot past in a spray of gravel. Though its several hundred residents were mostly Eskimo, Teller did not have the same immemorial presence as Wales. The feeling was decidedly historical: a few false-front buildings pressed into city blocks, along with the store and the school and other houses, an architectural cluster that vaguely recalled the days when a thousand white adventurers—miners, traders, and hangers-on—crowded the spit. A fuel delivery truck up from Nome blocked my way and I cut through an alley.

As Joe Garnie had predicted, I had no problem finding the small trailer at the landward end of town. Fifty hungry-looking dogs were staked out in a yard, each with a battered tin drinking cup, splintered plywood doghouse, and a personal radius of bare, worried dirt. The uproar that announced my arrival sounded like the howling of wolves.

Libby Riddles was alone in the trailer at her sewing table. She was a tall, pale woman with long blond hair. Though part of her post-Iditarod brush with fame had involved flying to New York to be photographed for *Vogue*, she had let most such opportunities slide and remained in Teller to look after her dogs.

The trailer was cramped but neat—Libby's sewing table and a television at one end, a stove and food jars on shelves at the other. There was a small vase of tundra flowers on the table, where she had been stitching a sheepskin jacket for a friend. Jackets hung from nails. Drinking water in a bucket came from a lake far away—in winter Joe and Libby kept their dogs in shape with ice-hauling runs.

In her lap, Libby was stroking her cat, a badly outnumbered feline named Danger. She got up to make me an egg salad sandwich, which I accepted bashfully.

"I've got a moose shoulder for tonight and some other good stuff if you're going to stick around," she said with a midwestern drawl.

Libby's unruffled, smiling manner suggested something of the inward-looking nature of athletes who compete in the annual thousand-mile sled dog race across Alaska. The course from Anchorage to Nome, veering northwest through the Iditarod gold district, commemorates the emergency transport by dog team of diphtheria serum to icebound Nome in 1925. In fact, the race, first run in 1973, commemorates a whole era of bush transportation. Before airplanes reached the bush, dogs were the only way to make long hauls of people and freight in winter. Dogs were still commonly used for village travel and work until the 1960s, when they were replaced by gasoline-powered snowmachines. The Iditarod has helped revive dog mushing in Alaska, though primarily as a sport. Iditarod racers travel as mushers did in the past, camping in the snow and packing guns to protect their dogs from startled and belligerent moose. Racers spend close to two weeks in the wilderness every March. Many give up somewhere along the trail.

The winter before my trip to Teller, a field of sixty had been winnowed to six leaders by the time the race smacked into a blizzard on the coast at Shaktoolik, two hundred miles short of the Nome finish line. From Shaktoolik, the race usually becomes a sprint across the ice of Norton Sound, but that night nobody wanted to take on the storm. Libby was the only racer to leave the checkpoint and push onto the ice.

She knew it was a gamble, but her dogs were used to the wind and ice from training around Teller; most of her competitors trained in the deep snow and quiet bottomless cold of the Interior. Under more stable conditions, Libby might not have had this home-stretch advantage. The temperature was ten degrees and the wind was blowing forty. In the ground blizzard her headlamp couldn't pick out the trail markers. She followed the lamp's hypnotic swirl, her lead dog plunging ahead in the blackness. The wind grew stronger. She was forced to stop. She hid inside her sleeping bag on the sled. The dogs curled up in drifts. But when the wind let up, she was out front, and she stayed there all the way to Nome.

Libby Riddles had moved to Alaska when she was sixteen. She'd grown up in Minnesota, and left home with a young outdoorsman named Dewey Halverson. For several years Libby and Dewey lived together in the woods just outside Anchorage, where Dewey started to get into dog racing. Libby helped him train for the Iditarod in 1977, and when they split up after the race that year Libby took along several dogs to start her own team.

She told me how she spent several winters alone in the Interior after that—"getting tough, I guess"—and then she entered the 1980 Iditarod. She finished eighteenth that year, not far behind Joe Garnie, who finished twelfth. They were running close enough to get to know each other along the trail. The following summer she moved to Teller and they became partners, combining their best dogs into a single team each year and taking turns running the race. In 1985, when Libby won the Iditarod, second place went to Dewey Halverson.

I asked about life in Teller. Dim as the limelight was here, she said she was inclined to move farther away from civilization.

Her neighbors in Teller were friendly and supportive—the local bingo game, the town's biggest weekly social event, had raised money to buy dogfood for her team, since she'd never been able to attract a commercial sponsor. At school they'd declared a Libby Riddles Day. But she had to worry about the dogs barking, and there were free-ranging village pets to drive hers crazy.

"I guess I feel more comfortable around dogs than people," she said.

It was the frozen landscape of winter that she liked best: the blank winter hills. Like many non-Natives who came to live in the bush, her feeling of being at home seemed provisional. Teller would do for now.

"The way I am, I'd just as soon live two miles out of town," Libby said. "It's good country for running dogs, though. Once the snow is hard-packed, you can go anywhere."

Joe Garnie showed up after lunch. He'd been out in a boat, checking their fishnet. He was a terse, dark, good-looking man with cropped black hair and a clever grin. He had a black mustache and a little hair beneath his chin; body-builder biceps bulged beneath a T-shirt.

"I saw a couple tourists out there snapping pictures and thought they was you," he said.

Tourists had started driving out the road from Nome, Joe said. It was different from being in a village cut off from any road. "People get conscious hanging meat in the village," he said. "You start feeling like you're a tourist attraction. It makes people just want to take care of business out at fish camp."

"You pretty much learn to ignore it," Libby said.

We talked about other racers. Joe mentioned a Canadian who'd won the big sprint races in Anchorage the winter before.

"I got to hand it to him," Libby said. "His dogs looked pretty good at the Fur Rendezvous. But I sure get tired of hearing him say he's the most eligible bachelor west of the Mississippi."

Joe went out to start a driftwood fire in the yard. When I joined him he was stirring a hot stew of seal meat and salmon in a drum over the fire. The dog yard was divided in half. Joe and Libby each minded their own. The animals were smaller than I expected, lean, long-legged, and eager. I wandered through the yard while dog racing's first couple ladled gruel. Each brought something special to the partnership: Libby a bookish knowledge of dog nutrition and dog economics, Joe a savvy about terrain and weather and how to compete in the tough country where he'd been raised.

I followed Libby like a puppy onto her half of the yard. Their dogs had different qualities, she explained. She bred hers for speed; Joe sacrificed some of that strength for fierceness and competitiveness.

"Out on the trail, every lead dog is named God-Damn-It," Libby said as she picked up a tin can of slop. "Joe told me I've got to be a better cusser if I want to be a winner."

Joe's side of the yard was boisterous and unruly. A thick-necked dog with a pink eye and a wolf's single-minded stare snarled as I walked near. Joe warned me to back off.

That evening I walked the quiet main street of Teller and hardly noticed the village I had come to see. My attention was drawn outward, toward the bare musculature of the Imuruk Basin. The mountains unfurled a bleak beauty about Port Clarence. I felt a familiar tug, that lure of open country Libby had spoken of. The wilderness! What was I doing here, surrounded by dogs and three-wheelers?

Others had come this way before. While the drift of the peninsula's Eskimo population had been to the towns, there had always been a few souls headed in the opposite direction, looking for gold, or for adventure, or just for a way to put some miles between themselves and the imploding civilization that drew all cultures and lives into itself. For more than a century, the trajectories of white and Eskimo had been intersecting in Teller.

Inupiat people had never settled permanently on the gravel spit. Storm waves were likely to sweep from one beach to the other, as they had in Teller one night in 1974—dogs had to be rescued by skiff and several drowned at their stakes. Inupiat hunters camped here, but the area was first settled by whites, just after the Civil War, when a local outpost appeared on maps, prophetically, as Libbyville.

In 1866 a Western Union survey party under Captain Daniel Libby made its winter camp here. Captain Libby was forward scout for the first of many grand industrial schemes envisioned for Alaska. Capitalists had proposed to run a telegraph line up through British Columbia to the Russian colony in Alaska, under the Bering Strait, and on across Siberia to Europe. Explorers and surveyors were dispatched. The advance party did not fare well that winter at Port Clarence. When the thirty-nine surveyors ran out of food, the region's Eskimo villages took them in. The following summer, just as U.S. Secretary of State William Seward was negotiating the purchase of Alaska, a telegraph cable was laid successfully across the Atlantic seafloor. The overland route to Siberia was abandoned. Lumber and supplies at Libbyville were bequeathed to the local Eskimos who had saved the surveyors from starvation.

White people kept a presence in Port Clarence from then on. Whaling ships anchored in the protected water in spring, waiting for ice to move out of the Bering Strait. And not all the white people were white. Inupiat stories record that the first "white man" buried in Eskimo country was a *doxivuk*, a black man. Left as a watchman at a whaling station, he drowned when his boat flipped in the surf, and his small son was looked after by an Eskimo family until the following summer.

There were more settlers on the spit during a gold boom in Imuruk Basin. The boom lasted less than a decade, and when it was over, the Eskimos inherited an entire town, which had been named for a turn-of-the-century U.S. senator and secretary of the interior.

Teller couldn't seem to unhitch its destiny from its white residents, however. After her Iditarod victory sent Alaskans to their wall maps in search of Teller, Libby Riddles received a call at her trailer from Bob Blodgett, the white storekeeper and former state senator. He was in Juneau, trying to convince his old friends in the legislature to restore Teller's earliest name. He hadn't checked with anyone else in town, but someone in Juneau convinced him he should at least get Libby's acquiescence. She forbade it.

I found a brass historical plaque on one of the oldest structures, a boarded-up false-front building of dark barnwood. The memorial recalled neither the mining boom nor Captain Libby's camp, however, but was a memento of an unlikely event in 1926 that put Teller in more headlines around the world than did Libby Riddles's Iditarod victory. It seemed fitting that Teller's moment of greatest fame was owed to the appearance of another white adventurer drawn to the open north, a restless explorer whose outward trajectory eventually would carry him into the polar void forever.

Roald Amundsen was a Norwegian veteran of many polar expeditions. Autocratic and driven, he had been the first to hammer through the Northwest Passage in a ship, reaching Cape Prince of Wales from the north in 1906 after three icebound winters en route. In 1909 he was planning an overland attempt on the North Pole; hearing that Robert E. Peary and Matthew Henson, two Americans, had gotten there first, he changed course and raced past the doomed British soldier Robert Scott to become the first man to the South Pole.

Fifteen years later he set out to achieve another first by crossing from one side of the North Pole to the other.

His initial attempts failed. He rammed a ship into the ice, hoping the curveball spin of the pack would carry him across, but the drift moved the wrong way. In 1925 he tried in a float plane, but engine trouble forced his "flying boat" down on an open lead in the ice. When the lead closed in, his crew worked several weeks to clear a runway across snowdrifts and ice ridges, and they made it back to Spitsbergen with only twenty-four gallons of fuel left.

In his fifties, bankrupt and discouraged, Amundsen was approached by an admirer, the young American heir Lincoln Ellsworth, who paid for construction in Italy of a 348-foot dirigible. The designer of the airship, Colonel Umberto Nobile of Mussolini's Military Aeronautic Corps, was the greatest dirigible pilot of his day, and Nobile became the third principal member of the expedition. With a crew of thirteen others, the airship *Norge* took off on a sunny day from Spitsbergen on May 11, 1926.

The *Norge* carried pictures of the King and Queen of Norway, an Italian madonna, and a four-leaf clover given them by the British. They had a solar compass—the pole's magnetism rendered useless any conventional compass—as well as a Marconi wireless direction finder powered by a windmill-driven generator. They had enough pemmican, chocolate, biscuits, and dry milk to last them two months.

The *Norge* reached the pole in a day. They flew at fifty miles per hour and watched their "whale-like shadow" trail over the ice beneath them, as Ellsworth later wrote. They dropped the flags of their three nations over the pole and celebrated with meatballs cooked in hot grease. It was 1:15 A.M. when they arrived, and moments later, starting south, it became 2 P.M. on the previous day. They continued in the direction of North America, finding "the same glittering surface" on the other side of the ice cap. But the weather deteriorated as they approached the north coast of Alaska. Fog, wind, and sleet enveloped the dirigible, and the wireless brought news of a cyclone over the Bering Sea. The sleet froze the windmill and the direction finder went down. Ice formed on the bow. The airship began to sink. Amundsen moved fuel and crew aft to get up above the clouds, and when they calculated they had reached the mainland, they dropped to three hundred feet, only to find themselves over ice—they had overshot Alaska. But now they picked up a radio call and turned east toward the Seward Peninsula. Seventy-two hours and 3,393 miles after their departure, they reached the "little trading post of Teller" and the news shot round the world.

It was Amundsen's final achievement and the explorer announced his retirement, but fate was to draw him out to the void one last time.

Soon after landing at Teller, Amundsen and Nobile began to feud in the press. The famed Norwegian was credited with the success of the crossing, and Nobile sought greater recognition for himself and his homeland. Amundsen dismissed him as an "epauletted Italian." Mussolini, fired by the challenge, financed a second expedition, this time controlled by Italians. On May 23, 1928, the dirigible *Italia* circled the North Pole while Nobile served eggnog to the crew and a gramophone played the Italian national anthem. Triumphal telegrams were sent. Mussolini declared: "The standard of Fascist Italy is floating in the breeze over the ice of the Pole."

Two days later, while the *Italia* was returning to Spitsbergen, fog rose from the ice cap and radio contact with the dirigible was lost.

For three weeks the world wondered what had happened to the missing expedition; an international search-and-rescue operation was launched. Amundsen was in Oslo when he received word of his former partner's disappearance, and on June 18 he set out in an airplane with five others from Spitsbergen to join the search. Amundsen's plane was never seen again.

Several days later Nobile and some of his crew were found alive on the ice by a Swedish pilot. The *Italia* had iced up and crashed in the fog. One of the two gondolas tore off and dumped Nobile. The other gondola, with eight men inside, bounced back into the sky with the balloon and vanished forever. Nobile, suffering severe shock, was flown out ahead of his men. When he reached Italy, Mussolini had him arrested for this apparently unforgiveable breach of naval protocol— coming as it did on top of the embarrassment of the expedition, which had cost seventeen lives, including the life of Amundsen.

Amundsen's name on the brass plaque brought me to myself with a sudden chill. The mountains around Teller offered no solace that evening, no promise of transcendence. Deeper than any aboriginal landscape, they seemed part of a void that made all escape attempts futile.

I walked on through the stillness to the last houses, where the gravel spit knifed out and caught gentle rollers from the sea. Two older Eskimo men on the inland side of the spit were loading gas tanks into a skiff. I helped push the skiff into the water. They cranked the outboard and started toward the hills of the Imuruk Basin.

I wondered who they were. How had they come to live in Teller? Where were they going?

W e dined that evening on red slabs of moose shoulder and then Joe invited me to join him for a sweat. The sweat lodge was a shed next door with a blazing woodstove inside. Once the beads of moisture started rolling, Joe relaxed. He told me one of the biggest problems in the villages was that the best Native girls wanted nothing to do with traditional bush life. Too much work for the women. They found some way to move to the cities, leaving the guys behind. Joe had it pretty good here in Teller with Libby, and knew it.

He admitted he was already feeling a little pressure about the next year's Iditarod. Being the champ's boyfriend and running with her team would really put the heat on.

"I'm thinking what to say when I go up to draw my starting number," he said, grinning. "I know they're going to give me a hard time."

Joe handled the team at checkpoints the year Libby won. He'd finished third two years ago. Several years before *that*, he'd hit a storm at Shaktoolik like Libby and tried to make a run for it on the ice, but that storm broke the dogs: he'd limped back to Shaktoolik and scratched.

Joe and Libby had raced each other only once: the previous New Year's Day, before the Iditarod. All the local teams had run in the Teller Derby that day. Libby won. As far as Joe was concerned, the question of whose dogs were best was still unresolved. The course ran across the frozen inner arm of Port Clarence and back, and the first half of the race happened to be the starting leg of Joe's long training route inland to the Imuruk Basin. His dogs declined to take off in a sprint, thinking they had the whole long route to go.

"I learned to run dogs from my granddad. He used to win a lot of sprint races out of Nome," Joe said. Other than a few years outside at an Indian boarding school in Oklahoma, Joe had spent his boyhood in Teller and at his grandparents' fish camp up the Tuksuk Channel.

"There was always a lot of famous drivers here, older boys. Teller never went out of dogs like some places. It was a poorer village since they didn't have commercial fishing. Nobody had money to buy snowmachines."

I thought of the exodus of the King Island Eskimos and asked who the Eskimos were who settled in Teller.

"There's people from all over," Joe said. "People from Wales,

Diomede, King Island, Mary's Igloo. A little bit of everything. A lot of them have more loyalty to the place they came from than here. My grandparents came from upriver. They were Kauweramiut. People of Kauwerak. People were called by the place they came from—you say the name of the place and add 'miut' on the end. Brevig Mission people are Sinramiut. My grandparents lived at Mary's Igloo, on the Kuzitrin River. We're supposed to be good dog drivers, us Kuzitrin boys."

He leaned over and shoved another log in the stove for Libby. I'd expected her to join us, but we were taking our saunas Native style, men and women separately.

"I'm the first generation born here on the coast. We're caribou Eskimos. Inland Eskimos. We're getting to be coastal people now— some of us are even starting to hunt walrus. There's those who want to move back, though."

"Back where?"

"Back to Mary's Igloo. They got land up on the Kuzitrin from the land claims act. Some of them old guys especially can't wait to get out of Teller. They're ready to move back and start a new village. They just can't agree where to put it."

"What about younger people? Are they serious about going back and living off the land?"

"The last few years have been fairly easy, but the economy's going down with all these cutbacks in state grants," Joe said, sounding like a mayor now. "They have to learn to live that way if they're going to stay around here. There's no way around it."

I said, "It's happened before, you know." I told Joe about the lost village of Chenega.

Chenega was a Chugach Eskimo village of eighty people in Prince William Sound, in southern Alaska, not far from the epicenter of the Good Friday earthquake of 1964. Moments after the earth shook, villagers looked out from the waterfront boardwalk to see their cove sucked dry. They could see rocks where they handlined for halibut.

Some ran for high ground. Others ran to the Russian Orthodox church. The water returned in a thirty-five-foot wave. Those who'd run to the church were never seen again.

It was the worst loss of life in the earthquake: twenty-three people were killed at Chenega. Every building was destroyed by the wave except the school, which sat back on a hill. A skim of wooden debris formed on the cove and drifted out that night with the tide, carrying away most of the bodies. The next day a coast guard plane sent out to scout for trouble returned to report their map was wrong because they couldn't find Chenega.

Government efforts to resettle the survivors in another Prince William Sound village failed—there was bickering between new and old families about hunting and fishing sites—and the survivors dispersed to bigger towns, Cordova, Anchorage. But the Chenega village council still met once a year in Cordova, where people went down by the fishing boats and threw a wreath in the water.

It took the government-in-exile two decades to find a new island in Prince William Sound and pry reconstruction money from government agencies, but finally Chenega was reborn as the village of Chenega Bay.

When I visited the new village, just before the dedication by a Russian Orthodox priest, I found the old weathered-wood village from the photographs had not been restored. What Chenegans got instead was a state-of-the-art bush package: airstrip, gravel roads, harbor, electricity, water system, satellite TV dish, and twenty-one modular homes with new refrigerators and linoleum floors. There was $5 million in the project so far and likely to be twice that by the time the building was done. The raw, scraped-earth look was to be expected in something so new, but the new villagers unpacking their goods after the flight from Anchorage were a little raw too. They admitted they were not the same people who ran into the woods on Good Friday twenty years earlier. They were hoping to make their house payments from commercial fishing, but even the fish weren't quite natural. The earthquake had wiped out the spawning runs in the local streams by lifting the land. Now they were catching pink salmon from a nearby hatchery.

Joe thought for a minute. "Well, there's folks around here who will tell you Mary's Igloo is just a land grab. You can go talk to Bob Blodgett, I guess," he said. "Maybe if we get a big disaster up here, Mary's Igloo will get that extra push."

We washed and dressed, and then Joe went into a storage trailer and dug through a box until he found a book. He handed me *People of Kauwerak*, by William Oquilluk. The author, Joe said, was the son of Mary—the woman with the igloo.

According to William Oquilluk, there were actually three great disasters that befell Joe's ancestors. Unfortunately, they all occurred in the time of myth—too long ago to stir compassion in the hearts of the state housing authority.

The earliest time that the old people knew about, he wrote, was a time of earthly paradise. "Northwestern Alaska was once a very warm country. Alaska was close to the sun. This continent had no winter and it was warm always. The Kauwerak Eskimos' ancestors were very large people. They were also healthy and very strong human beings. They lived long and were happy. They did not wear clothes. They never worried because they had everything they wanted. They did not work in their minds because they did not have to worry or think about how to survive."

The first disaster was an earthquake, followed by a three-day eclipse of the sun. The landscape froze. A few families survived by learning to make tools and to cooperate with one another. The ordeal awakened in them a spiritual consciousness and a sense of right and wrong. "They thought there might be someone who was punishing them and there might be someone or something that might help them if they believed in it."

The hero of the first disaster received two gifts from a prophetic apparition: the Power of Imagination, to see things "not present to your senses," and the Power of Wisdom, a practical, cautionary sense of accumulated knowledge that won him the honor of his people. The hero who returned to his people after this vision was named Ekeuhnick, which translates as "a glowing coal after a flame."

The second disaster was the great deluge. A few families believed a dream prophecy and built themselves a great raft. They alone survived. When the waters dropped, these Eskimos began to scatter across the North.

The third disaster occurred after the people of Kauwerak came to the Kuzitrin River. One year summer didn't arrive. There was a brief thaw, and then winter returned. Everyone except seven survivors starved. The descendants of these seven built Kauwerak village and became the dominant Eskimos on the Seward Peninsula. The people of Kauwerak hunted caribou by stampeding them toward corrals or into shallow lakes where they could be shot with arrows from boats. Their camps in spring and fall followed game migrations; in summer they moved to the coast for salmon. The more permanent winter villages on the Kuzitrin had to be shifted periodically, whenever silting filled in their boat landings and fishing holes.

The Kauweramiut were allied with Kingikin villages at Cape Prince of Wales in wars against invaders from Siberia. They traded caribou skins with the seafaring Kingikmiut and shared in the "messenger feast." But in the nineteenth century, the people of Kauwerak started to disperse. Several explanations have been suggested: a shift in the migration routes of caribou herds, or southward migration of Eskimos from Kotzebue Sound, either to escape smallpox in the north or to move closer to Russian trading posts. Few of the Kauwerak people were left by 1900 when gold miners pushed into the Imuruk Basin. The miners' riverboats ran out of navigable water at a small settlement on the Kuzitrin known as Aukvaunlook, about a day's travel by dog team inland from Port Clarence. William's mother lived there in a home made of sod and driftwood hauled from the coast. "Many's the poor fellow under obligation to this Eskimo woman for food and shelter during those severe winter storms," noted the *Nome News* at the time. "She has become one of the best and certainly the most favored member of her race among the whites." The miners marked the village on their maps as Mary's Igloo.

William Oquilluk was born in 1896 and learned the stories of the old disasters in the men's *qalgi* at Mary's Igloo. That was how the history was handed down: stories were told again and again, with listeners sometimes offering corrections if the teller strayed. Oquilluk worked with the village reindeer herds that had filled the niche on the tundra of the vanished wild caribou, and later found work at gold and tin mines on the peninsula, on river barges as a pilot, and on the docks at Nome. He began to record the old stories.

"The real bad times did not come until the miners came to look for gold," Oquilluk wrote. "Not too many years after that, the Fourth Disaster came."

A mail deliverer from Nome brought the flu to some reindeer herders, who carried it back to Mary's Igloo. Oquilluk's parents died, as did all his older relatives.

"The third day after the flu came there was no smoke coming out of any chimney in the village. . . . At Mary's Igloo, there were only seventy-five to a hundred people left. They were mostly children. While the flu was going on, people would be fine in the morning. In the evening, they would be dead. Five families in that village did not get the flu. All others did. Most of them died. The story was the same at other villages when there was someone left alive to tell about it."

Some children moved upriver to a Jesuit orphanage at Pilgrim Hot Springs. The remaining families were drawn downstream to a new village site—"New Igloo"—where there was a trading post and school. With the disappearance of the reindeer herds in the 1930s and the subsequent closing of the trading post, the last Eskimos moved out from the Kuzitrin Basin to the coast. The dispersion of the people of Kauwerak was complete.

"The Fifth Disaster is maybe now," Oquilluk wrote at the end of his book, published when he was in his seventies. "There are not many old people left. The rules and stories of our ancestors are being forgotten. The people do not know who their relations are. Many children lost their parents and grandparents in the flu and other sickness. They went to the mission orphanages and sometimes Outside. They did not learn about their forefathers."

Oquilluk died in January 1972, only a few months after passage of the Alaska Native Claims Settlement Act by Congress opened a new chapter in the history of the Bering Strait Eskimos. For a while, it had looked as if the aboriginal land claims deal cut in Washington, D.C., would be one more disaster for the people of Kauwerak, but in the end, thanks in part to the stories preserved by William Oquilluk, Mary's Igloo was one of 220 villages recognized by federal law as having ancestral rights to land. Most abandoned village sites were relegated to history in 1971 by a stroke of President Nixon's pen. The people of Kauwerak, through their Native corporation, received the right to select 92,160 acres of vacant and unappropriated federal land in the Imuruk Basin. The final disaster had been averted for the moment, but the effort to return to the Kauwerak country was not without its enemies.

When you have essentially a welfare community that has been provided with housing, a road, an airport, a water treatment plant, are you going to split half the population and duplicate it somewhere else?"

Bob Blodgett was indeed skeptical about the plan for Mary's Igloo. When I'd approached him in his store to discuss the matter, he invited me up the stairs behind the cash register. Now I was sitting on a couch in his homey living room above the store, my sock feet nestled in thick carpet, as his white-haired wife, Helen, joined us.

"You might tell him how many of those people have lived there in the twenty-nine years we've been here," she said.

He counted silently. "Ten people."

Blodgett told me it was always a pleasure having someone new to harangue. He complained about the provinciality of the Anchorage media and the heedless domination of the bush by ignorant politicians from the city. As an example, he cited the recent consolidation of most of Alaska into a single time zone. That move deprived him of two hours of daylight here in the far west. Coupled with skyrocketing insurance rates, the loss of flying light pushed him right out of the air charter business.

"Insurance rates are $3,000 per seat for air taxis. I said, 'We're not going to work for the insurance companies.' "

"I beg to differ, but it's $3,500," Helen said, addressing me again through her husband.

He turned his peroration to world affairs, claiming the title armchair secretary of state. "I'm pickled in the vinegar of my disillusionment up here," he said.

The Blodgetts had come to Teller after World War II, intrigued by what books said of the local mineralization. At the time Teller was a "wornout mining camp" in "the most highly undeveloped area in the free world." But the mining never worked out and they turned to other kinds of business and then to politics. Blodgett still owned the local power company and the telephone company in several villages, as well as the Teller store. He'd served ten years in the Alaska legislature until a rising tide of Native autonomy swept him away and elected a young Eskimo from Kotzebue in his place. Blodgett remained active in local politics, but was forced to make way when Joe Garnie led a voter-registration drive, got himself elected mayor of Teller, and started a recall petition, charging that Blodgett was getting his business and political interests confused.

Blodgett's face darkened when I mentioned I was staying with Joe.

"When you live in a small town of two hundred forty souls and you're a doer, there are always those on the sidelines who are sitting back going pooh-pooh," he said. "I said if they want to recall me because I have other business in the town, that's no problem. I'm far too busy a man to hassle an activity of this nature."

"We were doing the telephone before you were ever on the council," Helen said to her husband.

He was sour about the "young turks" in Teller, but then I mentioned Libby Riddles and he brightened again. "Never bet against a winner," he said. "Everybody in Teller loves her. She really has the qualities of a champion, doesn't she? I think it's a shame Joe is going to run next year. He's too much of a poker face. Personality is very important in sports."

Helen went into a back room and returned with a large yellow ivory tusk covered by a scrimshaw map of the northwest coast.

"Oh yes, that," he said. "It shows my Senate district."

"They gave it to you when you retired," Helen said.

"Do you know what an elected public official is?" he said. "A public pissing post."

Generally he'd got on well with his Eskimo neighbors, Blodgett said. "This is my home. I have an Eskimo daughter-in-law and two lovable Siwash [half-breed] grandchildren. We've put our lives into serving this community."

Helen turned to me. "We've worked like dogs," she said.

Bob Blodgett, comfortably fixed at the end of his driveway, was one of the few people, white or Native, who considered Teller home. The Eskimos who moved to town formed a lumpy mixture, hardly a community at all.

Native land-claims corporations from Wales and Diomede and Nome and Mary's Igloo clung to long-standing rivalries; the inland Kauweramiut and coastal Sinramiut kept a cool distance. Mary's Igloo maintained a separate village council, never joining in the Teller city government. A block of new government-built modular housing was split off from the rest of the town; one Igloo elder sniffed that residents there were "mostly Diomeders." Teller was like some international city with no transcendent identity of its own, a listening post full of refugees and plotters and pretenders to thrones.

Many grumbled about Blodgett and said they wanted to get out from under his influence. Some wanted to move on to Nome or Anchorage; others wanted to return to the land. Like the exiles of King Island, they looked back toward the horizon.

Older people in Teller still remembered which drainages each village was supposed to hunt in, and encouraged young people to go out and maintain the claims. Kauwerak elders kept a wary eye in particular on the coastal Eskimos from Brevig Mission, a small village across Port Clarence, who came and went from the spit by boat and had lately started netting whitefish and picking berries in Mary's Igloo territory.

"Them old guys around here are a crack-up," Joe Garnie said. "They think they should declare war or something."

Joe invited two of the old guys to come by the trailer. Philip Kugzruk was in his sixties and had bristly whiskers and square glasses. Paul Ablowalek was older, frailer, and more talkative. They sat on a step in front of Joe's trailer and counted off the many ways that the old Kuzitrin country was superior to the spit at Teller.

"There's nothing here," Ablowalek said with a dismissive wave of his arm. "All winter you eat only tomcod."

"Got to go long way to go hunting here." Kugzruk nodded.

They unfolded a worn topographic map and spread it out on the sand. Ablowalek caressed the Imuruk Basin with a dark knobby finger. "I like to stay there summer and winter," he said.

The map showed Tuksuk Channel leading inland from Port Clarence to a broad tidal bowl they called the salt lake. Beyond there the Kuzitrin River ran east and north into the steep contours of the Kougarok Mountains. Kauwerak country had stopped at the passes short of Mount Bendeleben, where in Oquilluk's stories the raft had come to rest after the great deluge. The people of Kauwerak had never hunted into the far drainages unless they were prepared for war.

The two old hunters used to catch seals in the salt lake with nets.

They chased beluga whales until the coast guard put listening devices at the mouth of Port Clarence after World War II, after which belugas stopped entering the channel. As young men they had been assigned to follow the Mary's Igloo reindeer herd across the tundra. They remained inland all summer, while their families moved out to the Tuksuk Channel for the salmon runs and cool breezes.

"Too hot up there," Kugzruk said.

"Hard to breathe because of mosquitoes," Ablowalek said.

"With reindeer we'd walk day and night to keep up with 'em," Kugzruk said. "Sometimes we'd run out of grub. No salt, nothing. Just eat meat. Only way to keep the mosquitoes off was build a big fire, plenty of smoke."

Now some Kauwerak families wanted to rebuild the village at Pilgrim Hot Springs, deep in the hot, mosquito-fogged interior. The only historical connection with the place was that some people had gone to a Jesuit orphanage there after the epidemic. But the hot springs were far enough inland that a highway north from Nome might be able to reach a new village there; then the Kauweramiut would have their own driveway. The two old hunters said it would be a mistake to build so far inland. They preferred the old Mary's Igloo site, with its access to fish camps and the subsistence resources of the coast.

"River is too dry, only deep up to here—" Ablowalek pointed to his ankle. "They're just going to spoil that ground up there if they make road to hot springs."

"I guess it's younger people want hot springs," Kugzruk said.

"Mostly older people want to move back," Ablowalek said. "Younger people just want to race around here house to house. They don't even know how to set a fishnet."

Joe and Libby were in the yard nearby, varnishing a dogsled. Joe looked up behind his sunglasses and smiled at the familiar turn in the conversation.

"Them younger people are going to follow as soon as their folks move up, though. They can't stay without their folks," Ablowalek said.

I asked if they expected the government to build them houses, as the government had done for Chenega.

They both said no. Kugzruk said he'd lived two years in new HUD housing and didn't like it. "Gotta have lotta stove oil. I see ice forming all along inside the house."

D on Lee presented himself as the pragmatic wing of the government in exile. The middle-aged chairman of the Mary's Igloo corporation lived in a wheelchair in a house behind Joe Garnie's trailer.

"I'm afraid these days we won't be able to live like we did in the forties." Don Lee wanted to see the village reconstituted at Pilgrim Hot Springs.

"They haven't had to deal with a cash economy," he said of the elders who wanted to go back to Mary's Igloo.

Since the village corporation actually owned the land, Lee had a strong voice in the matter. He spoke of the potential at the hot springs for geothermal power, tourism, and year-round vegetable greenhouses. A corporation had to be conscious of the land's money-making potential. I could imagine such talk stirring Blodgett's vinegar.

He wasn't eager to dwell on differences among the people of Kauwerak and blamed the lack of progress on opposition from Nome. "Special interest groups" didn't want to see a village start up in unoccupied territory—white hunters wanted the land for their sport hunting.

Don Lee didn't get up to the country himself. As a young man he had been shot in the spine in a hunting accident and he hadn't walked since. He carried on his letter-writing campaign for Mary's Igloo from the wheelchair.

"I'm probably never going to live there, but I want to do it for the younger people," he said.

He was tired, his voice strained. It seemed rude to stay and press him with skeptical questions, so I left and walked toward the boat landing at the end of the spit. I was feeling turned around by this talk of resettlement. For a lost people remembering their stories, the journey out had become a journey homeward. But I couldn't help feeling glum about how this saga might turn out. It was hard to imagine Don Lee in his wheelchair leading the way back from the diaspora, or the frail elders poling a boat up the Kuzitrin.

As I passed the village youth center, I looked in and saw half a dozen teenagers spending the sunny afternoon drinking Cokes and playing video games. It seemed a snapshot of the unfolding Fifth Disaster of the people of Kauwerak.

At the landing I helped a crowd of men roll a huge white septic tank into a skiff for a ride to Brevig Mission. The skiff rocked dangerously back and forth as it departed, top-heavy with the tank, which filled it like a giant marshmallow.

Nearby, one of the elders I'd met earlier was helping load a second skiff. Philip Kugzruk waved me over and introduced his son, a young man in a light jacket and torn blue jeans. Philip Jr. was about to head up to the Kuzitrin country.

We sat on the gravel and talked about the effort to return to Mary's Igloo. The young Kugzruk was thoughtful and modest, but it was apparent he'd grown tired of all the nostalgic dickering. "If I'm going to be here, I want to be doing something. I'm not going to sit around and say I'm caught, the future's bleak."

Philip Jr. had lived in Wales and Teller when he was small, but he'd grown up in Nome and gone away to college in Fairbanks and Seattle. When the claims act came along and he could choose which village corporation to enroll in, he chose Nome.

Later he became interested in his Inupiat roots and decided to move back onto the land for a time. He came to Teller in his mid-twenties with the idea of moving up to the Kuzitrin, but he'd been afraid the Mary's Igloo people would view him as an outsider and send him away. Instead, the older people whose permission he sought considered his interest cause for celebration.

As he told me the story of his journey out against the flow of history, I thought I saw in his determination the hard glint of an Amundsen. The decision to move up the river without subsistence and carpentry skills hadn't been easy. But it was the only way he could get started.

"I can't wait around to have everything handed to me on a platter," he said. His father smiled proudly.

Philip Jr. now caught most of his food. He commuted to Teller by skiff in summer for supplies and mail, and in winter he traveled by dog team. It was hard work. "Even if you don't want to go out and check your net after checking it a million times, you've got to do it."

He was thinking of going back to college next year, but now he felt he had a home he could return to.

"Every time I go up, there's a strange feeling I get," he said. "Just thinking about past gatherings, histories, wars, shamans. Especially when you have a dog team running up the Kuzitrin River in that evening light. Just to think you're there in the space age and that your great-great-grandparents walked right where you are going."

The next day I went partway up into Kauwerak country with Joe Garnie.

For Joe, the old country didn't have the same pull. He drove his dogs up through the Kuzitrin country where his granddad taught him to mush, but he didn't talk of moving back where his grandparents were born. He was the kind of bright guy who might be expected to leave the quiet of village life, but he didn't follow that route either. Somehow he managed to remain in Teller, not with regret and unresolved longing but with a jock's self-confidence. For now, perhaps, an Iditarod championship was ambition enough. I imagined dog racing and local politics—and Libby—kept Joe from being bored in the bush.

Still, Joe seemed happy getting his Boston whaler ready for a Saturday afternoon trip up the Tuksuk Channel to a cousin's fish camp. As a boy, he'd spent summer days there with his grandparents. A trip up toward the Kuzitrin was a trip into his own past as well as the past of his people.

Two teenage boys helped move boxes out of the skiff while Joe gave orders. In their eyes, Joe was a star. Shyly they tried to get him talking about dogs. They asked his opinion of other Native mushers. Joe was the only one of the top Native racers who didn't have a sponsor lined up for next year's Iditarod. That was all right, he told me. He knew mushers who got $50,000 a year from sponsors and needed only to make a respectable showing in the race.

"Keeps me tough," he said.

The day was again sunny and warm, and a breeze out of the tundra mountains barely clipped the water. Joe wore a T-shirt. I kept a jacket on for the dash across the inner reach of Port Clarence, but the afternoon was hot at the mouth of Tuksuk Channel. Joe said the last few weeks had been an uncommon streak of sun. Except for the ice water beneath us, this could have been Baja, California.

Where the deep saltwater channel narrowed to fifty yards and disappeared around a grassy cutbank, Joe throttled down. An abandoned wooden shack sat behind the beach. That was his grandmother's fish camp, he said. As a boy he'd spent his summers here, tending nets, cutting fish. Sometimes he even used to go for a swim.

Joe remembered where snow could be found even at this time of summer. There was a shaded spot along the bank where drifts piled deep. To a young boy in a rowboat, it had seemed a grueling distance from camp to snow on errands for his grandmother, but now he had a 115-horsepower outboard, and the few hundred yards blinked past.

He eased the whaler onto the beach, pulled out a long-handled shovel, and filled a bucket with snow.

"We can't just pass it by," Joe said.

The remnant snow was speckled with dirt from the cutbank.

"Lots of minerals," Joe said.

He pointed to a jut of land near his grandmother's camp where four seals used to hang out. Everybody hunted seals, but these four had become like pets to Joe as a boy because they stayed in one place and were so clever at avoiding the hunters. He used to laugh as he watched his frustrated neighbors give up shooting at them and continue through the channel in their boats. Joe still teased some of the elderly hunters in Teller about how old his pet seals were getting.

Current in the Tuksuk Channel pulses in both directions depending on the tide. For nearly ten miles, the channel snakes through a gentle canyon to the salt lake, which twice a day switches from being river's end to its beginning. The green slopes were frosted with cotton grass.

Joe told me about petroglyphs on a rock farther up the channel and identified sawtooth peaks from Oquilluk's book. There was a story about these camps from the old days that I'd heard in Teller. The Kauwerak men had gone off to fight Siberians, and while the men were gone, invaders were spotted coming up Tuksuk Channel. The women and children from the fish camps hid in a tunnel hollowed out of a dirt bank. The smallest children didn't understand the danger and they chattered and played, so their mothers fed them half-dried salmon eggs, an edible paste that the people sometimes used as a glue. The people of Kauwerak were saved because the children spent the time picking at their teeth.

My first night in Teller, looking toward this country, I'd thought it abandoned. Now each time we swung through a curve in the canyon I saw another fish camp. The landscape was not an empty wilderness, and yet it was. The fish camps we passed were abandoned in the heat, though the salmon were running. Finally we came upon a family just pulling away from shore in a battered aluminum skiff. It was Joe's cousin, Tom Ablowalek, going out for a cooling spin. They returned to shore and had cool drinks instead, mixing Joe's snow into their drinking water.

A small cabin and a wall tent were set where a creek notched the bank. With the tide out, six feet of beach were exposed. The water was mostly fresh at the moment, flowing to the sea. Their gill net was spread neatly along the beach, the white corks like marshmallows on a line.

Their driftwood drying racks were bare except for a few orange splits of salmon, hardly fit for dogfood. Seared too quickly by the blazing sun, they were blistered and oozing with maggots. There was no point fishing until the weather cooled, Tom said. Most of the camps on the channel were deserted because in such heat people had gone back to Teller for Saturday night bingo.

Carol Ablowalek threw Joe a smile and went in the cabin to make coffee. The men sat on the beach and took off their shirts. Too hot even for mosquitoes. Tom's two small children, bundled in pillowy life vests, were splashing in the water.

The laziness in the afternoon tugged at me like a current. I drifted along with the fish camp conversation until I felt like throwing in my own stories about fishing for bluegill as a boy in Michigan.

Joe spied seal meat hanging on a rack, black and dry as cardboard.

"I wondered what happened to Skipper," he said. "You shot him, huh?"

Tom Ablowalek showed several missing teeth when he laughed. He told about the day last summer when a gray whale showed up in the channel here.

"We're river Eskimos. We don't usually get a shot at a big guy like that."

He'd seen his neighbors come around the bend, shouting and firing their rifles, and he pushed off in his skiff. The rifles were too light and the outboards too slow. The river Eskimos had no harpoons, just long grappling hooks they used to pull seals into their boats. The gray whale sprinted all the way to the lake, turned under the boats, and led a chase back out to Port Clarence, where it escaped.

Tom said he'd be ready next time. He lifted a harpoon out of his skiff to show us.

"See what I mean?" Joe said to me. "We're learning to use tools of the coastal people."

"And white people too, it looks like," I said. The harpoon head was a slice of saw blade set in a yellow plastic screwdriver handle. The harpoon line attached to a snowmachine speedometer cable.

They said the old men might be right about coast guard electronics scaring off the whales today. There were plenty of whales here, Joe said, when MGM came up from Hollywood in 1933 to shoot a feature film in Teller about Eskimos.

It was the first I'd heard of the movie *Eskimo*. Later I saw it at a film archive showing and was surprised by the movie's sympathetic portrayal of a hunting culture that falls apart after the arrival of "the house that floats." The Eskimo actors spoke in Inupiaq, with translations interrupting the action as in silent films. The chastened hero's parting words were to his family: "Even if your bellies are torn by the Last Hunger—never go to the White Men." Apparently the actors had all been hired locally, though Joe said the pretty young women in the female leads had been Japanese.

The little Ablowalek son was pulling a small rowboat made of tin across the gravel on a string. Joe walked over to inspect the handmade toy.

"Is that the boat we used to play with here?" he asked.

"We used to sit in about an inch of water," Tom said. "We'd row all day and never get anywhere."

Joe stared down at the boat and finally shook his head. "God dang."

We thanked our hosts for the coffee and pushed off in the whaler. We were nearly to the salt lake but Joe had his mind now on feeding his dogs. The Kauwerak country had lost its pull.

On the way past his grandmother's fish camp, however, Joe stopped again at the snow. This time he set about filling the bucket to carry a load home to Libby.

After a few minutes Joe stood up and leaned on his shovel, shirtless, sweating, and gazed at the calm ice water where Tuksuk Channel emptied into the bay.

Like most people growing up on the Bering Sea, Joe wasn't much of a swimmer. It had been five years since the last time he'd been in a swimming pool. He stared for a long moment at the waters of many summers. Then he tore off his pants and dove in.

4. Return of the Native

*T*he weekly *Nome Nugget* had a story about an Apache Indian who lived in the bush not far from Nome. Apaches! The name leaped off the newsprint, reigniting long-ago debates over who was more bloodthirsty, the Apache or the Comanche, in which various television westerns were cited as evidence. My interest in Apache lore had faded along with my interest in toy guns and cereal box offers. Probably I'd never had a thought about the real Apaches and their aboriginal landscape.

His name was Tonashay—just one word. There was a picture of him in the *Nugget*, standing beside his pony. He was young and his hair was black and long in the way of a desert Indian, but he was dressed in a skin vest and leggings that would cook a warrior in the southwestern sun, and his pony was as shaggy as a grizzly bear.

The newspaper said the young Apache had come to the Seward Peninsula to work with the Eskimo owners of the reindeer herds. His goal was to persuade the Inupiat to give up snowmachines and helicopters used in modern reindeer roundups and return to the patient herding methods of old, methods brought to Alaska by Lapp reindeer herders imported from northern Scandinavia earlier this century to teach the indigenous hunters how to manage a domestic herd.

The university extension service agent in Nome, a reindeer specialist, sighed at the mention of Tonashay's name. He told me Tonashay had been staying most recently in the village of Golovin, seventy miles to the east.

Golovin could not be reached by road, so once again I sent myself out to the bush by air mail. A few years earlier I would have had to charter my own plane, at great cost; now, with federal postal subsidies, it was possible to travel via inexpensive seat fares on mail planes that fly from village to village every day, sometimes twice a day. As long as the subsidies lasted, they would make travel easier in the bush, though from my point of view they were a mixed blessing, because the added convenience was undoing some of what I'd come to see.

The single-engine plane stopped at the village of White Mountain, in a lovely valley of white spruce and birch, to unload several jumbo economy packs of disposable Pampers. The only other passenger was a small Eskimo boy who looked away whenever I turned in his direction.

We took off again and turned toward the coast. In the distance, beyond a broad tundra valley, an arm of the sea was salted by whitecaps. Two bare prongs of land shield Golovnin Bay from the winds of Norton Sound, making it the only protected water on the Seward Peninsula south of Port Clarence. The bay was a helpful anchorage for the first white explorers of Norton Sound, including the Russian sailor Vasilii Golovnin, whose name lost an "n" when affixed to the village Golovin, which later gathered around a trading post.

The people of Golovnin Bay were not sea hunters like the people of Bering Strait. Norton Sound is shallower than the Strait, and the great whales and the herds of walrus migrate far off shore, so the subsistence culture here grew up around summer salmon runs. The river pouring into the bay is called Fish River. Its vast watershed extends inland to Mount Bendeleben, on the divide with Kauwerak country, the Ararat of the mythic Eskimo flood whose Inupiaq name, *Aniyaayuq,* translates as "looks like a big one."

Flying east along Norton Sound, I was approaching a frontier between Alaska Native cultures. Across the north of Alaska and down to the Seward Peninsula, Eskimos call themselves Inupiat. The name means, more or less, "Real People." The Fish River Eskimos are Inupiat, like the Kingikmiut and Kauweramiut. Their language ties them to the Inuit of the Canadian Arctic and Greenland. South of Norton Sound, however, the Eskimos speak a different language, unintelligible to the Inuit. There the coastal people call themselves Yup'ik. The name means, roughly, "Real People." By calling themselves real people, the coastal Eskimos distinguished themselves from Indians living inland in the trees. The Inupiat called these Indians *Itqilit*, or "Louse Eggs" (while the word Eskimo was said, perhaps apocryphally, to derive from a demeaning Canadian Algonkian term for "Eaters of Raw Flesh"). Racially distinct from the Eskimos, descended from an earlier wave of migration across the land bridge, the Indian tribes of interior Alaska are Athabaskan, related to Indians as far south as the Navajo—and the Apache. The Athabaskans, northern and southern, call themselves by some version of the word Déné—The People.

Traditionally, the distinctions that mattered most in Alaska were the differences between groups of villages speaking different dialects of a common language. The major borders were seldom crossed until trade with whites provided an incentive. "Alaska Native" is a modern construct, a generic term emphasizing the political common cause among Inupiat, Yup'ik, and Athabaskan people as well as Aleuts in southwestern Alaska and Tlinget and other Indians in the Southeast.

Banking toward a peninsula where the few dozen houses of Golovin were bunched, I looked down and felt the generic definition of "Native" ratchet open yet another notch. Along a cuticle of white sand beside the bay, three horses grazed in the dunes near a canvas tipi.

At the airstrip, an old woman tottered out to meet the small Eskimo boy. She pointed to a knob behind the village. Yes, Tonashay was staying in the village right now, she said, up there in one of the new government houses. Ta-NA-sha, she pronounced his name.

I climbed a dirt road to the last house. My knock was answered by

Tonashay. The young Apache was short and handsome, tanned from the outdoors, with lustrous black hair to his shoulders and a body chiseled of hard rock. He invited me in and introduced his girlfriend, Laura, a slender and pretty daughter of Golovin.

"Want some French toast?" he asked. He spoke with the clear unaccented voice and pleasant manner of a kid from a middle-American suburb.

A pile of Tonashay's hunting gear emitted a gamy smell on the linoleum floor at one end of the house. When I asked about them, he sorted through the different pieces. Tonashay sewed his own boots and leather vests and leggings from reindeer hides he tanned himself in the old style, using reindeer brains and smoke. His winter parka was made of double-thick hides, hair side out, spangled with beluga whale teeth and Indian-head nickels. He showed me a rifle scabbard for his pony. It was made of the skin of the *ugruk*, the bearded seal, and was hard as thick plastic. *Ugruk* also provided a sturdy wrinkled sole for his skin boots.

"Old ladies in Kotzebue used to stop me on the street to ask who made my clothes," Tonashay said. "When they found out I made my own, they really used to tease their granddaughters."

Laura brought my plate to the table and joined us in front of the sunny window. She had met Tonashay when she returned to her village after finishing college. She smiled and said Tonashay knew all sorts of things she didn't. They hadn't offered skin-sewing classes at the university.

Over breakfast, Tonashay told how he had come to live beside Golovnin Bay. His parents were of Apache and Spanish descent. His journey started in southern California, in a small town where his father ran a store. San Diego had swept across the desert valley bringing housing developments and freeways, and by the time he graduated from high school, he didn't recognize his home country.

Tonashay set out in search of his Indian roots. He had learned his first bush skills as a boy, hunting in the desert mountains with his uncle, in country like the dry Sonoran highlands of northern Mexico where his Apache ancestors used to roam. He knew that the Apache had been great horsemen and stubborn fighters, famed for their endurance, so he traveled to the remnant reservations of the Southwest and spent time with Indian elders, learning about Apache traditions. He schooled himself in horsemanship and backcountry survival. An elderly grand-daughter of the great chief Cochise gave him the Apache name Ton-ashay, which means "He who is reborn."

Born again, but not into the modern world of the Apache. The cramped circumstances of reservation life depressed him. Tonashay set out for Europe.

"Really?" I asked. It was hard to picture the reborn Apache on the Grand Tour.

"I wanted to see it. But it seemed crowded. I decided I had to find some open space."

In Europe, the Arctic horizon of Scandinavia was as far as he could go. There he came upon the indigenous Sami people of Lapland and was impressed at how the Sami culture in northern Norway was holding together compared to that of the American Indians. For the Lapps, everything centered around their reindeer herds, which sup-plied a huge domestic meat industry. He learned the Sami language, lived with families, and worked with their herds, following the rein-deer overland, camping under tarps that were like tipis without the American Indian's wind flap. After four years, when his visa expired, a marriage with one of his host's cousins was arranged so that he could remain in Norway. The union would have tied together two of the biggest local reindeer herds.

"She was all right, but I wasn't ready to marry her," Tonashay said with a shrug. He returned to the United States and drove to Alaska in an old pickup with a hole beneath his feet. Sizing up the situation, he looked for a way into the bush. He might have sought out the Athabaskan Indians related to the Apache, but he moved instead to the open spaces of the northwest coast, where reindeer roam the tundra and Lapp surnames survive in a few villages.

I mentioned that I hadn't seen any reindeer when I flew to Golovin.

The project wasn't going well, he said. In his last big effort, he'd been paid by the University of Alaska extension service to set up an elaborate system of camps for one of the peninsula's privately owned herds. He had erected tipi poles at strategic locations in the tundra, where the herds grazed by permit on federal and Native corporation land, and then he followed the herds in winter, camping at thirty-five below, carrying a tarp on his Icelandic ponies. In Lapland, herders stay with the reindeer all year. If the Eskimos would do that, he said, they could prevent overgrazing of the lichen and drive the animals to better feed, guard against predation by bears and wolves, and fend off advances from bold caribou bulls, which stand a head taller and frequently sweep harems off to the wild herds that range to the east. The local practice of cutting animals loose all year and then chasing them in at roundup time with snowmachines and helicopters caused weight loss. Reindeer accustomed to the herders could be led easily to the corrals.

Tonashay had imported the Icelandic ponies as an experiment. The ponies were good-natured, big-boned animals that could graze on the tundra and plod across miles of wobbling tussocks in summer without panicking and breaking a leg. Tonashay had been working with Native corporations and the university for four years, shuttling between rangeland and the offices of the influential. "In Kotzebue, people could always tell when I'd been in because there'd be reindeer hair all over the furniture."

Everyone agreed Tonashay's scheme would provide employment and improve meat production. The problem, Tonashay said, was that most owners were less interested in meat than in "cutting horns": velvet antlers were worth ten times as much as reindeer meat per pound. Korean merchants flew to Nome during the harvest and paid eighty dollars apiece for the antlers, which were ground in Korea into aphrodisiacs and medicines. Tonashay was convinced the herd owners were interested in him and his ponies only as a free herding service from the university.

"Too many people are thinking about what they can do for themselves instead of the broader question of what reindeer herding could do for the Eskimo community up here," Tonashay insisted. "What they need is one guy to show them what a difference he could make. But I can't find that one guy."

There was a knock at the door, and Laura went to open it. Tonashay said across the table to me, "It's hard work to keep on a herd's back. People here get a lot of things for free and they get used to it."

Laura's father, who lived next door, joined us with his coffee cup. David Amuktoolik was a thin man with hollow cheeks and a David Niven mustache. They wished him happy birthday.

David Amuktoolik had lived in Golovin fifty-eight years, long enough to remember the old days of reindeer herding. He'd been a herder himself, and was full of disdain for these days when the only part of the reindeer Eskimos used to throw away had become the only part anyone was interested in.

"Reindeer used to be meat. Now they're money," Amuktoolik said with a gummy smile.

"In Kotzebue, the price of reindeer meat was higher than beef," Tonashay said.

"Nowadays," Amuktoolik said, "they can't even find the herd if you want to buy one. When the boys took over, that's when they went away."

Lately he'd had to go out and learn to hunt caribou, he said, like his ancestors. He recalled old hunting stories he'd heard as a boy, about animals changing form in order to escape.

"Squirrels to trout. Tomcod to voles. Killer whales to wolves. That's what them Eskimos always said. I don't know how true that is."

This was a good region for hunting, he said, though he had to travel far on a snowmachine to reach the caribou. He was used to long winter distances—when he was younger, before they had television, he and his wife used to mush a dog team three hours to White Mountain to see a movie.

"I like living right here because you can get almost anything you feel like having. I wouldn't leave this place. If I do I'm going to starve."

He said he tried to time his trips to coincide with hunting seasons, but like most local Natives he sometimes had to go when his freezer was empty. "I won't starve for Fish and Game. If Fish and Game catch me and stick me in jail, I'll tell the state to go out and give my family chicken and beef."

Amuktoolik used to keep white-spotted reindeer for breeding because he could see them a long way off in summer, when the animals tend to scatter. He wanted to know Tonashay's opinion regarding proper herd size these days. The old reindeer herder and the young one talked about how a good rangeman gets to know his animals as individuals.

"Some got short nose. Some got long nose," Amuktoolik said. "Once you stick around with them for a while, they get different faces, just like human beings."

It was apparent that he liked his daughter's boyfriend. When Tonashay had first come to Golovin, "burned out on the politics" as he put it, he'd pitched his tipi on the beach at Amuktoolik's fishing site. In return Tonashay was helping Amuktoolik during the commercial season when Fish River Eskimos make cash to pay for what subsistence can't provide. Now he was spending most of his time here in the village at Laura's. I wondered if Tonashay's long wanderings might be coming to an end.

"We better go now," Amuktoolik said. The Japanese processing ship anchored in Golovnin Bay would be leaving that night, bringing the fishing season to an abrupt end. Amuktoolik said I was welcome to join them. He thanked Laura for the coffee and headed home to get his oilskins.

"I've gotten along better with the older people here than the younger ones," Tonashay confessed.

Tonashay and I walked through tall stems of fireweed on the crest of the hill and followed a steep dirt path down to the village. Small children yelled out "Tonashay! Hi!" as we passed. David Amuktoolik's skiff was on the beach just beyond a large wooden trading post from gold rush days. The trading post was boarded up now except for one wing, outside of which the current residents had strung their laundry. Someone had nailed an oval sealskin to dry on the weathered wood.

A knot of Eskimo boys sat on the steps of a house nearby, hanging out, the younger boys listening and the older ones talking. The topic was dog mushing and a particular racer from White Mountain.

"When one of his dogs dies he just cuts it up and throws it in his cooker," said the tallest of the group, who wore a ratty jacket with the stuffing exposed. "He told me two puppies of his climbed into his cooker one time."

The younger boys grimaced with pleasure.

"He just boiled 'em up and fed the others."

They said hello to Tonashay, who turned to one of the younger boys and thanked him for his help that morning. The boy had brought word when the ponies forded the river next to the village and were found among the houses.

"They don't like to cross that creek, but sometimes they get restless," Tonashay said.

"Hey, I'm glad you got them horses here," the boy in the ratty jacket said. "I might run out of food for my dogs next winter."

He looked around at the others, then back at Tonashay. "I jokes," he said.

The wind on Golovnin Bay was picking up. The surf crashed along the beach in front of Tonashay's tipi. David Amuktoolik said he wouldn't be out in weather like this if it wasn't the last day of fishing. He kept the skiff just outside the breakers.

Amuktoolik's gill net was draped perpendicular to the beach and anchored at both ends. As the two fishermen worked out toward deeper water, the corkline taut across the gunwales steadied the beat-up wooden skiff against the lift of the rollers. Occasionally they stopped to withdraw a fat seven-pound chum salmon from the tangled webbing and drop it at my feet.

Salmon ran close to the beach so the net lay shallow and picked up fish off the bottom as well. Amuktoolik peeled the sandpaper skin of a small flounder off the nylon threads and flipped it twenty yards. "Waste-of-time fish," he said.

In the old days he had fished this beach site just to get food for his family, but when processors came to buy fish he started sleeping in a tent and checking the net with each tide. He built a small plywood shack, but the shack had blown away in a storm. He hadn't rebuilt. He wasn't in shape to keep after the tides that way anymore.

It was hard to untie knots these days, Amuktoolik said, now that he had lost all his teeth. He shouted this out to me—most of his hearing was gone, too, a result of his early years as a boat mechanic, when he used to sleep between thumping twin diesels for warmth.

"It's my fifty-eighth birthday," he shouted, "and I'm falling apart."

A silvery salmon, choked dead hours ago and already stiff, slid out of the net and sank beneath his outstretched arm.

"Uh-oh, he went down," Amuktoolik shouted. "Gonna become a scarecrow for other fish now."

Tonashay worked quietly beside him. He was clad in yellow rubberized overalls and a blue bandanna for a headband. I could not tell if this was just the way he worked, quiet and serious, or if the desert Indian was unhappy as a sailor.

Amuktoolik had told me he was thinking of turning the fishing over entirely to Tonashay the following summer. If it worked out, then, this would be the last day of Amuktoolik's last fishing season.

"Pretty good wind, hah?" Amuktoolik said. "Keeps the mosquitoes away. White Mountain is mosquito hole. Golovin is wind hole." He paused to untangle another salmon. "Tougher to live up there in White Mountain. Got to have snowshoes all the time. You sink in snow up to your bellybutton when you go out to find wood."

A pile of bloody fish filled the middle of the skiff. Tonashay dropped the net anchor back over the side. Amuktoolik cranked the 55-horse Suzuki and pointed us into the oncoming sea. Out beyond a paw of tundra, the Japanese processing ship was a small silhouette on the serrated horizon.

The sky was clear and blustery, the slippery green waves hard as steel. Each slam rattled bolts in the plywood. Amuktoolik could no longer fish during big storms: he was afraid he would shake his old bones loose, if the skiff didn't fall apart first.

"Some way to celebrate my birthday, hah?" he shouted.

A soup of fish blood and seawater covered Amuktoolik's ankles; more water splashed in over the sides. He bailed the boat with a crimped coffee can while his other hand held the outboard on course.

"This is where I need fiberglass boat," he shouted.

He'd once owned a big new fiberglass skiff able to cruise the bay in most weather, but several years ago he took it outside the bay on a firewood-gathering trip. While he and his nephew were on shore, their boat's anchor line frayed and broke in half. They returned to the beach to see the new fiberglass boat blowing away in an offshore wind, its two new outboards perched proudly on the stern. His nephew had wanted to swim after the boat. Amuktoolik wouldn't let him dive into the icy water. Instead they climbed a hill and made a fire to attract rescue. The next day he chartered a plane from Nome and flew the coast all the way west to Solomon, but the boat had disappeared.

Amuktoolik had told me he never regretted the decision to hold back his nephew. He mentioned the story I'd heard in Tin City, about the postmaster from Diomede who'd drowned in the Bering Strait.

"The things that man makes will always come back," he'd said. "Human beings won't come back."

Tonashay and I were hunkered in the crashing bow of the twenty-five-year-old wooden skiff, where Amuktoolik had sent us to balance the load of fish. Waves rained on our shoulders and ran cold down our necks. Tonashay gazed at the horizon without comment, a meditating warrior.

"How long this boat going to last?" Amuktoolik yelled to me. I shook my head.

"One time my wife and I came around from Moses Point. All whitecaps across bay," he shouted. His sentences were clipped short, punctuated by the boom of the plywood bow.

"People sure were surprised to see us show up. Had a preacher in boat. He had tarp over his head. We never seen him the whole trip. Praying, I guess. Preacher is supposed to be happy. I'm a sinful man and I wasn't scared."

He was keeping an eye on the big red Japanese ship and pointed so I'd turn to see the deckhands lined up along the railing.

"They look like cormorants on a cliff," he said.

Tonashay tied the skiff in the lee of the ship as Amuktoolik climbed up a ladder. The Japanese clapped him on the back. He told me they were his long-lost cousins. Somebody lighted his cigarette and handed him the lighter, the third Japanese lighter he'd received that summer.

The salmon were unloaded by crane and weighed, and from the deck we made a noisy procession to the bridge: Amuktoolik shouting his gummy English, the Japanese officers shouting their own few English words in the direction of his hearing aid.

Japanese candy waited in a box by the door to the bridge: party favors for fishermen. Everyone pulled off his rubber boots and stepped in sock feet to the purser's desk to settle for the delivery.

"Clean people," Amuktoolik said to me.

At less than two dollars per fish, the load amounted to something under one hundred dollars, but the run home in front of the wind was swift as sailing.

That evening David Amuktoolik's wife and daughters made a birthday cake with chocolate frosting.

After dinner I walked back down the hill to the beach where I'd pitched my tent in the sand by the creek. I crawled in my sleeping bag to read. Just before midnight I heard the ringing of an outboard and looked out. The whitecaps had turned a creamy color in the late sun. Amuktoolik and Tonashay were passing in the skiff, going to check the beach one last time.

The next morning cold gray clouds had moved in over Golovnin Bay. The dome of high summer had finally disappeared. The water had calmed and the Japanese processing ship was gone.

I stood in the deep sand outside my tent and stretched and looked across the bay. Shafts of light moved on the tundra hills. The emptiness seemed forlorn. I was leaving the Seward Peninsula, and it was sad to think about everything that was passing, the older people I'd met, the last generation to have grown up in a world wholly unlike our own. I knew I'd never again be able to cruise so calmly through my newspaper's obituaries—those brief paragraphs that marked the passing of men and women in their eighties, the elders of distant villages that were not so timeless after all.

I pulled out my pack and began to stuff my sleeping bag. The mail plane would reach Golovin by midmorning, and I wanted to be ready. As I worked, I saw Tonashay coming down the beach from the village, leading two Icelandic ponies on a rope.

One pony was cinnamon colored with white shanks, the other piebald brown with a blond mop hanging in its eyes. The animals were short and strong, scaled to their owner and the stocky reindeer.

Tonashay said they had gotten restless again and forded the stream during the night. They were found foraging among the houses, and once again a child had been sent trotting up the hill to fetch their owner. I'd gotten the feeling that some villagers were beginning to sour on the distinctly untraditional practice of having horses around.

I asked how the fishing had gone the night before. Tonashay sounded unenthusiastic.

"I don't really like to fish commercially, to tell the truth," he said.

I thought that David Amuktoolik would probably be disappointed to learn how deep was Tonashay's disaffection with the world as it is.

"You've got to keep on top of it," Tonashay said. "I prefer to hunt. If I fish, I like to fish for food."

He wished me well and I did the same to him. Calmly, he who had been reborn led the ponies down the sand and across the frigid belly-deep stream.

I turned and began to take down my tent. Autumn comes early to the Norton Sound coast. In not too many weeks, moose season would open. The hunters of Golovin would be housebound, unable to travel into the mountains on their three-wheelers and snowmachines until freeze-up, but Tonashay the Apache would cinch a bandanna around his head, strap his *ugruk* rifle scabbard on his pony, and set out across the tundra.

The picture that came to mind was more cowboy than Indian. I had a feeling that once Tonashay started riding toward the lonesome sunset, he might just keep on going.

5. Indian Country

*T*he Glenn Highway sailed across a lake-spotted plateau toward the mountains and Canada. A road sign warned to watch for caribou. Occasionally a commercial truck or fat waddling recreational vehicle would meet me going in the other direction, heading toward Anchorage. The scrawny bog spruce on the plateau seemed less a forest than a crowd scene, a cast of thousands, trees milling and staggering this way and that. The northwest coast had been so exposed—a landscape for religious zealots awaiting the apocalypse of their choice. Here everything felt comfortably midsummer, midcontinental. A day of high, spotty clouds. The open road! It was like being back in America.

I wasn't really breaking my rule of staying beyond the highways. My destination was an Indian village near the Canadian border—a community of the Déné, Athabaskan relatives of the Apache, some miles back in boggy woods from the Alaska Highway, where it could not be visited by picture-snapping tourists. In some ways it was even more isolated than the places I'd been: the Inupiat villages outside Nome had been churned up by the gold rush at the turn of the century, while history and geography had kept the village of Tetlin cut off. Even today, relations between the Tanana River Indians and the encroaching white world were in a raw frontier state, to judge from the sketchy reports I'd heard the previous winter of an armed showdown between Tetlin villagers and state troopers over hunting rights on Indian land.

The Glenn Highway tipped forward as it descended to the Copper River. Dead ahead were the icy self-absorbed peaks of the Wrangell volcanoes, rising to sixteen thousand feet. I squinted to erase the yellow line, trying to imagine the valley as it was when only Copper River Indians lived here, as it must have looked to the first white explorers.

The trailers and evangelical Christian radio towers of Glennallen brought me back to the present. In the grass outside a red log cabin, a wingless airplane was rusting like an old truck. Through a field of propane tanks I saw the Trans-Alaska Pipeline, a gleaming silver worm slipping underground to cross the highway.

At Glennallen the route turned north and the highway became an undulating ribbon of blacktop that rose and fell over a sea swell of frost heaves. At times my car seemed ready to leave the ground. I slowed, then stopped at a gravel turnout to look at the silty glacial river. The Copper was the color of iced cappuccino, wide and swift and frothy. South from where I stood, the river had slashed an exit through the coastal range to the gulf. I thought again of the early explorers, for whom the Copper River had been the only route into this country. I didn't even have to squint.

One hundred years ago the geography of Alaska was still a riddle—the discovery of gold in the Klondike would produce libraries full of maps and books about the North, but that was more than a decade away. In 1885 Americans knew only two geographical bands of the former Russian colony: the Yukon River valley and the mountainous southern coast. The two were separated by a wall of ice (including an unclimbed twenty-thousand-foot behemoth north of Cook Inlet that would be named a decade later for President McKinley). The U.S. Army wanted to know if a route could be found through that apparently unbreachable rank, a route that would make it possible to reach the upper Yukon River without a sea voyage through the Aleutian

Islands, should it be necessary to go there and keep the peace among the Indians.

This old-style military expedition into Indian country was the work of General Nelson A. Miles, commandant of the Northwestern Department of Columbia, Division of the Pacific. Miles had to go up against the opposition of Congress and civilian scientific agencies, who were assuming control of the nation's exploration efforts; the historian Morgan Sherwood called it "the dying gasp of original geographical discovery by the Army."

Lieutenant Henry T. Allen, a dashing aide to Miles who saw Alaska as the last place on the continent to attain an explorer's glory, started up the Copper River with three hand-picked companions in March of 1885. A large, unwieldy expedition had failed to get more than a few miles upriver the previous year; the last Russian attempt to explore the Copper, in 1848, had ended with the massacre of all twelve Russians at the hands of the Indians.

The ice was just going out on the shallow river as Allen departed. The soldiers tried pulling and shoving sleds through sleet storms for a week, then dropped clothing, their tent, beans, rice, flour, bacon, tea, and chocolate—more than half their provisions. They resolved to travel light and live off the land. Unfortunately for them, the Interior proved to be what old-time sourdoughs called "a hungry country." For months they struggled through the alders without seeing a living moose or caribou; they wounded one small black bear but it got away. The soldiers survived on boiled rabbit, the rotten meat of a moose killed by wolves, and dried fish purchased from Indian caches that were nearly empty themselves. The Copper River Indians, Allen wrote, were "the thinnest, hungriest people I have ever seen." At one camp a lone Indian with a shriveled leg sought to join the white men's party and was turned away, but when he showed the soldiers how to dig for roots he was allowed to limp along after all. A few days later he was in the lead. On May 30 Allen wrote in his journal that an Indian boiled up a meal of moose meat "from which he scraped the maggots by handfuls before cutting it up. It tasted good, maggots and all."

Paying each Indian chief in turn to lead him to the next, the first explorers reached the Mentasta Mountains three months after leaving the coast. The low-slung link in the chain of mountains looked gratifyingly "insignificant when compared with the lofty white masses to our south and east." They had reached the pass to the Interior. As they were climbing out of the Copper River watershed, the summer's first salmon splashed into a spawning creek. The explorers halted and ate their fill.

Allen's route through the Mentasta Mountains is crossed today by the highway between Glennallen and Tok. I made another stop at a log roadhouse near the pass for blueberry pie and coffee, then cruised on toward the Tanana River.

The Tanana flows northwest from the Mentasta Mountains to the Yukon River. Two years before Allen got there, on an expedition of the Yukon dispatched by General Miles, Lieutenant Frederick Schwatka got a glimpse of the Tanana and thought it the longest unexplored river remaining on the western continent. Of the Tanana Indians, Schwatka had written: "They are always opposed to any exploration of their country."

When Allen descended from the mountains, the Indians of the Tanana "assembled to gaze at a sight never before seen." All the way north, the party had paid dearly for food, and now at the village of Chief Tetling they gave up the last of their money, along with coats, shirts, and pocket knives, in exchange for the skins of three caribou, which they used to fashion a riverboat. They floated out the Tetlin River, then traveled three hundred fifty miles down the Tanana to the Yukon. Allen would continue north on the Koyukuk River to the Brooks Range that summer before beating the ice to the Bering Sea and home.

The army officer had breached the Interior. It was the start of a brilliant career for Allen, who went on to command the 90th Division in World War I and later the United States occupation forces in Germany. General Miles called his 1885 journey the greatest feat of exploration since the Lewis and Clark expedition. The drawback was that anyone less hardy than Lieutenant Allen attempting to follow the route was liable to perish. Most Klondike gold rushers found easier ways, and the upper Tanana River valley remained one of the most isolated regions of Alaska. As late as 1939, a traveler to the upper river counted three hundred fifty Indians and twenty whites. Not until World War II, when the military built the Alaska Highway through Canada to Fairbanks along the Tanana, did the valley's indigenous people come in regular contact with the outside world.

Descending to the Tanana flats, the hills to my right were Indian country still. Somewhere below, down there in the muskeg swamps where Lieutenant Allen visited, was the village of Tetlin. Ahead, the bald mountains of the Fortymile country rose from the far side of the Tanana. I was heading down a long razor swipe through the woods toward the Alaska Highway, approaching the first intersection in 140 miles. That single stop sign had made the town of Tok the biggest and most powerful community in the Tanana valley. A new town, Tok is mostly non-Native, settled after the highway came in. I recalled that ten years earlier, when I arrived in Tok from the Lower Forty-eight, the town had been the remotest bush settlement I had ever seen.

The day I arrived in Alaska was one of dark, shredding clouds and rain squalls. Black pipecleaner spruce flickered behind the wipers through twin arcs of windshield. Our car was a speckled trout, spattered with mud. I'd spent a week driving the Alaska Highway with friends, and the forest through which we rode was endless and mysterious. Tok, the first town inside the border, had been less a town, really, than a chain of clearings linked along the highway. The few inhabitants were weathered and good-natured. They took American dollars at the public shower, which seemed a comradely gesture. Up here, we all would learn to hang together.

Next door to the laundry in Tok, beyond a pitted parking lot, there had been a shop selling tacky postcards and earrings of dried moose turds to the hardy few like ourselves who made it up the muddy road. Bucky the Moose had been sequestered nearby in a whimsical corral of burled spruce logs. Bucky's taxidermist had pitched his head forward beneath a five-foot span of antlers, and the boreal animal looked ready to rear up like a bronco. I climbed aboard for a photo opportunity—a saddle with stirrups was provided. Now I was embarrassed to recall the dopey pleasure of the moment, but there had been something endearing about Bucky. Given the hardships of life in the North, it had seemed a brave frontier joke. However tenuously these Alaskans clung to their clearing, they could laugh back at the wilderness with impunity.

Ten years later, as I pulled up to the stop sign at the center of Tok, the joking no longer seemed so funny.

The clearing in the wilderness had grown considerably. Tourism was booming. Gas stations and new hotels straggled for several miles along the highway, where mock-rustic signs beckoned to drivers. In a freshly scraped and graveled lot, a crowd of elderly tourists hung near their glass-browed bus, waiting for an escort to lead them across the highway. Some trees of the mysterious besieging forest were still about, but their days were probably numbered. Or, worse, the trees themselves were numbered—preserved as props in a frontier panorama.

I sat behind the wheel at the T-intersection, transfixed by a vision of Alaska's fate. Naively I'd imagined Alaska was somehow too "natural" to succumb to such artifice, to the arranging of experience for the traveler's behalf. I blamed the road leading directly from that stop sign to Disney World. Now that the highway through Canada was being paved, the number of RVs and air-conditioned tour buses crossing the border increased each year. At Tok, fifty empty miles inside the border, the highway forked toward Fairbanks and Anchorage. For entrepreneurs, Tok was a great fishing hole, the only place tourists making the loop tour were sure to pass twice.

Business could not have been all *that* great, however, because I sat at the intersection several minutes before a horn startled me. The grillwork of an RV filled my rearview mirror. I turned toward Fairbanks on the Alaska Highway. I was suddenly desperate to get away from the highway and back to the bush—though how long would even the bush be immune to tourist traps? I already knew of fly-in tours of Nome and Kotzebue that featured Eskimo dancing performances.

A mile or so north, a ten-foot-high red Eskimo boot made of fiberglass compelled a stop. It turned out to mark a small amusement park known as Mukluk Land, where I'd just missed a poetry reading. Every afternoon a local woman read from a book of poems about her family's first winter in Tok and described the experience for customers. The family had lived in a canvas tent and nearly froze. The flimsy tent was pitched nearby, a monument to their gritty pioneer determination.

Later, at an RV campground where I stopped to ask directions to the airport, I mentioned the tent family to the woman at the counter.

"At the time, people just said Dick was too lazy to build his family a cabin," she said. "Now she's written a book and Paul Harvey even talked on national radio about the Tent at Sixty-nine Below. If we'd known we could be famous, we all could have lived in tents."

Her answer gave me hope. I went searching for the Tok I remembered best. But Bucky had vanished, and I felt a funny, sentimental twinge at the sight of his empty burlwood corral. Why should Bucky the Moose be any more endearing than Mukluk Land? There was no logical reason, except memory's prerogative. Bucky may have been part of the general perversity of Tok, but he was an authentic piece of Alaska as *I* discovered it.

I pushed into the souvenir shop, past the plastic Indian dolls and painted gold pans to the counter, where two white-haired women were discussing ivory billikens with the saleslady. They decided against Things as They Ought to Be and moved on. I stepped forward and asked about Bucky.

"They just hauled him off to Anchorage last week in a trailer," the saleslady said. "Bucky's hide was getting a little wore out. He had to get himself reupholstered."

I had been given the name of a woman who could tell me what makes Tok tick. The Terwilliger house was set back from the highway in a little historical eddy, behind some bushes. I knocked on the screen door, and Fred Terwilliger, sitting in cool shadows in the rear, called me in. The living room was full of books and paintings and stacks of papers. Fred told me Mellie had gone to lunch in town. I was welcome to wait.

Fred was quiet at first. We talked about the weather and a few things, and then he started telling me about old times and I decided he was happy for the company after all.

Fred Terwilliger had come north from the Black Hills in the 1920s. Now *that* was a time to be in Alaska. The Interior was quiet then, between booms: The gold rush had receded, leaving the country to Indians and a handful of tough old whites. A man could go from place to place, inventing occupations as he traveled. One winter Fred lived in the bunkhouse of a coal mine and shot porcupines with a .22 for a living. He'd skin the porcupines where they fell so he could pack them home more easily. A fur farmer bought the meat to feed his silver foxes. Terwilliger gillnetted and packed herring in Halibut Cove, a rocky narrows long since fished out, its dark-green waters appropriated these days by artists and vacationing Anchorage dentists. He'd slogged through the thorny underbrush of the southeastern forests, working in rainy logging camps. In a Haida Indian village down in Southeast, the oldest person when Fred visited was a white man who spoke no English. A rotund, happy man, sitting back in his house and receiving callers, he'd been stolen by a war party as a baby.

In the Fortymile country, when Fred mined gold on Napoleon Creek, there were still remains of log fences from the days before rifles. The Indians used to stampede caribou through gates in those fences and snare them. Fred kept pounding the arms of his chair as he talked, as if he were ready to abandon his sedentary present and resume his adventures.

"Wolf, bear, moose, caribou, Indians—they all got along back then," he said. He smiled with droll sympathy for those of us who had to keep Alaska sorted out these days.

One year he'd teamed up with a gnarly old-timer named George Matlock, who had been a prospector since "before they struck the Klondike"—it sounded, from the way Fred expressed it, that he knew who "they" were, personally. Fred served as old Matlock's apprentice and mule, listening while Matlock told stories of an even earlier epoch in Alaska.

Matlock had known an Indian up on the Chandalar named Chief White Eye, who played chess on a set carved from fossilized mastadon ivory.

"The pieces were all animals. Now I can't remember for sure but they'd be maybe caribou, and the king and queen would be grizzly bears. That Chief White Eye must have got down on the lower Yukon and learned to play from the Russians down there."

We were suddenly back to the Russians. Next I expected to hear about the time somebody ran into Lieutenant Allen stumbling through the alder.

"One time early in the fall of thirty-three, we were stopped and camped, and he looks around and says, 'Today I've been in Alaska for fifty years.' He died right soon after that. Dropped dead of a heart attack, packing a moose out of a muskeg. I could kick myself for not writing down all the things he told me."

Now Fred Terwilliger was eighty-four, retired to a house in a growing town. Like Natty Bumppo in James Fenimore Cooper's tales, Fred was living his last years hemmed in by new hunting regulations and wooded lots for sale. Through the screen door I could hear traffic headed for Fairbanks—the trucks shifting gears for the last leg of a long haul up from the States, the big tourist RVs cruising more slowly, looking for some sign of the last frontier.

That winter with Matlock, Fred was saying, they'd lived in a cabin on the Middle Fork of the Fortymile.

"I noticed on a hill back away from the river what looked like old, old beaver cuttings. They were about two feet high, all dried out, and they looked like they'd been chewed all the way around. I says that's funny, beavers don't usually like spruce. They're interested in birch and poplars along the rivers, you know. And George says that's not beaver cuttings, those are Stone Age stumps."

The hillside had been cut by Indians in the days before steel ax blades, probably for building logs. The base of each tree had been chipped away with a mallet and stone chisel.

How many years had it been, I wondered, from the time of those Stone Age Indians to Terwilliger, and from him to me? Not many at all.

Mellie Terwilliger arrived driving a pickup truck. She was lean and crackly, and at seventy-four lived as much in the present as Fred lived in the past. She'd been a bush schoolteacher and kept store, and during the Vietnam War, when they first moved down to Tok from their mining claim, Mellie was elected by antiwar delegates as state Democratic Party chairwoman. A bumper sticker on the truck's tailgate said "A Nuclear Freeze is not the end of the world."

She'd been to lunch that day at the governor's new hotel in Tok. There was a story about Tok that in the days after statehood there were three hotels, two owned by Democrats and one by a Republican, and whenever the Democratic governor passed through town he stayed at the Republican hotel because if he didn't he'd split the party. This was not a problem anymore—the current governor owned his own hotel chain. Recently he'd trucked an old Trans-Alaska Pipeline construction camp to the stop sign in Tok, where the trailer shells were remodeled in *du jour* tones of mauve and green.

The afternoon passed with Mellie talking of the present and Fred of years gone by. When Mellie described a power struggle on the Older Alaskans Commission with an elderly Republican, Fred snorted and said that's what she deserved for getting mixed up in politics. Mellie asked about the political season in Anchorage, eliciting another curmudgeonly snort from Fred. Every once in a while, he said, somebody would rob a bank in Anchorage and get picked up by the troopers in Tok, speeding for the border in a stolen car.

"Must be the dumb crooks who come up here," he said. "There's only one road out. If I was them, I'd stay in New York."

Mellie said they didn't have many souvenirs from the old days because Fred was never one to keep things.

"When I married him he was forty," said Mellie, "and he owned a sleeping bag, a rifle, and a suitcase with a change of clothes."

"It was a duffel bag. I never owned a suitcase."

As for Tok itself, the town was a puzzle, Mellie said. You couldn't assume it was only what you saw along the road. Back in the trees, some even within hearing distance of the highway, there were young people living without electricity or water, drawn to Tok by the availability of land and the chance to live a bush life-style within range of a day's work.

"With some folks, if you say Tok's the bush, they get mad," said Mellie. "Others, if you say it's *not* the bush, they get mad."

The Terwilligers invited me to spend the night in a log cabin they owned, located down a gravel road, deep in a wooded subdivision. The land had come cheap from the state in a discount program for pioneer Alaskans, a program later thrown out as unconstitutional, though that evening, as I admired the large irregular logs Fred had cut and peeled on the spot in his eightieth year—the ridge pole and purlins were big enough to be masts on sailing ships—it was hard to begrudge him the prize of a few acres toward the end of the trail. Even if he had cleared the trees with a chainsaw rather than a stone adze.

I pushed open the door to a single large room that looked empty and cold. A comfortable warmth gathered me in. Fred and Mellie had dropped by and left a fire burning. A cot and small table were pushed up by the woodstove. The cabin had a familiar fragrance, a faint spice of resin and woodsmoke that made me homesick for my own cabin. The night was bright as a cloudy afternoon. I sat on a folding chair near the stove and opened a book, happy not to have ended up at the governor's hotel. I was far away from the highway—alone on the Fortymile, maybe. Waiting for Matlock to get back with that moose.

I unstuffed my sleeping bag, thick and warm, and spread it on the cot. A gauzy green curtain softened the light. Pulling the bag up around me, I admired the roof beams once again. The fire could go out. I closed my eyes and gave in to the tugging of a slow current, drifting slowly down a river through a Stone Age forest.

D riving into town the next morning, I passed a sign with the tactful designation, "Tok Community Limit." It was the only official acknowledgment of a highway settlement that had grown in a decade from two hundred residents to a thousand, eclipsing the local Indian villages that remained invisible to passing tourists.

In more conservative parts of Alaska, especially where the predominant voices were Native, state land sales stirred vehement opposition. Not in Tok. New land brought new settlers, more business, more work in winter. At the same time, people acted as if it were coincidence that neighbors now lived just through the trees. Each family was still surrounded by an acre or two of the bush.

The people of Tok refused to incorporate as a city. They wanted no taxes, no zoning, no local government, which made certain community undertakings difficult. Recently a boy on a bicycle had been hit by a truck, and Tok residents were trying to figure out how to get state money for sidewalks and bike paths along their main street, which happened to be the Alaska Highway. There were only nonprofit groups to take charge of such improvements: the volunteer fire department, the cable television committee. The dog mushers' association was trying to convince the state to give them money for the sidewalk job.

"But they still want someone to answer the phone when they're calling for an ambulance," said Sergeant Mike Dowd, the young commander of the state trooper detachment in Tok. Dowd was responsible for law enforcement at the border and throughout a backcountry half the size of New England, and seemed more amused than alarmed by the violent pretensions in certain local precincts. "Up there in the Fortymile mining district, everyone tends to be armed against each other as much as against the wilderness. They have shootouts where they stand back and shoot at each other just like in the Old West."

Sitting on the step of his family's state-provided apartment after work, Dowd recalled a showdown the previous year, when three suction dredge miners up the Taylor Highway near Mount Fairplay caught local teenagers vandalizing their truck. They held the kids at gunpoint, even made them smile and wave when a tourist bus drove by. Then they pistol-whipped one of the kids and sent him off to his father's mine for three ounces and four pennyweight measures of gold—just enough, they calculated, to pay the damages. To make sure he returned, they held on to his friends. The next day state troopers arrested the three miners at the bar in Chicken and charged them with kidnapping for ransom.

"That kind of behavior by a person on the Taylor Highway did not shock the jury in Tok," the sergeant said. "They acquitted the miners. I had five of the jurors call me up to say I should charge the kids with vandalism."

I asked about law enforcement in the Indian villages, and Dowd said that several communities in the valley were pretty good at policing themselves. Under a new state program, a Village Public Safety Officer was trained to handle local cases. The program had a high turnover—some VPSOs had a problem arresting troublemaking relatives again and again—but it eased the troopers' burden in the bush without surrendering the state's jurisdiction. The jurisdiction question was important, he said. Increasingly, they'd been hearing young militants talk about Native rights and about the land being sovereign "Indian country." There were Tetlin villagers who felt the only authority they had to recognize was the federal government, not the state. If the state started to cede its authority, the villagers might as well write off law enforcement in the villages, Dowd said, and he told me about the case in Tetlin the previous winter that had called everything into question.

Someone in the village was supposed to have shot a caribou out of season, a not-unheard-of offense in the bush, where patrolling by state enforcement officers is impossible. This time, however, there was some evidence. The game warden from Tok flew to Tetlin with a partner and a search warrant, but villagers wouldn't let them off the airstrip. If the militants wanted to make a test case, Dowd had been ready to oblige. A show of force in the bush has to be convincing because reinforcements are a long way off, he said, so when Dowd and several other state troopers flew to Tetlin at dusk to back up the warden, they were carrying rifles. The search was carried out without further incident. He couldn't talk about the case beyond that, he said, because the village had filed a civil rights lawsuit against the state.

But most Indian problems came out of the bars in Tok, Dowd said. He acknowledged it was probably easier for a jury here to convict an Indian of assault than a white. If some people in Tok thought badly of Indians, he said, it was because all they saw were the young rowdy ones in town for a party.

"I'm not sure it's racial bias. People don't say, 'That Indian.' They say, 'That drunk.' They see it all the time. The white folks do their drinking behind closed doors."

"Do you get Indians on the juries?" I asked.

"That's another difference. When a friend of theirs is accused, white people always say they want to be on the jury. Indians almost exclusively say they don't want to be on the jury. They say they couldn't give a fair verdict."

On my way to the airport I stopped to see the informant in the Tetlin caribou-poaching case. Tony Conrad was a gruff, outspoken white man with bushy black eyebrows and gray hair. He reminded me of nineteenth-century backwoodsmen, at once admiring and contemptuous of Native ways of doing business. He'd worked as village game warden in Tetlin, keeping white hunters off the village reserve. Then, he said, the village wanted to *sell* hunting rights on their land to sport guides, so they fired him.

Conrad had been painting a sign in front of his chain-saw repair service when I arrived. Last winter, he told me, shortly after he parted ways with Tetlin, a villager named David Sam had brought in a chain-saw with a bent bar. Conrad noticed blood and hair on the blade; the saw looked like it had been used to cut up frozen meat. He'd mentioned this to the local Fish and Wildlife Protection officer, but Conrad said he was as surprised as anyone by the furor that followed. Everyone in Tok knew the Indians hunted when they felt like it.

"You bet it disturbs people. You're a taxpayer, and they go out and hunt every time they want. But what are you going to do? I know what goes on over there. If I wanted to I could have had 'em all in jail a year ago."

Tetlin may be as close as the Alaska bush ever gets to a highway. The village was a twenty-mile hop in a small plane from Tok over a range of bare hills and out across the forested flats of the Tetlin Reserve. Without an airplane, however, this Indian country would have been as difficult for me to reach as it had been for Lieutenant Allen. I suppose I could have gotten there by boat: like most old Native villages, Tetlin was located for transportation purposes on water, in this case a tributary of the Tanana. But there were no boats in Tok. The spot on the highway where Tok had popped up, selected by a different logic, was several miles from the river. In the Tanana valley, Indian and white realms did not readily intersect.

Below the plane, a sodden taiga spread east into Canada and south to the white buttress of the Wrangells. My map was full of evocative names—Gasoline Lake, Porcupine Grass Lake, Long Fred Lake, Old Albert Lake. There were mystifying Athabaskan names for lakes too: Dathlalmund, Taltheadamund. The spruce and muskeg flats of the reserve were good for trapping, fairly good for moose. Whitefish and pike filled the lakes. But no salmon run this far up the Tanana River, and caribou migrations veer through only in rare years. It is still a hungry country.

The question of who had the right to control hunting on Tetlin land was by no means clear. For one thing, Congress hadn't quite made up its mind about aboriginal hunting rights in Alaska. The 1972 Marine Mammal Protection Act, of no immediate consequence in Tetlin but important to Wales and Teller, allowed a Native preference for subsistence hunting of certain species. The 1971 Native land claims act had seemed to do away with Native hunting rights, but a decade later the Alaska National Interest Lands Conservation Act insisted that rural Alaskans be allowed to continue to hunt and fish for subsistence on federal land, in new national parks and wildlife refuges, for "cultural" reasons. Since two-thirds of the land in Alaska is federal, the state had tried to oblige Congress with a rickety legal system to provide a degree of priority preference for rural subsistence hunters, Native and non-Native alike. Even so, the rural subsistence priority was under constant attack from hunters in Anchorage and Fairbanks, who said it amounted to special treatment for a few citizens—an unconstitutional privilege, whether based on residence or race. For their part, the more radical Native activists told the state to butt out with its hand wringing about who should be granted special seasons because hunting rights had always been not a racial question but a *political* matter between their sovereign forebears and the U.S. government. Nothing was settled, and no one was happy.

In Tetlin, the case was further complicated by the issue of Indian country. Indian country was what cartographers once called the blank spaces west of the American colonies. To protect their country from encroachment by land-hungry settlers, Indian tribes generally appealed to the center of power farthest away from themselves. The tribal government of the Iroquois allied with the British during the Revolutionary War. Later, tribes sought to preserve areas of Indian jurisdiction by making treaties with the federal government rather than the enveloping territories and states, whose interest invariably lay in getting the Indians out of the way of settlement. Furthermore, Congress was supposed to "regulate commerce with foreign nations, and among the several states, and with the Indian tribes," and so a government-to-government relationship with some tribal groups was established. But treaties were subverted and broken. With time, "Indian country" came to refer to smaller and smaller enclaves, until for most Americans the term conjures remnant reservations where non-Natives go to play bingo and buy cigarettes without paying state taxes.

The nation had nearly two centuries' experience expropriating Indian territory for the greater good by the time aboriginal land claims in Alaska became an issue. Because relatively little settlement had occurred in Alaska, awkward questions of Native jurisdiction had been pushed aside until the discovery of oil at Prudhoe Bay. Suddenly Congress was called upon to sort out who owned the pipeline route.

Non-Natives saw no reason to complicate the administration of modern Alaska by introducing Indian reservations—sovereign enclaves of Native self-government—to the bush. In the 1960s many Alaska Native leaders considered Indian reservations to be destitute rural ghettos, products of a discredited federal paternalism. Congress sought an alternative that would hold out greater hope of Native self-sufficiency, and so the 1971 Alaska Native Claims Settlement Act awarded land (44 million acres) and money ($962.5 million) not to tribal governments but to new Native-owned corporations.

The stated goal was economic assimilation, but the act reached beyond economics to the heart of Native self-government. In the Lower Forty-eight, tribal councils held jurisdiction over all land established as Indian country, but in Alaska there were now multiple local powers. The old tribal councils still had some authority over their members, but traditional lands were controlled by boards of directors elected under state law by corporation shareholders. Whether Native corporation lands could be called Indian country was a legal question several Alaskan villages wanted very much to test.

Tetlin felt unusual proprietary interest in its lands because of a unique twist in local history. In 1915 chiefs from the Tanana River villages were invited to meet with the territory's nonvoting delegate to Congress to discuss a new federal law affecting Alaska Indians. Under the law, Indians had the right to apply for individual land allotments or village reservations. Judge James Wickersham, the delegate who made his reputation cleaning up gold rush corruption in Nome, asked the chiefs which they wanted. The Tanana chiefs told him the whole country was theirs and they didn't prefer either alternative to the present arrangement. Two decades later, though, at the request of Tetlin's chief and a trader with exclusive rights to local furs, a "vocational" reserve was approved on Tetlin's traditional trapping grounds by executive order of President Hoover. By the time of the 1971 land claims act, the village controlled an area the size of—well, nearly the size of Rhode Island. Tetlin transferred the reserve to its new Native corporation.

Plainly, the village corporation had authority to control hunting access on its land. But did villagers have any authority to set their own hunting seasons? Was the former reserve just like private land anywhere, or was it still Indian country? Did the old government-to-government relationship give the tribal council power to set its own laws and govern its own people? Such racially charged questions were being debated throughout the bush, but I knew of few instances where the state had flown in with rifles to enforce its view of the situation.

The difficulties of bush law enforcement that plagued Sergeant Dowd had been envisioned a century earlier by Lieutenant Allen.

At the conclusion of his exploration narrative, Allen discussed the chance of an uprising among the Tanana Indians and the obstacles the army would face in such an event. The country was nearly impossible to reach on foot, and steamboats would be useless on the shallow glacial rivers. "To get a force into the Interior marching would be necessary, and [marching] could be accomplished more easily than the party could be subsisted after it arrived at its field of action." He did not predict trouble from the Indians, though his assessment of the people who helped him survive was surprisingly cool: "Gifted by nature with the skill and cunning of their southern relations, and inhabiting a much more inaccessible and foodless country, depredations and other crimes could be committed with correspondingly greater impunity."

Tetlin remained peaceable. The army never had to march. But neither had the Indian way of life been seriously challenged until Tok's growing population made a conflict over hunting inevitable.

The plane set down on an airstrip in the willows at a bend in the Tetlin River.

This time I had called ahead but failed to reach the mayor. I wondered what kind of reception an unannounced visitor might get on the reserve.

Two young men with long black hair met the plane on three-wheelers, but they were interested in several large cardboard boxes and ignored me. I asked where to find the mayor. They said I wanted the tribal council chief, and pointed helpfully toward the far end of the village.

I shouldered my pack and started across a footbridge to the settlement of one hundred fifty people. Unlike the houses of Tok, each set off in its own parcel of bush, the small houses of Tetlin were crowded together, marshaled in erratic lines. At the time of Lieutenant Allen's visit, the people of Tetlin lived in cabins of upright logs, with doors too narrow for bears to walk through. Now there were log and plywood cabins with piecemeal sheet metal roofs, evoking memories of the rural poverty that inspired the federal housing programs in the 1960s, though soon I noticed newer houses built by the Bureau of Indian Affairs. The grassy underbrush was planted with empty oil drums and rusting propane tanks. A canopy of power lines emanated from a generator.

The first person to take an interest in me was a boy in his late teens. He did not seem happy to see me and demanded to know if they'd checked my bags at the airplane. They checked his bags for booze whenever he flew in—why didn't they check a white guy's?

A village elder came to my rescue.

"You've been drinking, that's why you're talking smart," the old man said.

When the young man repeated his protest about baggage searches, the old man let him have it.

"You shouldn't be drinking that way. Little kids see you drinking and they never forget. You keep drinking, pretty soon they'll carry your body out of here. You younger people, it's like I'm already gone, but I got a few more years."

The young man drew himself to attention before this barrage. He shook my hand and slurred an apology before lurching off into the bushes.

The elder, a tall bony man with a face of shellacked copper, turned out to be Titus David—chief of the tribal council, eighty-one years old, descended from Chief David, last of the old traditional chiefs of Tetlin, and from Chief David's nephew, Chief Peter, who built the first school. It was Chief Peter who told the soldiers in 1941 they could run the Alaska Highway across the Tetlin Reserve as the Indians' contribution to the war effort.

I told Chief Titus I hoped to learn something of Native hunting on the reserve. He took me home to his bare kitchen and fed me moose stew. As if exhausted by his confrontation, he sat back and said nothing until I slurped up the last of the meaty broth. Then he offered more.

"When we hunt, we use everything," Titus said. "Even hang feet in tree, come back and make soup in wintertime." I sat through a brief sermon on the evils of white men's trophy hunting. Titus said people in the village hunted to survive; families shared game with old and sick people. They followed the state's hunting seasons, but not when somebody ran out of food.

"If white man live here, he starve." My host smiled and offered a third bowl.

The chief didn't want to see a year-round road built to Tetlin. A road would bring outside hunters and bottles of booze. He wasn't angry at Tok. He had friends there, he said—"new people, just come in a short time ago"—but they didn't always understand about the way people live on the reserve.

"Native people sometimes need to hunt when it's time to make potlatch," he said.

Potlatch was the traditional Athabaskan feast that culminated in the giving away of possessions, thereby establishing the host's prestige. Chief Titus had started to tell of his recent efforts to organize a village potlatch when we were interrupted by a knock at the door.

A young man the size of a football lineman came in. He had a drooping black mustache and wore a greasy checked shirt. Saying he'd heard a visitor was around, he settled himself at the table. Danny Adams was one of the village's new generation of leaders, active in the village's Native corporation. I got the feeling he wanted to be sure I didn't form my opinions of Tetlin solely on the basis of the genial old chief and his potlatches. The object of the Native corporation was to accumulate money, not to give everything away.

Danny reminded me that after the land claims act passed, Tetlin transferred control of the reserve from the tribal council to the village corporation. Danny was inclined to call the whole land claims act a fraud intended to pry land out of Native hands by pushing them into bankruptcy—"Give Lee Iacocca a million dollars and send him out here and he'll file Chapter Eleven in a year." But he was full of money-making notions, hoping to beat the odds. A road might bring in tourists; logging trucks could get at the trees. Hunting guides would pay for the right to take rich white clients onto the reserve.

"We've got to get grant monies for capital projects, set up regional connections," he said. "We're twenty years behind here. Twenty years from now, we'll probably see moose in a zoo. Things are changing and we've got to change with them."

Chief Titus had fallen silent. He did not seem in disagreement— merely detached, as if the talk of corporation business did not concern him. But when I asked about the trooper raid, both men grew equally animated.

That day the game wardens came with the search warrant, Danny said, was the first time villagers had ever seen such a piece of paper. The village took care of its land and its own people, he said. If some family shot too much game, the village council would make them stop. If somebody caused serious trouble, they would call in the troopers. When the troopers arrived at David Sam's house with so many rifles, people were frightened. They thought there must be something really terrible going on, maybe a murderer holding hostages. But the troopers were laughing.

"The thought of that thing happening is never going to leave the village. The fright will always be there," Danny said.

The incident had aroused strong proprietary feelings in Tetlin, but their lawyers couldn't tell them whether transferring land from the tribal council to the corporation had done away with the tribe's sovereignty over the old reserve. Danny was truly perplexed. It was still the same people who owned the land.

"I think people look down on us for having land of our own," Danny said, turning the thought over slowly. "Do you think so? What did they say in Tok? I wonder what it means that we have a reserve. Nobody can ever tell me. Is it something the government protects for stupid people? Or is it for people who are smart and want to preserve their heritage? In the Lower Forty-eight, reservations were forced on Indians. In Alaska we asked for it. I don't know. It's something I always wondered."

He looked at me as if I might have an answer.

We talked late into the evening, and eventually I asked if anybody was going out hunting or fishing. I hoped to get out and see some of the reserve. Danny replied, "Everybody's leaving tomorrow."

Chief Titus gave a serious nod: "Baseball game."

Danny said the village had a team in the valley's fast-pitch softball league. Everyone would be going to Tok the next day for a game.

It was rotten luck—I'd hoped to hang around a few days. The one person I'd particularly wanted to talk to was the hunter who was busted for shooting the caribou.

"What about David Sam? I'd like to meet him."

"I think you should," Danny said.

It was dusk, approaching midnight, when we stepped out, but people were sitting on benches in front of a row of rough log cabins, the village's oldest houses. The Tetlin River was a noiseless channel with brushy woods on the far side. Lieutenant Allen had said the lake country around Tetlin recalled lower latitudes and was "more pastoral in its nature than in any part of the Territory." It seemed pastoral still. Villagers sat in shirtsleeves on the warm night, as if they were on the porch of a feed store in Mississippi or a door stoop in Brooklyn, smoking cigarettes, talking just a little. Small children chased each other, oblivious to the hour. Danny said they stay out late in summer, eating away from home and sometimes sleeping where they drop. The adults gazed south from their benches, across the reserve toward the distant Wrangells, the "smoking mountains" where legend had it the dead danced in craters. Squadrons of swallows swooped overhead—taking care of the mosquitoes, a woman said. "They're our guardian angels."

Danny introduced me to the Village Public Safety Officer, a petite young woman who had been trained at the state trooper academy in Sitka. She'd been away from the village at the time of the raid and was glad of it.

"It's hard for me to bust my own people. I live on that stuff, too," she said shyly when I pressed her with questions. I was treating her like a public official, not like one of my hosts in the village. "If I had been here I would have had to side with the state and it would be against my utmost feeling."

What else could the troopers have done? I asked. If they called the village council first, wouldn't that give a hunter time to hide the evidence?

"They're my people, too, and I'd rather not say. It was not tactful," she said, her voice growing still quieter. "It was very stupid. I felt shame."

Danny led the way to a dilapidated house with a steep-pitched roof. The house was painted a faded Haight-Ashbury purple. Danny knocked and swung open the remains of the door, which looked to have been chewed to pieces by porcupines on an acid trip.

The room was furnished with a torn-up plastic chair, a table, and a small color television in the corner. Dried moose ribs lay atop a plastic bag on the kitchen floor beside a stove and an old refrigerator.

David Sam rose from his bed in the back room. He padded out and spoke in a faint wheeze. I leaned close to his face to hear him repeat the words: "I have flu."

Sam was a short, sickly man with muttonchop sideburns. He offered a timid smile, and I reached out to shake a spongy stub at the end of his arm. Twenty years ago, he said, he lost five fingers to frostbite. His voice froze in the same accident. He said he hadn't hunted since.

"The troopers never did find the caribou meat they were looking for," Danny said over my shoulder. "Only moose. A judge threw the search warrant out when they came back with the wrong meat."

Village dogs and children had followed us through the open door. A big black dog leaped onto the chair and David Sam jumped back, startled.

"People share moose around, like the Eskimos up North with their whales," Danny continued. "The funny thing is the moose meat they took that day was from the Alaska Highway. A road kill. The warden himself gave the carcass to Fred Demit, who passed it on to old people who don't hunt."

David Sam had gone to his kitchen shelf to make toast for a child who called him Grandpa. Reaching for the toaster, his clumsy hand pulled several pans clattering to the floor. The man accused of hunting big game illegally had a hard time making a cheese sandwich.

"We just want them to show more consideration and respect," Danny said.

I asked David Sam why he thought the troopers had come for him that day. He said he didn't know.

"I think they don't like that we got reservation," he said.

The visit was brief. David Sam returned to his sickbed, and Danny led me back to the dusk and the benevolent swallows.

The next morning, while we were loading flat-bottom boats at the riverbank with softball bats, my disappointment over the imminent departure of the village I'd come all this way to see gave way to awakening delight.

Softball is a serious matter in the upper Tanana valley. The men's league is a fastball league—no friendly lobs. Most teams are made up of brawny construction workers or government employees posted near the border, and the team from the Indian reserve had always been a pushover—until this year. Now they had a sandy new practice field by the village airstrip, new black-and-yellow uniforms, a new attitude, and a league-leading record of six victories and one defeat.

The elders of Tetlin were worried about alcohol and indolence and their young people, so the team's success, its newfound scrappy confidence, had everyone delighted. Chief Titus himself had contributed wire screen and two-by-fours for the new backstop.

I climbed into one of two snub-nosed riverboats reserved for players and found a place among the bats. A half-dozen grinning teenagers sat opposite in the stern.

A third boat was overflowing with spectators. From his high seat in their midst, Chief Titus lent the occasion a regal air. The fans' boat was pushed into the current amid loud predictions that ours would reach the highway first. Their outboard popped into gear and the boat leaped into the far riverbank. Old people held tight and the younger ones were trying to push free from a snag as we disappeared around the first turn.

The players were dressed in blue denim and sneakers for the trip to town, ball caps flipped backward so they wouldn't blow off. They crowded the rear of the boat, and Danny, the team's 280-pound designated hitter and inspirational hothead, settled amidships next to me. On his other side was a red duffel bag of ball gloves and a bear pistol.

We swerved quickly along the narrow curves of the channel, Lieutenant Allen's route of "many windings" out from Tetlin to the big river. Spindly spruce pressed to the banks and reached across the water. The Stone Age forest. Open muskeg revealed cottonwoods and birches and sprays of pink fireweed. Danny described black-water channels leading to lakes where families had their ratting camps and pointed to a bluff where he scouted for moose in the fall. It was the old Tetlin Reserve that prompted this proud narration, not the assets of the village corporation. He pointed out the route to Fish Lake, where he'd spent every spring as a boy, packing in with his grandfather to hunt ducks and muskrats.

Danny's survey culminated in a thoughtful gaze at his feet, and with a curse he realized he'd left his sneakers in the village. He'd have to play ball in heavy-soled hiking boots. His spirits sank. Tetlin's dream of a perfect season had been dashed in their most recent game, when the team from Tok Lodge flew to the village and knocked off the league leaders by a score of 35 to 5. Danny blamed the team's collapse on "attitude problems" and offered no further explanation.

To instill discipline, the coach was benching several of their best starters for today's game. This was risky: the little village didn't have great depth.

"They're waiting for us today," he said. "I can feel it."

Where the clear Tetlin poured into the murky glacial rush of the

Tanana, the landscape opened. Rain squalls were blowing across the valley. The broad gray Tanana shoveled through gravel banks and sandbars. The river's surface boiled and swirled; dirty brown foam skittered past. Behind us, the fans' boat emerged from the forest.

Danny sat forward, shouting directions. He was a few years older than the teenagers and seemed to have a better feel for the Tanana's shifting channels. He pointed to a far shore—"Keep it open!" he cried—but the outboard threw up a shower of black mud and died. We sat motionless, silent, on a sandbar in the midst of the broad rippling river as the fans' boat shot past. Chief Titus, riding low, smiled and waved. While his smirking teammates moved to the bow, Danny stood with an oar and single-handedly shoved us back to deeper water.

A black cloud was dumping rain when the steel bridge of the Alaska Highway appeared in the distance. The team was huddled under several jackets.

"The things we've got to go through to play softball," Danny said. "Some days we're on the edge of not making it."

Tetlin's leading capitalist had brought his pickup truck to the bridge. After years of running the village store, Donald Joe had moved to Tok and bought a trading post. Don's Store and the trailer he lived in behind the store were the main gathering places for Tetlin villagers when they went to town. The Indian souvenir business helped make the store a success and now Donald Joe was helping get the village corporation on its feet. He was a quiet, diligent man who seemed, when I had the chance to talk with him, a bit grim about the burdens placed on him by the rest of Tetlin. One responsibility he relished was sponsorship of the village softball team.

Chief Titus and several elders got in an old green sedan parked by the bridge. Everyone else climbed over the tailgate of Don's pickup truck. We sat quietly while the truck fizzed down the long rainy straightaway to town.

With its backstop and bleachers, the ball field behind the Tok Lodge could have been a municipal park anywhere in America. Fans were scattered in the stands, Indians on one side, whites on the other. The sun had reappeared and the Tetlin Eagles, having changed into their yellow-and-black bumblebee uniforms at Don's Store, were looking sharp.

Donald Joe found a place on the bench and settled his manager's scorebook in his lap. The Boundary Bandits took the field. Leading off the game for Tetlin was a young man who had his ball cap tied to his head with a bandanna and long black hair flowing out beneath. He held his bat cross handed, a technique his teammates said seemed to improve his control. The underhand pitch rocketed toward the plate, and the lead-off batter stroked a single into left.

I sat in the stands with Bill Hanley, the only non-Native in a Tetlin uniform. A sandy-haired, long-legged first baseman, Bill worked with Donald Joe as a business consultant for the village. He said Don's attention to the kids was widely credited with turning the team around—that, and the development of Don's young cousin Ronnie into the fastest pitcher in the league.

"The baseball team is the most successful thing they've got going," he said. "We want to use the team as an example for other things—to work hard, overcome shyness, stand firm, not to fight each other. All those things."

Bill was friendly and eager to share what he'd been learning of Indian ways. Flattering me by assuming we shared a concern for the best interests of the village, over the next few innings he gave me a new picture of Tetlin politics. Chief Titus was looked up to in the village, accorded the respect of an elder; his duty was to tradition. Lately he'd concerned himself with alcohol: the baggage searches at the airstrip were his idea. He held the elective position of village council president, but Titus wasn't a chief in quite the same way his ancestors had been. Power was now dispersed.

If anyone these days could assert his authority through the kind of potlatch display the village knew in the past, it would be Donald Joe. In many respects Don was the real leader, and Danny Adams was his acolyte. Together with Hanley, they were working to make money for the corporation, because if it failed, they might lose the reserve to banks.

Tetlin had Native rights activists with a defiant attitude toward state authority, who thought it had been a mistake to transfer the reserve to the corporation in the first place. Ironically, Bill Hanley said, the radicals had been pushed off the village council shortly before the trooper raid. It was unfortunate that no Kremlinologists in Tok cared enough to track the shifts in power on the reserve.

"When my message has been we've got to meet the world, and then the world comes in and slaps your face it's really maddening. It made Donald Joe look bad. It made me look bad."

The new council members had turned, as usual, to Donald Joe for help after their election. They wanted him to be council president, but the storekeeper didn't want to leave Tok. I gathered, then, they had settled on old Titus David as a figurehead.

On the playing field, the Eagles had followed the lead-off single with three runs in the first inning, but it wasn't enough. Blooping singles by Boundary and sloppy fielding by Tetlin's second-string starters helped the Bandits pull ahead.

I paced behind the Indian cheering section, watching the score mount. "Too many chiefs on our side," a middle-aged Tetlin fan said.

An argument was raging over whether to put in the players who'd been benched. From what I could hear, Bill Hanley was for sticking to the game plan. Danny's goals were more short-term: forget the disciplinary lessons; they were losing the game. Donald Joe leaned toward his consultant's view.

Up in the stands, Chief Titus remained above the fray, a ball cap on his figurehead. He grinned and waved me up.

"You going to pull this one out?" I asked.

"Don't say if you're going to win," the chief said. "Old people always say that, say you shouldn't brag. Maybe we win today, though. I sure hope so."

Boasting brought bad luck to the traditional Tanana Indians. It was *endji,* taboo. *Endji* was the work of dark powers. I wondered if any of the shaman spells for hunting success could be prescribed for late-inning rallies.

I asked Chief Titus if he ever played baseball. He said they used to play their own ball game in Tetlin when he was young: Indian ball. They used a moosehide ball filled with dirt and decorated with ribbons and beads. Men and women played together on teams, trying to keep the ball up in the air, batting it with snowshoes as they scrambled through deep snow. They used to keep the game going a long while if they didn't tire from laughing too much.

Nobody was laughing on the baseball field. Despite Ronnie Joe's mean rising fastball, Tetlin had fallen behind 14 to 9 by the sixth inning and the Eagles finally made some substitutions. John Joe, another cousin of Donald's, tagged a bases-loaded triple into the left field corner and Tetlin pulled to within one run. An infield single and a walk loaded the bases again, with Bill Hanley at the plate. The first baseman popped out. Boundary held on to win, 16 to 15.

Danny stormed off the field and gave the backstop such a ringing kick with his steel-shanked hiking boot that the bleachers shuddered.

"I like to win. I don't know about you guys," he bellowed at his teammates.

"I think we had too many coaches," Bill said. He scurried off to corral a couple of discouraged outfielders migrating in the direction of the Tok Lodge bar.

Donald Joe leaned against the hood of a car in the parking lot, studying his scorebook. "We should have pulled those kids out earlier," he said.

A green sedan drove up. Leaning out the passenger window, Chief Titus looked up at Donald Joe. The chief was still wearing his ball cap, still smiling his snaggletooth grin.

"Too much air, hit up in air," he said. "Got to hit ground balls."

6. Animal Powers

A t the end of summer, I flew to southwest Alaska with two friends for a camping trip. We landed at the mouth of the Nushagak River, at Dillingham, the principal fishing town in Bristol Bay. In a few weeks of twenty-four-hour fishing every July, one-third of the world's salmon catch is landed by small fishing boats in Bristol Bay. By the end of August, however, the spawning run had ascended to lakes in the tundra uplands and Dillingham had quieted. The people of the region, especially the Yup'ik Eskimos in villages up the Nushagak, had turned from the commercial harvest to subsistence hunting and fishing.

We took a floatplane to a chain of wild mountain lakes above a tributary of the Nushagak, where we camped on mossy granite ledges and paddled about in fold-together, snap-tight wood-and-canvas kayaks. Though I planned to stay on and visit the villages downriver to see what I could of the subsistence season, these were a few days given to myself. Time alone at the tranquil center, at the source of the harvest.

One evening we glided between craggy peaks down a fjord of polished black marble. The alders on shore were bent and grabby like the evil roots in fairy tales. My previous kayak trips had been on the

Alaska seacoast, and it felt strange to have a tidy foot of gravel beach here and not a raked-over twenty feet of bare intertidal rock. There were fish in the clear shallows, schools of spawning sockeye salmon turned a blazing orange. The salmon were the color of carp, and as we passed above them, unheeded, I had the illusion that we had been shrunk and set to paddling in a Japanese garden pool. The hand of the gardener was concealed in the setting's perfect naturalism. A light rain began to fall, and the lake became a plaza of round tiles. All we could hear was the creaking of our boats, the dip of paddles, and waterfalls above making a sound like the wind.

That night a porcupine urinated in my kayak. It was a useful reminder that while the traditional relationship of Native Americans to the animal powers was one based on respect and reciprocity, my own tended to veer between extremes of the sublime and the slapstick.

I'd left my boat tipped upside down. The rubberized canvas was too heavy to be pierced by a quill, but the intruder gnawed through a wooden rib, tasting the salt of past ocean trips. Alerted by a sound of steady scraping, the three of us tumbled to the beach in rubber boots and long johns, shouting and waving flashlights. Finally we lifted one end of the kayak and rolled the porcupine onto the sand, where it bristled and waddled away, leaving splinters, quills, and a faint smell of the urine we'd scared out of it.

A few days later my friends flew home to Anchorage and I took the mail plane from Dillingham back up the Nushagak River. The long autumn rains had begun. Clouds tumbled low to the tundra so my plane stayed just above the twisting river. We passed the village of Portage Creek and the Nushagak grew narrower, the bluffs on either side higher. We rounded a bend and two floatplanes were flying at us. One passed between our right wingtip and the bluff, the other to our left. The pilot cursed. He said they were pilots from fishing lodges, too green to know they should keep to the right when flying in a tunnel.

The Nushagak is unusual among Alaska's rivers: short, clear, and powerful. Its route down through bands of forest from the bare high country is only some two hundred forty miles; more than one hundred rivers in North America are longer. But in the volume of water it carries, the Nushagak ranks twentieth.

At Ekwok, second of the four villages on the river, I spent a night with a man responsible for keeping an eye on the Nushagak's extraordinary flow. Paul Romie measured the water level for the state twice a day, "to a gnat's eyebrow." He was a skinny man with a beard of white bristles who described himself as a Johnny-come-lately, having arrived in the Nushagak country only in 1929 as an eighteen-year-old stowaway on a cannery boat. The varnished wood walls of his cabin were hung with calendars dating back to 1978, open to various months, the days crossed off with occasional notes on the weather. He proudly showed me a school district calendar of local elders, mostly Natives except him. Each write-up contained a favorite quote; his was, "If whiskey gets in the way of your business, give up the whiskey."

"The teacher must have missed part of what I said," Romie said. "Actually the saying was 'give up the whiskey or give up the business.' "

Romie started pouring coffee and we sat up past two on kitchen stools as he recited ribald miners' verses and talked about the Red Spot of Jupiter, Solzhenitsyn's gulag, and the historical basis for the biblical flood.

"Did you hear the story about the prospector who went up to Heaven?" he asked. "St. Peter tells him, 'Sorry, there's no room. You'll have to wait for a vacancy.' He sees the other guys are all lounging around in their bunks inside, taking it easy. So the old prospector yells out, 'There's a strike in Hell!' Everybody takes off, just like that. St. Peter shakes his head and tells him, 'Well, I guess you can come in now.' So he goes in but after a while he kind of misses the other guys and says, 'By golly, there might be something to that,' and he grabs his pack and takes off too!"

Romie had trapped for years around the lakes where I'd been kayaking, then married a Yup'ik woman and settled in Ekwok. He'd fished Bristol Bay in the days when the commercial boats still used sails, and was postmaster in the village for twenty years.

"If you stay up here two years, you can't go back. You're gone," he said.

He took his high-school equivalency exam at age fifty-nine and was taking college correspondence courses now, including one on Bristol Bay history, in which he was able to answer exam questions in the first person. He was glad he had never lived in a place where he needed a steady income to make payments—"Someplace where it's pump or sink," he said, in the language of Bristol Bay fishermen—but he regretted he hadn't pursued an education earlier. "If I'd kept at it I could have been a doctor or a shyster, heh? I'd probably been dead by now, too much prosperity."

I finally fell asleep on a cot covered in a bearskin. In the morning Paul Romie took me to see the river gauge. The shed in his yard was full of old tools and Indian-made snowshoes—"forty years of gathering"—and an old wooden skiff was surrounded by willows that had grown up since the boat was overturned and left there. The day started calm and gray, with a mist across the quiet water. The river was running high from all the rain, which resumed by the time I took off.

The watershed of the Nushagak is the size of southern New England. The river runs clear because, unlike most of the big rivers in Alaska, its sources are in lakes rather than glaciers. The country is rich in game animals as well as salmon, and trappers have worked its tributaries for more than a century. The first whites on the river, in 1829, were looking for furs—Russian scouts, they no doubt recognized Siberian taiga and tundra in such a landscape. The Russians had a fort at the mouth of the Nushagak, among the coastal Yup'ik, and as they ascended the river they met the "inland people," the Kiatagmiut, whose seasonal camps once ranged as far into the mountains as the state park where I'd been kayaking. Russian Orthodox missionaries convinced the Kiatagmiut to throw their ceremonial masks into the river, and they built churches that survived the transfer of power to the United States. But the inland people continued to live off the land.

In New Stuyahok, the largest of the four villages on the Nushagak today, with a population of three hundred, Russian Orthodox elders were holding a church feast when I arrived. The riverbank was crowded with aluminum skiffs from other villages but deserted in the pouring rain—everyone was in the steamy school cafeteria. An archpriest from the Kuskokwim River, delivering the annual message from the Kodiak bishop, inveighed against smutty videotapes in rollicking guttural Yup'ik from which an occasional phrase of English—"X-rated," "parents' guidance"—tumbled like a coin of a different currency. Meanwhile the elders sat at lunchroom tables built for their grandchildren, eating moose and caribou and salted salmon heads.

I took a place in line and filled my plate eagerly. The Eskimo food seemed a kind of extracurricular communion, and I skipped the anomalous string bean and chicken casseroles. I paused, however, at a tray of "stinky head": salmon heads buried in the ground until they mold into a ripe Yup'ik blue cheese. My hesitation drew a smile from an elderly woman, who dragged a ladle through thick gravy and pulled up stringy chunks of porcupine meat. The porcupine was not bad, though it still wanted salt.

Subsistence hunting and fishing have been called the hidden economy of the Alaska bush. Forty million pounds of food are harvested every year, according to Department of Fish and Game estimates. A survey in the 1980s found harvests of wild foods ranged from ten pounds per person in Anchorage to four hundred pounds in Tetlin and nine hundred in New Stuyahok, to more than one thousand pounds in several Brooks Range villages. None of it shows up on any economic balance sheet.

Not much about the subsistence harvest seemed hidden during that week along the Nushagak. In Koliganek, split salmon were draped like laundry from drying racks. A fresh run of silvers was hitting subsistence nets in the eddies. An elderly couple was unloading fish when I was dropped off by boat from New Stuyahok, and kids worked the shore with rod and reel, adding to the cache for winter. Entering more than one kitchen, I had to step over the carcass of a moose. Men rolled fuel drums to their houses with eyes cast outward: they were watching a clutch of caribou across the river, wondering if a boat could get close enough to make a hunt worthwhile.

Rain swept down day after day. It was the season of early darkness, of discovering flashlight batteries are dead. The first coins of gold appeared on poplars by the river. Old women with buckets toddled into the dripping woods, where they could slap huckleberries off shrubs like bears. In every house I was offered heaping purple mounds of *akutaq*, the traditional "Eskimo ice cream," a confection of berries and sugar and, as a modern replacement for seal oil or caribou fat, Crisco shortening.

Salmonberries, like plump red and orange clusters of fish eggs, were in short local supply that fall. A band of women had chartered an airplane to fly to the Kuskokwim where they had relatives, timing the visit by the ripeness of salmonberries over there.

"You can catch fish through the ice all winter, and you can poach a moose if you have to," a Koliganek resident said one night in a steambath. "But you only get one shot with the berries."

Every night, in every village, there was a steambath. In a country where many houses still have no running water, the *maqi* (mock-HEY), as modified by the Russians, is the traditional way of getting clean, but it is more than that. Steam time is the evening social hour, especially now that satellite television has curtailed the custom of neighborly visiting. In Yup'ik country, men steam first, then women. The *maqi* is a chance to slow down and put the world in perspective. It is a beer with the boys, a gossip session. It is a rite of initiation.

They really cooked you good in Charlie Nelson's *maqi*, took your untested city flesh and steamed it mottled red, poured water on the sizzling rocks until you jumped to your feet and burst out the door.

"One good one," Charlie Nelson said, picking up a long wooden handle with a tin can crimped on the end. He was my host in Koliganek. Until that moment he had seemed a kindly old gentleman.

Charlie Nelson had been born seventy-six years earlier on the shore of Bristol Bay. His mother was Yup'ik, his father a Swedish fisherman who packed him off to a Methodist foster home in the Aleutians. Charlie returned to the Nushagak country in his late teens and though he started as a trapper, he became a schoolteacher by virtue of being the only high-school graduate on the river. Now he was a respected elder, a taciturn, white-haired businessman who looked after the village store and the Koliganek Native corporation, and whose approval was sought before any village undertaking. He held court every evening in the plywood shack behind his house. Charlie could think of only two nights all year when he had failed to take a *maqi*.

There was no talk at first. The barrel stove roared, sucked air, boomed like a drum. Steam exploded off the rocks, crowded the corners, and crawled down the walls. On a low bench beside the stove, four men pressed wet washcloths to their faces and bowed their heads like monks. Breath came in short gasps.

"*Ak-qa*," one said. It hurts.

"Feels like a woman kissing your back," hissed another.

The room was low and dark, blackened by years of woodsmoke, the only light coming through a small window. The barrel stove was set low on gravel and covered with rocks. Beneath a bench were aluminum wash pans, each containing a dole of water. Cool water in a plastic bucket waited outside the door. More water hit the rocks. I fled.

A few moments later the others joined me in the outer room. This was the rhythm of the *maqi*: here the atmosphere was as relaxed as the inner room was tense. By the light of a single bulb, we faced one another on benches, leaning against the plywood walls with scraps of carpet underfoot. A heavyset man tucked his washcloth under a roll of stomach to shield his private parts. Cans of cold beer were handed around. One of Charlie Nelson's grandsons opened the door and planted himself where a wreath of steam off his shoulders caught light from the setting sun.

In the *maqi* that evening, talk was of hunting, the summer's fishing, women.

They told of someone from Koliganek who'd introduced steam baths to a tundra village on the Yukon delta, where they were now addicted to nightly steams, though they had to scavenge driftwood for their stoves. Somebody told a story from breakup the previous spring. Villagers who lined the bluff at Koliganek to watch ice move out of the Nushagak spotted a small tree of dead, dry wood coming downstream on a floe. A young man ran to the river's edge, hopped on one floating block of ice, hopped on a second, and in this fashion reached the tree. He dragged and rolled and tossed the tree back from floe to floe. One slip and he would have been lost beneath the ice. But he made it to shore, and when he did he looked up toward his audience with a subsistence hunter's pride and shouted, "*Maqi* wood."

We climbed back through the door for one last steam and then the men dispersed. Charlie Nelson threw a few more logs into the stove and shuffled up to the house with his towel over his arm. His grandson and I were digging into fresh-baked white bread and homemade blueberry jam. Charlie went to the corner of the living room, where a CB radio hissed and crackled all day (village homes had no phones) and spoke into the mike; a woman's voice replied.

"Steam time, you women," he said.

Later in Koliganek I met a latter-day Paul Romie prowling the area between the village store and the Koliganek school.

"You didn't see a big brown dog, did you?" the tall white man asked me. "A Chesapeake, kind of shaggy?"

I didn't think so.

"He would have been dragging a walrus head."

Definitely not.

Don Winkelman pulled out his pipe and shrugged.

"Pulled it right off my porch. I'd sure hate to lose that head."

He invited me into his house by the school. Winkelman seemed a Jimmy Stewart character landed in the bush, an abashed, gangly, pixilated man in his forties. He was new to the Nushagak River, but he had lived in Bristol Bay on the coast for five years. He and his wife moved north from Tacoma after she got a job teaching in the village of Togiak; now she was the Koliganek principal. Winkelman loved the bush and admired the Eskimos. He'd grown up in Wisconsin, running a trapline along dirt farm roads, and in Togiak he'd taken to trapping otter and mink—the local trappers were only taking beaver, he said, so he got their tacit permission. Now he was scouting traplines on the upper Nushagak for the coming winter, asking about spoken-for territories as any careful newcomer should. The country there was rich in wolverine, fox, and beaver, but hard to work: it snowed every day, so you had to go over your route constantly to unbury and reset your traps.

In summer, Winkelman said, he planned to return to the coast. He had a business in Togiak, ferrying visitors out to an island in Bristol Bay, a state game sanctuary for walrus.

Knowing that non-Natives weren't allowed to hunt walrus or buy raw ivory, I asked about the walrus head.

He said he'd spotted a dead walrus on the beach of an island while returning from the sanctuary.

"Whew. When they've been dead awhile, that first cut really takes your breath away," he said. "You have to find the vertebrae to get the head off. Chopping the neck with an ax is like trying to chop a tire. It bounces right off."

A disarming tone of wonder came into his voice as he spoke of the sanctuary on Round Island. "They've had ten thousand walrus hauled out on the beach at one time," he said. "You have to camp on the island, and sometimes when I take people out I stay and camp myself. It gets so noisy you can hardly sleep. There are more than a million nesting pairs of seabirds on the cliffs. The island is just alive. You should come out next summer. You realize what amazing country this is."

Once the amazing country had been Eskimo country—as Tetlin had been Indian country, as Yup'ik and Athabaskan peoples, in the eyes of Congress, had once been sovereign, indigenous, "real" people. But not even Yup'ik hunters are allowed to hunt for walrus on Round Island. Given the changes brought to Bristol Bay by commercial fishing and a growing population, by increased Eskimo hunting, and now by the prospect of offshore oil development in the area, the State of Alaska wanted an island where walrus could haul out and rest undisturbed. The sanctuary was a small island of a western conservation ethic circumscribed by subsistence hunting country. I wondered how the local Yup'ik people felt about it.

"Togiak is a pretty militant village, isn't it?"

"There were a lot of misconceptions in Togiak about the island," Winkelman said. He paused to light his pipe.

"They know the place well. They call it Walrus Island. They like to hunt walrus off the beach there. At first they thought white people were going out there to shoot walrus, when *they* weren't allowed to. That didn't make sense. I couldn't figure out how you could go out and shoot walrus in a sanctuary. Fish and Game finally came over and explained it. Even then, not everyone believed them. Some of the older people, their way of life is to make use of everything. They have a hard time figuring that anyone would go out there just to take pictures."

It is not an easy island to get to, for either photographers or hunters. There is no safe harbor. Round Island is so far offshore that most days the water is too rough for floatplanes. Fish and Game had wanted somebody in Togiak to offer boat service for tourists, but the village people kept saying it was too rough out there for the fishing boats of Togiak Bay. So Winkelman, who already had the teasing nickname Great White Hunter, bought one of the fishing boats, reinforced the bottom for the bigger waves, and got a new nickname, Walrus Man.

Still, there were misunderstandings.

"I have some good friends in the village," the Walrus Man said. "But after a while it seemed like a better idea to move across the bay and run my trips out of the cannery."

Drifting gray clouds pressed low to the tundra on the day I flew out to Togiak Bay the following spring. Some fifty miles west of Dillingham we squeezed through a low mountain pass that was an airplane graveyard. Pilots navigated by landmarks like "the Otter wings." My pilot was fighting a stiff wind, but dipped and swooped to improve my view of one such signpost, which looked like the ashes of someone's campfire on the tundra. The pilot said that was how the wreck looked when searchers found it. Dust to dust.

The small plane descended from the pass to a black-sand airstrip on the shore of the bay. On the opposite shore, the houses of Togiak village were like boulders along the beach. Big sky, big wind country. I pulled out my gear and started through the rain toward the cannery, which was humming with industrial life in the storm.

The Walrus Man's summer home was a small silver trailer staked out amid the cannery dormitories. Ropes stretched over either end of the trailer and knotted to airplane tie-downs held down the trailer during big blows. Inside, the atmosphere was steamy. Several other travelers waiting to go to Round Island were crowded around a table: three schoolteachers from Dillingham and a doctor from Fairbanks. I hung my rain gear on the porch and squeezed in at the table. Our Fish and Game permits for the island were valid immediately, but it was up to the Walrus Man to tell us when the weather would permit a trip.

Don Winkelman sat beneath a dripping window, brown pipe in his teeth and a tide book jutting from the pocket of his blue wool shirt. He was telling the others about getting caught in a storm like this.

It was flat calm the day he dropped a party off at Round Island and started home—"more like swamp water than Bristol Bay water." Forty-five minutes out, a biologist on the island called on the VHF radio. She'd just heard a weather report: a cold front was coming in fast. She was too late. In no time he was surrounded by twelve-foot waves. For ten hours he rode like a surfer in a curl of green water. Above the cabin of his little boat, wave tops were shearing off in 55-knot gusts. There are several other islands near Round Island, but they were all "shaped like footballs" and offered no place to hide.

"If you climb on top of one of those waves, suddenly there ain't nothing under you for ten feet. The floorboards fly up at your feet when you hit. Three or four of those and there'd be nothing but pieces of plywood floating around. A little wooden boat like that won't take much."

The trailer shuddered in a blast of wind.

He had tacked back and forth in the troughs, following his compass and never glimpsing land, though he knew he was close.

"Finally I noticed the water getting choppy, more like washing machine water. So I rode up on top of a wave, and there I was coming around the point into the bay here."

We looked at one another as he sucked on his pipe. Any impatience we'd felt was gone.

I told about meeting Winkelman in Koliganek and his search for a walrus head. Somewhere near the trailer, Winkelman said, he had another walrus head buried in the sand. Bacteria and sand fleas were scouring off the meat as we sat there. Soon the skull would be clean and white, with ivory tusks the size of forearms thrusting from deep sockets.

He led us out in the rain to see his boat, which was tied up by the cannery dock. It was a Togiak bowpicker, a twenty-seven-foot plywood boat with the fishing gear removed, but where most Togiak boats were painted a dull gray, Winkelman's boat was brown with red trim and a white wheelhouse. He'd named the boat the *Puffin*, and on the side of the cabin he'd painted the squat eponymous seabird with its clownish orange beak.

"At first I thought, 'Puffin, that's a sissy name, I ain't going to name my boat the *Puffin*.' But the older ladies in the village, they all liked it. They talked me into it.

"Those ladies used to be real shy around me—a lot of the older ones don't speak any English—but I got to teasing them a little, and now they act more like little girls than older ladies. One day when it was real calm, I took some of them out to the island. The only walrus they'd ever seen were dead ones brought back by the hunters. They had a real good time. It was good for the sanctuary, too, having them come back and talk about the island. You know, when people in Togiak hear an elder talking, that's just like hearing words out of the Bible."

I remembered a story I'd been told by a Yup'ik woman from the Kuskokwim River. The first time she saw a seal, she said, was behind glass in a California aquarium. She had grown up eating seal meat and seal oil, but hunting seals had always been men's work in her village. What she remembered about the seal was the look in its eye. The life within. Gee, she had told me, they must really have felt guilty for killing that seal. The traditional Yup'ik way was to show respect for the animal by using all parts of the seal except the bladder, where the seal's spirit resided. The Yup'ik called the spirit *yua*, like the Inupiat *inua*. At the time of the annual bladder festival, following a week of singing, dancing, and feasting, hunters returned the bladders of seals through the ice, releasing the *yua* to return again as a new seal. With such an act of reciprocity they washed the blood from their hands.

To pass the time, Winkelman took us on a tour of Togiak Fisheries. It was not the sort of wilderness experience any of us had come for: a dry-docked barge, a freezing plant on a dock, fuel tanks, power lines, forklifts, a scrap yard of rusting assembly-line equipment cast off during the recent conversion from cannery to freezer plant. The local herring season was already over, the big herring fleet had come and gone, and workers were busy getting ready for the Bristol Bay salmon season. There were segregated dormitories for older Eskimo ladies, roe technicians from Japan, and the college students who made up the bulk of the workforce. A sign by the door of one dorm said "Animal House."

With an awe in the face of nature's wonders that we were beginning to see as characteristic, Winkelman swung open the heavy steel door of a blast freezer.

"It's equal to being out in seventy-below weather with a forty-knot wind," he said. "A human being would last three minutes."

In the evening the rain let up and we walked down the beach to investigate a rumor of a dead gray whale. The tide was out, baring a half mile of slick, sucking mudflats. Behind the dunes, wild marshes were littered with pop cans and plastic trash dumped overboard by herring boats.

The whale was piled on the beach, twenty feet long, fresher and more intact than the gray I'd camped near at Wales. Heaved up by the storm to feed the bears and sea gulls, the whale had drawn other scavengers as well. We saw strips of exposed black meat where they'd peeled away blubber, and the knobby tracks in the sand of their three-wheelers.

A small plane pitched down on the runway the next day. Ken Taylor, a state wildlife biologist who had stayed at the cannery overnight, went out to talk to the pilot and recognized the single passenger, a young Native activist from Togiak named David Nanalook. The two were old foes. David Nanalook refused to acknowledge the state's authority over the walrus sanctuary. A few years earlier Taylor had faced down Nanalook on the beach of Round Island when the young Eskimo came out in a skiff to "claim his birthright." After some tense words, Nanalook had climbed in his skiff and left.

"Hi there, Ken," Nanalook called from inside the plane, all smiles now. "Got any walrus out there for me?"

"Lots of walrus, but none for you," Taylor said.

The storm held over Bristol Bay. The rain had let up, planes were flying, but the seas were still too rough for the *Puffin*. The air taxi flew David Nanalook off to Dillingham, and when it returned I caught a ride across the bay to the village of the walrus hunters.

Togiak, population six hundred, was the biggest village I'd seen. A tidal slough snaked behind the houses, creating at high tide an island tethered to the mainland by a footbridge wide enough for three-wheelers, which turned out to be a handicapped ramp from the city hall, installed according to federal regulations and then put to use elsewhere. From the air I saw that the tundra was littered with rusting oil drums scattered when fall storms pushed water across the dunes.

The runway funneled into a gravel street through the heart of town.

There was an old cannery, several stores attached to homes, and a small snack bar, the Green House, painted red, white, and blue inside. A Madonna poster hung on the wall, and two teenagers *ping*ed at video games in a side room. I ordered an expensive cheeseburger and a vanilla milkshake made of soft ice cream. They were out of chocolate. The snack bar had been started by the village corporation as a local diversion; before, the cook said, kids had worn a rut in the gravel two feet deep walking in bored circles around the school.

Past the school, a construction project with a bulldozer and backhoe was underway. The beach was being shored up with a wooden wall. The state was building a girdling seawall, based on a design from the Netherlands, to keep out the storm waves. The design called for imported ironwood, scraps of which, I later learned, had become prized for long hot *maqi* fires.

I looked off across the choppy bay, remembering that small settlements used to be scattered all around this country and up the broad valley of willows to the north. The Togiak River came down from summits with such names as Pistuk Peak and Nuklunek Mountain. Nearly every feature on the map here had a Yup'ik name—except the four Walrus Islands: Summit, High, Crooked, and Round.

The small settlements around Togiak Bay were mostly gone now. Commercial fishing had made Togiak the principal surviving Yup'ik village in the region, and the ironwood was going to make it more or less permanent. But commercial fishing had also brought an unusual number of outsiders to the area, and that was one theory used to explain why Togiak had developed an unfortunate reputation as a village where non-Natives did not get a friendly welcome.

Unlike Tetlin, Togiak was a place where conflicts over subsistence hunting and fishing rights sometimes went beyond surreptitious moose kills to acts of outright civil disobedience. I'd heard of one Togiak duck hunter arrested for turning his shotgun on a patrol plane. Several months before I arrived hunters on snowmachines had apparently cleaned out a small caribou herd that was expanding its range into the mountains to the north. At the urging of state biologists, other Yup'ik villages had been leaving the animals alone in hopes of building a local herd. News media coverage of the caribou killings reinforced the reputation of Togiak hunters as the bad boys of Native subsistence.

In Alaska's political climate, such incidents seemed a dangerous provocation. Subsistence rights for rural people were controversial enough already. Some urban residents felt preferential rights should be granted, if at all, only to Native hunters who agreed to revert to bows and arrows and fishing nets of sinew or shredded spruce root. The courts and legislators were trying to develop narrower and more manageable definitions of what "subsistence" means, while rural Native communities defended it as a practice tied to every aspect of their cultures' traditions. Subsistence advocates argued that even if some of the forms had changed, reliance on the bounty of the land was still integral, economically and socially, to village life. Anthropologists tended to support this idea, noting in particular that adaptability is more deeply characteristic of Eskimo societies than is any particular technology.

Some Natives went further, arguing that indigenous people have a right to the resources of their homeland, whether it is Native corporation land or not—a premise that in Togiak, as in Tetlin, had yet to be settled by Congress and the courts. What was plain in Togiak was that government policies and changes in the regional economy were putting more pressure every year on local subsistence.

It was not that the population had grown. Seven villages were counted on the Togiak River when the area was visited in 1880 by Edward W. Nelson, an ornithologist dispatched to Alaska by the Army Signal Service to collect weather observations (and who produced some of the most important early volumes on the natural history and Native people of Alaska). Togiak Bay's fish and game supported several thousand people, by Nelson's count. In addition, most families had large dog teams that required fish. Traditional harvest methods such as caribou fences and fish traps were more efficient than modern snowmachines and bullets. Today fewer than half as many people live in the Togiak River country. But Native subsistence was being cut back.

Villagers had watched the spring herring runs, which they used to catch for food, disappear in the seine nets of million-dollar commercial boats. Efforts by the state to preserve a small share of the commercial catch for local boats had not dispelled the impression in Togiak that the big fleet came for a few weeks, took the resource, and left the beaches covered in plastic trash.

Even more rankling, oddly enough, were the sport-fishing tourists. At least the commercial fishing boats worked from motives the Yup'ik had come to understand. Every year more sport fishermen came on floatplanes with guides to fish the Togiak River for trophy-size rainbow trout and salmon. As most of the river ran through the Togiak National Wildlife Refuge, created in 1980, villagers had little control over its use. Many of the sportsmen considered themselves good conservationists because they practiced hook-and-release fishing. Some even used barbless hooks. These fishermen, who sometimes felt the local hostility, would undoubtedly be confused to learn that hook-and-release fishing was offensive to Yup'ik tradition, which held that it was disrespectful to play with animals and catch what you didn't want to eat.

Another source of friction was walrus. Though less important to Bristol Bay Yup'ik than to the northwestern Inupiat around Wales or the Siberian Yup'ik of St. Lawrence Island, the walrus had been a traditional part of the diet of Togiak, particularly important as dogfood in the days of sled dog transportation. When the federal government, under the Marine Mammal Protection Act, tried to turn management of walrus over to the State of Alaska, it was the village of Togiak that successfully sued to preserve the Native hunting preference in the law. Critics claimed that in Togiak, and in other walrus-hunting villages, the disrespect to animals that Natives found so bothersome in hook-and-release fishing did not prevent headhunting for ivory by at least a few villagers. White hunters opposed to subsistence preference rights could find common cause here with animal protectionists who argued that walrus hunting was no longer subsistence, that Native handicrafts made for tourists are not sufficiently "traditional" to justify hunting walrus for ivory alone.

It was a terribly difficult and sensitive issue. For the government to take away Native hunting rights by fiat would be a bellicose act by an outside power, unenforceable in the bush and utterly destructive of efforts within the Native community to adapt to the changing world and police itself through guidance of elders and organizations like the Alaska Eskimo Walrus Commission. On the other hand, the introduction of a cash market drew Natives inevitably into a world of regulation and laws against wanton waste—laws that were occasionally used to convict Eskimos caught wasting meat, in violation of their own canons. Those who watched over walrus populations today, Native or white, had to be conversant in matters of sustainable yield and the scientific management of resources: given the pressures on animal populations apart from Native hunting, the observation of old taboos alone might not be enough to ensure that the spirit of the walrus continued to return. The modern world was shrinking, and even indigenous populations were being forced to think globally.

In Bristol Bay, on Round Island, an uneasy truce prevailed.

The chief of the Togiak elders' council was at home in his one-story plywood house, sitting in a stuffed chair watching television. He looked up at me solemnly, stone-faced as an ancient Mayan god, and spoke in Yup'ik to his wife, who called someone on the telephone. I waited quietly, watching the movie on television, in which a handsome English-speaking Indian brave was kidnapping a damsel in a white petticoat. After a few moments a woman in an apron came through the back door of the house.

"I was vacuuming my house. Sorry," she said.

I repeated my introduction to the chief's daughter, who translated for him.

"He says he's busy right now," she told me. "He says to write down your questions and they'll talk about them at the next elders' meeting."

I wrote some questions on a pad I carried. What do you think about the Round Island sanctuary? How does commercial hunting alter the relationship between hunter and prey? Is headhunting for ivory acceptable to the elders? Spelled out so bluntly, the questions seemed impertinent, even to me. I was not surprised that in the weeks to come I never heard a word.

Given the reticence of its traditional leaders, Togiak owed its reputation to young firebrands like David Nanalook, whom I'd seen that morning at the cannery airstrip. I'd met him before, at political gatherings in Anchorage: a clever speaker, usually good for an inflammatory quote. He called the land claims act genocide, and he could cite arcane United Nations resolutions to prove that the State of Alaska is a figment of the white man's imagination. There were others like him, a new generation of Native radicals with an intriguing critique of Native capitalism. But as a journalist in Anchorage I had been reluctant to portray them as leaders, uncertain whether they had any genuine following in the bush.

Now that I was in Togiak I went to see David Nanalook's sixty-year-old father. Though less fluent in English, he turned out to be just as adamant on the subject of Native hunting rights. Dan Nanalook led me to a bucket of bloody brine outside his house and, with each hand around a tusk, hoisted out a dripping walrus head. Short, strong, and narrow-eyed, he thrust out his chin and insisted that I get a picture of him there beside the head.

"We have rules and regulations for how to hunt," the elder Nanalook said. "We kept hunting until there's no hunting anymore at walrus islands. Their own people, the herring boats, they're the ones chasing the walrus, disturbing it. I know it—I'm telling you—the Fish and Game doesn't. First they said the population is declining. Now they say it's overpopulated."

He walked back to the outboard motor he'd been working on, but kept talking. "We know our rules, but our laws somebody is attacking."

Once when he found fly-fishermen casting into a pool on the river

where he liked to fish, he set his gill net across from them and filled it up
with rainbow trout. He laughed at the hook-and-release fishermen with
their #2 wooly worms and black maribou flies dangling helplessly.

In the presence of the village chief I'd cringed at my own forward-
ness, but now I felt I was being goaded. What about the caribou in the
Kilbuck Mountains last winter? I asked.

"It hurts me that sports hunters just take horns," he said. "That's
why I told the Native people to keep hunting no matter what the
seasons are, to keep populations low."

"You mean you'd kill the animals to keep outsiders from coming to
hunt and fish?"

"I guess you got it, man."

He turned his back and resumed working on the outboard.

Over the next two days it came to seem that the antic cynicism of
the Nanalooks was out of proportion to feelings in the rest of the
village. In fact, I was told young David Nanalook had got himself into
trouble locally and lost his job translating for Yup'ik elders at public
hearings. His command of English and familiarity with legal precedents
made him useful, but his translations had tended to swerve off course
and become orations for Native sovereignty.

Still, the cause of sovereignty—the claim that Yup'ik people held
political power over Eskimo country, however that might be defined—
was gaining adherents in Togiak. People were frustrated. The village's
young mayor, Moses Kritz, said the elders were particularly concerned
about how cynical young people were becoming. It had reached the
point, he said, where some young hunters respected neither the laws of
the state nor the laws of the elders, and hunted for tusks they could
trade for joints or a bottle of whiskey.

I would have liked to ask Moses Kritz more, but he spoke from the
doorway to his home, holding me at bay. He said he had to get ready for
fishing season. Others were busy, too—especially when I started
asking about fish and game management.

The mayor let me put my sleeping bag in a city office. But as it was, the village chief's stony stare became the emblem of two days spent in Togiak: a souvenir mask from Eskimo country.

Not having brought along a fishing rod, I decided to hunt up some nonsubsistence food for dinner that night and stopped by Nick's Yup'ik Store, one of the private businesses. I knocked on the door of a small house to gain admittance to the adjacent store. The shelves were dusty and half empty, but I managed to find a pack of cookies. Moses Nick stood behind the counter, an Eskimo in his late fifties with a shock of long gray hair off his forehead. When I mentioned the name of a friend of mine in Dillingham who did his taxes each spring, he invited me into his house.

I sat by a window in the kitchen and he offered me tea and half-dried salmon and hard-boiled eggs. The eggs were small, green with brown speckles, fresh from a tundra nest. They tasted rich and delicious.

I asked about walrus. I said I'd heard walrus weren't particularly good to eat because they were bottom-feeders.

Moses Nick scowled. "They taste good if you know how to cook 'em. Taste like a big clam."

Walrus was the food for big families, he said. "You got to overcook 'em, long time boil 'em, like two and a half hours."

When I said I was heading out to Round Island, the scowl deepened. He said Eskimos used to hunt where the walrus hauled out on the island so the animals wouldn't sink after they'd been shot. He talked about white people and hunting restrictions. He used the plural form of "you."

"If you guys give us permits to use for hunting for what my family used to hunt, I'll give you permits to use for your farmland. What you think of that?"

Moses Nick felt it was disrespectful for people to go to the island just to look at walrus, and he spoke bitterly of anglers who came from all over the world, from Germany and Japan as well as Anchorage, to play with their fish.

"Those people should be arrested and thrown in jail for sport fishing," he said. "Our forefathers tell us not to play around with the animals or the fish, unless you want to eat 'em or save 'em for winter. Because when you're hungry, you'll think of what you've done."

I was afraid he was beginning to regret inviting me into his kitchen. Looking for a way to get him off the defensive, I remembered that my friend had told me Moses Nick played the accordian.

A smile creased his face at the mention of music—I think he, too, was relieved at the change of subject. He went into a back room and returned with a Hohner accordian, black with gold trim. The instrument was much bigger than I expected an accordian to be.

He'd first heard an accordian when he worked in a Bristol Bay cannery as a teenager. Later he bought an instrument and taught himself to play by ear. One year some German sport fishermen came through Togiak and they became friends. Later the Germans sent him a tape with tunes that he managed to pick out.

"I play you German's waltz," he said. The tempo shifted a bit until he got in step. He played with obvious enjoyment. A daughter in her twenties emerged from the back and grinned as she headed out the door.

"Do you like polka?" he asked. "I play 'Floating Down the River.' "

The rest of the evening we floated down the Danube, not the Togiak.

Finally the storm broke. We loaded the *Puffin* under shifting skies and pushed off the beach. Chugging straight out the bay, keeping to the invisible channel of the river, we passed the inner Walrus Islands, with big grassy slopes above jutting sea cliffs. Round Island lay on the horizon, wreathed in a menacing cloud, like King Kong's lair. The bow banged through the chop as we reached open water. Up front, the passengers pulled on their rain gear.

"I've got a new boat on order," Don Winkelman was saying in the wheelhouse. "A twenty-eight-foot welded-aluminum semi-V. Twice the horsepower. It will take the water here a lot better. But I'm going to miss the old *Puffin*."

The trip took three hours. The sanctuary rose out of the ocean as a single mountain, three miles long and a mile wide, clear of its cloud by the time we got there, still the color of straw, though summer would turn its slopes green before long. Winkelman pointed to a line of rust on the beach at the north end. Walrus, he said. We asked him to go closer but he said he couldn't—boats are supposed to stay in an unmarked corridor two miles off and hold the throttle steady, to keep from spooking the animals. Fifteen minutes later he turned toward a rocky cove where grass instead of cliff descended to the surf. A Zodiac raft with an outboard, piloted by the two Fish and Game technicians who spend the summer on Round Island, was on its way out to meet us.

In sunshine and bright slapping water we transferred our gear and said good-bye to the Walrus Man. He said he would return for us in two days. Our eyes were on the cliffs—we'd practically forgotten him by the time he turned and started for home. We had no way of knowing it was the *Puffin*'s last happy voyage.

A curious transformation took place the moment we stepped onto the rocks. In Alaska there are still certain places and times where it is possible to encounter wildlife in the mythical profusion we associate with the Great Plains buffalo and the herds of the Serengeti. Such spectacles are often seasonal, a function of migrating patterns: the post-calving aggregations of caribou on the Arctic coastal plain in spring; hulking coastal brown bears gathered on the Alaska Peninsula at the mouths of salmon streams; nesting geese on the Yukon-Kuskokwim delta. In early June Round Island is such a place. We could see a few walrus hauled out beyond the cove, near enough to make out an occasional white flash of tusk but too far for them to be bothered by our voices. Our whispers were instinctive, as if we'd entered a chapel, uncertain whether we belonged, a bit worried about being expelled. It was the same hushed feeling that had come over me in the spawning lakes above the Nushagak River, a feeling of being close to the source.

The grassy bench of land above the cove where we set up our tents, scooped as if it had been shelled by battleships, was the site of an ancient hunting village. It evoked a time when humans were less ambiguously part of this wild landscape. Yup'ik families made the long voyage out just once a year, establishing a summer village on the island, then beat the fall storms back to Togiak Bay with *umiaks* full of hides and meat and ivory.

Round Island's modern summer inhabitants lived in a small cabin sunk in the sod on a higher bench. Judy Sherburne and Bob Lipchak were graduate students from the University of Alaska and were here with research projects, but they were on the island mainly to keep animals and people apart. They represented the new, more distant relationship between mankind and environment. Fish and Game recognized it was impolitic to keep all taxpayers off Round Island—the department needed publicity and budgetary support for its policing effort—so when authorized visitors with permits showed up, Judy and Bob had the additional jobs of shepherds.

"Don't step off the trail," Judy cautioned as we started up the steep mountain slope the next morning. "We want to limit the human contact with the island to as narrow a band as possible."

Judy had her brown hair tucked inside a sporty cap. She was in excellent shape from climbing the island every day. The morning was clear and blue. Twenty minutes later we came to a high precipice and Judy crawled cautiously to the edge, waving for us to stay low. From our bellies we peered out at a sea cliff hundreds of feet high. It wasn't fear of heights that prompted Judy's caution, however. We had come upon a vertical avian city. Every niche on the cliff was noisily occupied. A steady traffic of birds flew out to sea and back in a din of birdcalls that echoed like the roar of a stadium crowd. At first it was hard to sort out any single bird. But soon I picked out the bright parrot beak of a tufted puffin. Judy looked through heavy binoculars and helped us identify others: common murres, cormorants, kittiwakes, parakeet auklets.

The birds of Round Island are not particularly rare, but are rarely seen. They spend most of their lives on the open ocean, coming to land, or to islands near land, only at breeding season. One must go to sea to meet such pelagic birds halfway.

Immediately before us was a colony of black-and-white murres, clumsily erect on their narrow ledges. The murres looked like small versions of their southern relatives, the penguins. Unlike penguins, northern alcids like the murre can fly, but with their webbed feet and small wings they are better swimmers. They nest on cliffs for protection from predators: wild foxes that roam the island and ravens that dance hungrily on the cliff tops. Another alcid, the tubby little puffin, was a natural scene stealer. I'd seen the brightly painted clowns before, thrashing across the water in attempts to take off; now, from on high, we watched airborne puffins fly in furious ascending circles to reach their burrows, their orange beaks loaded with small fish, while others tumbled off in a long free-fall and set course to sea. These gay birds were once part of the aboriginal harvest: Aleut hunters used to climb to their burrows at night and set garrottes of sea lion sinew that would hang the puffins when they burst forth in the morning. It took the skins of forty puffins or twenty-five cormorants to sew a parka, which was worn feathers-in as a coat of exceptional warmth but feathers-out on social occasions.

Judy's research involved black-legged kittiwakes. The sleek gray-winged gulls with wing tips dipped in black ink are wild birds that live far out at sea—not the kind of gull to hang around a cannery dock or garbage dump. Her particular project involved habitat quality as a predictor of breeding success. It seemed appropriate that part of Judy's job was to remind visitors of their own contribution to habitat degradation.

"We already think that murre production may be falling off here at the observation point," she said. "It's a good thing there's an in-built limit to how many people can get here, because of the cost and dealing with the weather. The island couldn't handle a lot of visitors peeking over and flushing the birds. When anything causes them to fly off their nests quickly, you can hear eggs falling off the little ledges and cracking on the rocks below."

Judy and Bob rousted us onward, up around the cliff and down a long hogback ridge toward the rocky north point of the island. The mountains of the mainland rose hazily beyond a wide moat of blue. Descending to a notch barely a hundred feet above the surf, we suddenly caught wind-carried whiffs of a barnyard.

The walrus were massed on the beach directly below. Packed flipper to flipper, they covered the pebble beach with a writhing mat of wrinkled, rust-colored leather. Bob said there were probably two thousand walrus present. They did not look happy being wedged so close together, but at the same time walrus with broken tusks were the ones who sat alone, excluded, in the least favored spots. The others jammed together, argued, butted heads, belched, roared, defecated, dozed off hangovers, and woke up grouchy whenever another one-ton walrus decided to drag himself across the top of the heap. As the tide came in, the squabbling intensified. I could not imagine how a Native hunter would view such a scene. To me, it was sublime and slapstick both.

The tusks clacked like baseball bats when the big bulls clashed. Walrus use their tusks, which are really long upper eye-teeth, to haul their mass onto ice floes—their generic name, *Odobenus*, is Greek for "tooth walker"—but the tusks are primarily for display. On the beach the gleaming weapons would have been deadly but for the thick hides of the walrus. Young bulls with smaller tusks tucked their heads submissively, trying to wedge open a place to rest, and were prodded along anyway.

All the walrus were bulls. In summer, cow walrus drift north with the ice past Cape Prince of Wales, taking the young with them. Left alone, bulls grow grumpy and listless. They feed at sea, dredging clams off the bottom and sucking out the meat with muscular mouths, then look for a beach where they can haul out with their own kind and be unsociable.

Judy laughed and pointed to a bull that had evidently broken his tusks not long ago—there was blood on the ivory stubs. He hadn't figured out that life was going to be different from now on. He was making the usual snail's charge up the beach, shaking his head in what he took to be a menacing manner. The other bulls were unimpressed and refused to budge.

"It's a lot of fun to watch, but for biologists it's not all that interesting," Judy said as we opened a picnic on the ridge. "A lot of male-to-male aggression. You could do better work looking at female-calf interactions farther north. There's still a whole lot we don't know about walrus. Where they go to feed, for instance. If we had the money, we could get radio transponders and bolt them on the tusks of a few walrus. We could track them by satellite."

Bob said there had been seven times as many walrus on the island at one time. In recent years the numbers were falling off, though, and the state's biologists were worried.

In the Bering and Chukchi seas, the Pacific walrus population was believed to have climbed to 250,000, about what researchers say the population must have been to support the harvest rates of the nineteenth-century commercial hunts (as well as the Soviet commercial hunt from 1931 to 1956). That's welcome news—the smaller Atlantic walrus, which once ranged as far south as Massachusetts Bay, has never recovered from its decimation—but there is some concern it's a false boom based on a food supply built up during decades of low walrus numbers. Hypothetically, a crash could come even without the pressures of Native hunting and habitat loss. Alaska Native hunting doubled between the mid-1970s and the mid-1980s, so that 4,000 to 5,000 walrus are taken every year and several thousand more lost in the water. Ship-based hunting takes that many and more on the Soviet side of the sea. Researchers say the hunting totals need to be watched but are not yet a cause for alarm, given the size of the total population.

Judy showed no great sympathy for those Eskimos who wanted to hunt on Round Island, but she made it clear that local Natives weren't a threat to the walrus here. Local hunters kept away. Nor was poaching by non-Natives the danger. Tusks were bringing $35 a pound on the black market (for a tusk weighing perhaps nine pounds), and scavengers could get much more for a pair still set in a noseplate. Fishing boats had tried to stampede walrus deliberately, hoping a younger walrus would be crushed and left—a hunting technique used farther north by polar bears. But taking ivory from the island's beaches, even off a dead walrus, is illegal and seldom attempted. To discourage scavengers, Judy's predecessors used to patrol the beaches and dump loose tusks in deep water.

The Fish and Game guardians kept hunters away. Today it's more likely to be naive curiosity that brings boats into the forbidden zone. Herring fishermen on a day off want to get close enough for Instamatic photos. Vulnerable on land, the walrus are easily panicked into a waddling stampede. Animals can be injured in the down-slope shinnying, but the more serious problem is that once in the water, walrus generally swim away on another feeding expedition rather than struggle back to land. A full stampede will leave Round Island deserted for days. Disturbed too frequently, the walrus look for another haul-out beach—and beaches outside the sanctuary tend to be disturbed even more.

The worst stampedes Judy had witnessed in two years had been caused by tourists. Once a pair of planes buzzed the island; another time a cruise ship launched a flotilla of Zodiac rafts straight for the main haul-out beach. Sightings of cruise ships are still rare in the Bering Sea, but this general increase in human activity was Judy's biggest concern. With the growth of the Togiak herring fishery in recent years, more fishing boats and spotter planes were passing by for a look each spring. Now huge factory trawlers had come to the sea, and they were starting after yellowfin sole in Bristol Bay, generating a steady underwater drone with their props, dragging nets through the walrus food supply. And the federal government was preparing to sell offshore oil leases in the bay— a stacking of priorities that Judy, along with most of the commercial fishermen and Natives of the region, considered demented.

"My bottom line is that I feel this area is going to see a lot of development," she said. "The islands will be affected, from oil pollution to helicopters going overhead to more people gaining access. If you don't have a baseline on what's here before all that takes place, how do you know what the effects are? Right now this is a wonderful laboratory for learning about Bristol Bay. You can follow things from year to year without a lot of outside disturbance."

She looked off toward the peak on the island, where her nesting plots were laid out.

"A person could stay real busy around here for a long time."

Judy lifted her binoculars from the grass and excused herself. Leaving Bob behind, she bounded up the grassy hogback into the sun, ascending into the company of her kittiwakes.

The rest of us remained on the ridge in a summery swoon. We spent the afternoon just watching and listening. Far offshore, I could see more walrus, bobbing up from the deep. Swimming just below the surface, they trailed a rippling wake and popped their heads up for loud husky breaths.

The sanctuary was here for the walrus, not our viewing pleasure. If visitors were ever confused on that point, Judy and Bob—guards as much as guides—had made the priority clear. But even this gesture of respect, I was thinking, contributed to a larger effort at control. The biological reserve was a hedge against exploitation everywhere else—a pristine component in some large, inchoate effort by modern man to keep the ecosystem of the Bering Sea from spinning wildly out of balance.

The Yup'ik hunters, who had believed themselves to be at the mercy of the animal powers, considered the walrus unpredictable, occasionally malevolent spirits. The island's guardians sometimes felt that way, too. Bob told us a story of walrus and carpenter. A few years ago a young carpenter had come out to build the Fish and Game cabin on Round Island. He spent the summer alone, ordering supplies over a radio and exploring the island when he could. One sunny morning he decided to take a day off and paddle around the island in a folding canvas kayak. On the back side of the island, as he passed beneath the island's highest sea cliffs, he was attacked—tusks ripped open the canvas between his legs. No one knew he had gone out that day. The isolation he'd enjoyed all summer was suddenly turned against him. Why was he attacked? Possibly the kayak looked like a seal, which walrus sometimes kill for food. He paddled the swamped boat for shore and made it, luckily, washing up beneath a steep headland—a castaway. The tide was high, cutting off the beach in either direction. He tried to climb the cliffs, but his feet kept slipping off the seabird guano. Finally he tied his boots around his neck and waded into the ocean, swimming around the rocky points when he needed to, and walked home.

I was thinking I wouldn't have wanted to swim in those waters. Even the walrus looked cold when they arrived from a week of feeding on the sea bottom, pale white as they rolled up in the surf. Unlike sea lions and seals, walrus have little hair, so they retain warmth by withholding blood in the body's core—a walrus at sea is seventy-five degrees warmer inside than on the surface. Once they have dragged themselves up the shingle, the new walrus stand out like albinos for several hours, until the blush of color returns—as a red glow was coming to our faces that bright afternoon, as color was returning in that season to the whole island sanctuary.

But on the day we were to return to the mainland, I saw how the carpenter must have felt.

Rain tapped at the tarp. I stuck my head outside the tent and saw a dark, heavy sky. A few walrus lay on rocks in the cove, inert above the crashing waves. One was awake and looking around, his head shoved back into the rolls of his neck to give the tusks room to swing free. Groggy from sleep, I felt I was looking into a mirror.

I started up through wet grass to the biologists' cabin. The higher I hiked, the stronger the storm was. From a bluff below the cabin I watched a parade of long ground swells emerge from the lee of the island to be slashed by whitecaps. I zipped up my jacket and wondered whether the *Puffin* would show up that morning after all. Winkelman had warned us to bring extra food because we might find ourselves marooned with the walrus.

Inside the tiny cabin, the oil stove was pumping and the atmosphere was snug, if not up to steambath standards. Bob and Judy were down from the loft, drinking coffee and making supply lists to send back with the charter boat, their only link to the mainland.

"Don's on his way," Judy said. "He's trying to beat the storm. He said to have all your gear packed and ready."

They kept the VHF radio off most of the time to save batteries, but now it was hissing like a radiator. I poured a cup of coffee, lingering in the warmth and wondering about how bad a real storm could be. Two of my fellow campers showed up, and we agreed we should take down the tents even in the rain.

Winkelman's voice came over the radio. Judy looked up from her writing pad with surprise.

"Yeah, Round Island? I must have broke something. I'm taking on water pretty bad. I don't know—can you get the Zodiac ready?"

His calm tone of voice made it hard to register the danger in what he'd just said.

Judy grabbed the microphone. "What's wrong, Don? Do you have power?"

"I guess I hit something. Water's coming up through the floorboards and the bilge pump isn't keeping up with it."

"Yeah, Don, we're heading down to the cove." Judy set the microphone back and started pulling on her rubber boots.

"I'm not sure we can lower it in those swells," Bob said.

Judy headed out the door. One of the other campers stayed behind to listen to the radio and the rest of us followed into the storm, our feelings not yet caught up with the sudden change in fortune, wondering what qualities of character might be called upon before the day was through.

Bob and Judy shot down the trail. I stopped on the bluff and ran my binoculars across the water toward the empty mainland coast. The mountains we'd been admiring the day before were gone. Dark clouds pushed toward us. The sea was a sickly pale green with racing streaks of white.

My hood rattled and rain stung my face. The wind rushed through the grass and across the mounds of the old village. I remembered that Knud Rasmussen was once told by an Inupiat shaman that the wind was the voice of the great weather, the spirit Sila, telling man not to fear the universe. The stronger the wind, the more insistent the call to faith.

I looked again through the binoculars for a sign of the *Puffin.*

The wind blew harder.

Thirty minutes later the tiny boat could be seen from the cove, cutting inside the two-mile limit on a rude beeline. The Zodiac dangled above the water from a suspended cable. We dropped it beyond the rocks and Judy scrambled into the stern. As she pulled on the legs of an orange rubber survival suit, Bob leaped into water to his waist and pushed the raft away. Judy started the outboard.

When she reached the *Puffin,* we relaxed a little. She circled nervously until Winkelman entered the cove and threw her a line from his stern. Judy maneuvered close to the suspended cable and flung the stern line over and tied it off. Winkelman let out slack until the boat stopped, just off the wet rocks where the rest of us stood in rubberized rain gear like curious, brightly colored seabirds.

Winkelman came around to the bow in black hip boots and navy watch cap. He smiled and lighted his pipe, then gazed at the floor of the boat and pointed to a vertical crack that ran down both sides of the *Puffin,* just in front of the cabin.

"I thought for a minute I was going to get my pipe wet," he said.

"Gee, Don, we thought it might be serious."

"The boat acted like it was on a hinge," he said. "The back end was going straight up the waves and the front end was pushing down the other side."

Bob was pouring seawater out of his boots. "I've got a come-along," he said. "We could jack the two halves together."

"Wouldn't hurt, would it?" Winkelman looked for daylight through the crack. "I've still got to get these folks back to land."

"Got any aquatic epoxy here?" somebody suggested.

"How about duct tape?" said another.

"If the tide leaves her on the rocks when it goes out, maybe I can make repairs tonight," Winkelman said.

"Did you see any walrus?"

"I was kind of afraid I might spook them," the Walrus Man said. "I had a box full of life preservers ready in case I went down, but I didn't want to be in that water with a bunch of angry walrus."

The distance between the boat and the rocks seemed to shrink as he talked.

"Maybe I could have got one of them to give me a ride to shore."

"Don, I think your boat is moving."

He turned to pull on the stern line, but an especially big swell was already heading into the cove. The wave picked up the *Puffin* and dropped it with a splintering crash into rocks and white foam.

Winkelman gazed again at his floorboards.

"She's not going anyplace now," he said. "There's rocks coming up through the bottom."

We lashed the *Puffin* to shore and unloaded several boxes of supplies. Mixed in the sounds of hammering waves were the booming and crunching of wood. Bob and Judy were opening their mail on the rocks when Winkelman finally stepped to shore.

"Now how are we going to get out of here?" he said.

We had to drag the details of his adventure out of him. Seas running fourteen feet. Waves crashing across the windshield, and it took five sweeps of the wiper before he could see again. Each time he came down off a wave and landed, water squirted up between his feet as if from a drinking fountain. He couldn't speed up because he was afraid he'd hit the waves harder and snap in two. He couldn't slow down because he was afraid the split sides would yawn open and more water would pour in.

We were sitting around a pot of soup in camp that afternoon. Shipwrecked. We sang the theme to "Gilligan's Island" and tried to remember the names of all the castaways. The name nobody could remember was the millionaire.

Winkelman, gazing out to see, suddenly heaved to. "Thurston Howell the Third, wasn't it?" he said.

"Do you suppose anyone in the village would be willing to come out and save some marooned conservationists?" I asked.

"Maybe if we let them have one walrus? A small one?" somebody added.

It did not reach the point where we had to contemplate taking a walrus ourselves, or tie up Judy to get some of her kittiwake eggs. The manager of the Togiak cannery called on the radio to say he'd send a tender in the morning. He had heard Winkelman's call when the boat was starting to break up.

Winkelman descended to the cove when the tide went out. He patched the floor of his boat with plywood and epoxy and splinted the sides with two-by-fours. With any luck, he announced, the boat would float on the morning tide long enough to be lifted to the deck of the tender.

The *Puffin* broke in two just after dawn.

Winkelman had been standing at the helm in his hip waders, running the bilge pump as the tide came in. The battery was low and the pump quit. Water rose like inside a bathtub. Lines snapped. Waves came pounding in and the boat split along its hinge.

When I got to the cove, Winkelman was back on the rocks. It was another gray morning, and the cove was full of a green light. Walrus heads bobbed curiously in the jade water, just beyond the two barely floating halves of the wooden boat. Winkelman watched, thinking perhaps of that new welded-aluminum semi-V he had on order. The painted puffin on the side of the cabin was still above water. When the stern half slapped against the rocks, Winkelman climbed on the roof, shattered the windshield with a rock, and pulled out his radio. He hopped back to the island with a bleeding thumb and said, "I wish I'd pulled the engine."

The cannery tender arrived with a deep chuffing sound that chased the walrus out of the cove. It was a big work boat with a crane in the stern that hoisted the *Puffin*'s pieces onto the deck like driftwood. Judy ferried the rest of us out in the Zodiac. Our departure from the island, in doubt for twenty-four hours, was now all we thought about, and there was no ceremonial leave-taking from the walrus.

The Walrus Man was the last aboard. The tender hacked up a ball of black smoke and headed out of the cove. "This might turn out to be a pretty expensive subcontractor," Winkelman muttered. He turned to his customers.

"I said I'd get you back, didn't I?"

We went to thank the skipper of the tender. As we climbed a metal ladder, a deckhand squeezed down excitedly with an Instamatic camera in hand. From the wheelhouse we saw we weren't leaving the island quite yet. We were chugging straight toward the north beach.

"I promised these guys I'd run in and see the walrus," the skipper said.

Through the smoky gray morning, we could see the beach was already nearly empty.

7. Red Devil

SLEETMUTE

Apart of me hadn't wanted to go to the bush in winter. I could have happily restricted my travels to the season of long daylight and riverboats and returning salmon. January in the villages conjured a different sort of place, the primitive Alaska I would have imagined the one or two times, as a boy, when the place might have crossed my mind: a land of igloos and shivering, starving people. To judge from the stories I'd heard of hard drinking and violence, winter in the bush could indeed mean a struggle to survive. There was little hunting, especially among the young, and there were no jobs; nothing to divert the mind from a long dark turning inward. The season played to the weakness of life in an empty place, and I didn't want to look—fearing, I suppose, to find that when the rivers freeze and animals disappear, exalted ties to landscape don't count for much.

But summer in the bush was only half the story, and so one morning I found myself gazing down on the eerie stillness of the frozen Kuskokwim River, turned inward already, floating on my own soft cloud of goosedown. The cold had sent me smartly in retreat the moment I stepped from the Aniak air terminal into the morning darkness. The air had spent the night out at thirty below, and at the first gulp my throat choked shut. I pressed my lips together and my nostril hairs turned brittle with ice. Inside the mail plane, I pulled my knees up toward my chest. The drone of the engine and the faintly nauseating exhaust shut down my other senses. I wore earplugs now after a summer in small planes, and a balaclava of thick gray wool was pulled to my earlobes. I did my best to burrow into a place where nothing could touch me.

Dawn came slowly as we flew through the Kuskokwim Mountains. Above the wing, rounded Appalachian ridges rose to wind-crusted knobs where snow picked up the first blue tinge of day. It was getting on toward midmorning—in Anchorage the rush hour would be over, stores and offices would be busy. In the river canyon below nothing moved.

Snow, cold, cold, snow—January weighed on me as a single heavy fact, a bloc impossible to break apart and examine. I longed to have at my service a multitude of nuanced Yup'ik expressions, sharp as ice picks, but part of me wanted to stay bundled up and forget the whole thing.

I looked again at the canyon's snaking course. There was life in the landscape, I told myself bravely. Beneath that frozen track, a great river moved.

Outside Alaska, the Kuskokwim is virtually unknown. It lacks the epic historical resonance of the famous river running parallel to the north, yet among Alaskan rivers, the Kuskokwim is second in size only to the Yukon and its tributaries. Its source is in the glaciers that run west from Mount McKinley. Highpower Creek, Swift Fork, Windy Fork, Big River—silty rough-and-tumble tributaries carry the ground-up Alaska Range southwest into a broad interior valley, where new rivers—the Stony, the Holitna, and the Hoholitna—come up from mountains to the south. Fully assembled at last, the Kuskokwim pushes into these aging mountains where the names on my map were mostly the names of ghost towns: Ophir, Tolstoi, Iditarod, Flat. From Mount McKinley to the canyon where I was flying, and on, all the way through the mountains and out across the delta to the sea, in 724 miles the

Kuskokwim never passes a dam or a bridge or even the dead-end turnaround of a road. The Kuskokwim retains an intact wildness the Yukon can no longer claim. In an overcataloged age, its obscurity seemed a sign of grace.

The most remarkable feature of the Kuskokwim is its delta, a vast tundra plain that the river shares with the Yukon. More than four hundred fifty miles of coastline wrap around a marshy plain the size of South Carolina. The region's one big town is Bethel (1985 population: 3,681), which sits atop the river's long tidal mouth, but there are more than fifty small Yup'ik Eskimo villages scattered across the delta and up the river canyons, among them some of the most isolated and traditional communities in Alaska. When Knud Rasmussen finished his crossing of the Arctic in 1924, he was intrigued by what little he saw of the Yukon-Kuskokwim delta. The whaling fleet had passed its shallow coast by, he wrote, schools and missionaries had hardly penetrated the pagan country, and "as a result the people there are most interesting." The delta remains home to the largest concentration of Eskimos in the world. It had also become the center for a growing "self-determination" movement whose aim, so far as I had been able to make out from Anchorage, was to go back to living by ancient Yup'ik precepts without sacrificing the right to be a people of the modern world. In a week the villages that called themselves the Yupiit Nation were going to meet in the delta settlement of Akiachak. I planned to be there, but first I wanted to spend some time on the Kuskokwim, traveling downstream through this traditional part of Alaska. In winter.

We flew into a basin filled with sun: the Holitna River valley. The Holitna fastens onto the Kuskokwim in a braid of channels, and on the first big bend below we flew above the small village of Sleetmute.

Yup'ik hunters had been pushing into this Ingalik Indian valley just when Russian fur traders from Bristol Bay arrived in 1830. All three cultures left parts of themselves in Sleetmute. Russians crossing the mountains from the Nushagak had built the first fort on the Kuskokwim close by. Within the unsteady grid of Sleetmute's houses and log cabins, I picked out the tin roof of a Russian Orthodox church.

We buzzed the snowy airstrip to make sure it was clear, and banked sharply. A beguiling thread of chimney smoke across the river told a story of peace and wintry contentment. A visitor wouldn't have guessed that Sleetmute's reputation for epidemic alcoholism, broken families, and violent death had marked it as one of the most miserable places in the Alaska bush.

One year there was a husband and wife who were drinking hard," said the mayor of Sleetmute. "They pushed their skiff into the river and started up the outboard too fast. He had a cast on his arm. They both fell in and the boat was just going around in circles. Their six kids were standing there on the shore, watching."

Andrew Fredericks, the mayor, and Pete Zauker, the traditional chief, were surprisingly eager to talk about the village's problem. There were a hundred people in the village altogether. They could name only two families who kept away from alcohol. Everyone else drank to get drunk. Sometimes it seemed like everyone in the village was drinking at once.

"They look right at you but they won't know who you are," Andrew Fredericks said. "When everyone is drinking you wouldn't want to be here."

Pete Zauker said he stopped drinking a few years earlier after he saw that his oldest son was afraid of him.

They told of rapes, beatings, suicides, deaths by hypothermia, all owing to alcohol. In one family the father had been sent to prison, the mother stayed drunk, and the children had been taken by the state. Six months earlier at a party, a young man had shot his uncle to death with a rifle. The year before an older man froze to death in a skiff, wrapped against the cold in a sheet of clear plastic.

Such stories were not unique to Sleetmute. As they spoke, I

stretched their stories over a familiar skeleton of statistics. Alaska Natives, 16 percent of the state's population, accounted for 34 percent of state prison inmates—and for nearly every serious crime in the bush linked by state troopers to drinking. If the bush was a dangerous place to be around when people were drinking, it was even more dangerous a place to be drunk. There were so many violent "accidental" deaths and injuries that the state epidemiologist called them "our new plague," and statisticians were being forced to redefine the category of "suicide." Even under the standard definition, the suicide rate among young Alaska Native males was ten times the national average. Alcohol was working its curse down the generations not just in broken families but in the birth defects and mental retardation of fetal alcohol syndrome, found among Alaska Natives at a rate two and a half times the rate in Seattle.

In Anchorage you could see lost faces in the crowds outside the Fourth Avenue bars, and it was easy to feel sympathy as you drove by. In the bush, however, sympathy gave way to fear in the presence of open liquor bottles. I remembered a night in Fort Yukon when I'd been invited into a small trashed-out house to share a plastic bottle of whiskey with six Indian teenagers. I took in the eyes back in the shadows, fumbled a lame excuse, and fled—for once, I had no wish to see the world from their side.

What the general theories about the boredom of the unemployed and loss of self-respect in a community funded by welfare checks failed to account for was how twists of fate and geography allowed some villages to rise above the troubles and consigned others to unending misery. I was surprised, when I sought out Sleetmute's leaders, to hear them spill their stories so readily. A natural reticence compounded by grief and embarrassment makes the subject difficult for many rural people to talk about, even among themselves. The traditional way of handling deviant behavior through silent disapproval and social shunning had poorly prepared Native people for epidemic alcoholism. But a sobriety movement was beginning to spread, with dozens of villages voting to ban sale or importation of alcohol. There was even talk of a new state law that would allow villages to vote in prohibition and ban possession.

Then I realized that perhaps the leaders of Sleetmute were so ready to talk because they had an explanation for their troubles. They started to tell me about Red Devil.

It happened that the biggest liquor store outside an incorporated town in the bush was located two bends down the Kuskokwim. There were only a few dozen people living in Red Devil, an old mining camp named for the ore that had produced mercury. The Mercury Inn opened as a bar and package store to serve the mine thirty years ago. After the mining stopped in the early 1970s the bar closed, but booze continued to flow through the Red Devil package store to the communities of the middle Kuskokwim.

The village of Sleetmute had voted itself "dry"; people weren't supposed to bring in booze. But the liquor store was only twenty minutes away, and the chiefs said they couldn't check every skiff or snowmachine coming up the river.

Recently they'd put together a list of all the alcohol-related deaths in the past thirty years in the tiny communities along the middle Kuskokwim—Crooked Creek, Red Devil, Sleetmute, Stony River— and came up with eighty-five names. The closer a community was to Red Devil, the more violent crimes and deaths it had. Thirty-one of the dead had come from Sleetmute.

This winter had been one of the calmest in a long time, Sleetmute's leaders said. They attributed the improvement to the dry law, but more to an airplane accident that resulted in the Red Devil store being shut down for a while.

"Why do they keep selling it, even though so many died, so many are in jail, so many families are broken up?" asked Moxie Alexie, a younger man and staunch former drinker who had joined us upstairs in the village's two-story office. "The only people that can answer it is them."

Sleetmute's leaders wanted the state alcohol board to revoke Red Devil's liquor license, though apparently not everyone agreed with them. Someone was circulating a petition in Sleetmute to overturn the village dry law. They already had thirty signatures.

"People who just got out of prison for alcohol-related offenses, who are still on probation, signed the petition," Alexie said. "It makes you wonder what they are thinking."

They said there was no binge in the village at the moment, but there was a plane coming in that afternoon from McGrath they weren't sure about—it might have a load.

When I asked about a place to sleep, they suggested the lodge across the river.

I walked around the cold lanes of the village for an hour, terrorizing myself. In each smiling stranger I thought I perceived, if not an assailant's glare, at least a threatening glint of an unpleasant truth. I stayed burrowed in that place where nothing could touch me—I myself might as well have been drinking. I spoke at length to no one and learned nothing more about Sleetmute than I could divine from my own heart.

I caught a ride on the back of a snowmachine as the snowy hills were turning pink. The quick trip across a half mile of ice turned my cheeks the same color. The temperature, already below zero, was sinking fast.

Nixe Mellick lived in self-imposed exile in a small cluster of wooden buildings opposite the village. His father was from Yugoslavia and had owned the trading post in Sleetmute, and his mother was a local Native. Nixe was active in the local Native corporation and ran a fishing and hunting lodge in summer, flying his customers himself. Because the Holitna entered the Kuskokwim just above his lodge, his side of the silty river ran clear in summer.

His guest cabins were deep in snow and closed for winter, but he invited me to stay in his comfortable home and share dinner with the family.

After the meal his wife and kids faded from the room, and we sat up talking past midnight. Nixe was a big-featured man with thick black eyebrows and an air of self-assurance. He told me of an old Eskimo from the area who'd had a window seat on his first flight out to the Lower Forty-eight: when the jet banked, he turned to his seatmate and said, "We're passing the moon." The last two truly traditional people in the region, he said, were an old woman on the Holitna who still trapped for a living and a shaman who had successfully sweated his own cure for his kidney problem.

Showing me a collection of prehistoric artifacts that he kept in a glass case, he made the region's early Natives sound more like mysterious and fascinating strangers than his own ancestors. Nixe was an amateur archeologist. He helped researchers in the area, locating old village sites along slough channels of the Kuskokwim that were now filled in, visible only from a small plane—"You've got to go way up high. I tried to tell them but at first they wouldn't believe me."

He told me how early Native hunters were able to kill a bear with a spear: walk right up to the bear, stare him in the eye, let him know you're going to kill him. Then show a sudden flash of fear, to make the bear drop his guard, and that's when you make your thrust. Hunters wrapped leather around the spear handle at a bear's arm's length from the point, so they would know not to let their hand slip too close. But Nixe said he, too, believed animals could talk to you, and if one outsmarts him on a hunt he lets it go.

He was disappointed I knew nothing about his newest interest, the forced collectivization of Siberian Natives as described in H. P. Smolka's 1937 book, *40,000 Against the Arctic*.

Nixe was an active Republican—in the Democratic bush, it seemed a further way of disassociating himself. But he defended the local state legislator, a homesteader from up the Holitna River who had been mocked in the press after billing the state $13,000 in moving costs when he returned from Juneau with fifty sheets of plywood, three outboard motors, three airplane wheels, and a bathtub.

Occasionally Nixe lifted his empty coffee cup in the air and his wife appeared with a refill.

Nixe described himself as a social drinker. It was his opinion that every village should have its own bar: better to have drinking in the open than behind closed doors.

I doubted his idea had much future, given the bush's spreading prohibitionism.

"A bar you can control," he insisted. "A package store you can't. We've had too many people fall out of boats between here and Red Devil. My brother was one. He disappeared in the fall. There was a lot of ice running on the river at the time."

Later I learned that Nixe's own son, a pilot like him, had been buzzing boats on the river and crashed into a bluff two years earlier. He and a passenger were killed. The autopsy showed his son had been drinking.

"You know, I owned the trading post at Red Devil for a few years back in the sixties," Nixe said. "One night I had a Tin City miner who died at the bar—fell asleep with his head in his arms and never woke up. Another old gal left and we found her the next day, froze by the door. I sold the place soon after that. It was a hard way to make a living."

He gazed into his glass reliquary.

"You've got to be able to live with yourself," he said.

The last census of Red Devil had put the population at thirty-nine, mostly non-Native. The post office was on the closed-in porch of somebody's cabin. A young woman behind the counter said she'd taken my message over the village phone and passed it on to the Vanderpools. I'd called to be sure they were around when I stopped by. It was a mistake.

She told me how to find the Mercury Inn. A road passed through the piles of plowed snow by the airstrip and followed the river. The morning was clear and still, the temperature twenty-one below. Snow squeaked beneath my boots. When I reached the two red buildings at the end of the road and knocked at the trading post, nobody was inside. A hand-scribbled note said the store would be closed all day "for inventory."

The other building appeared to be a lodge, shut for winter, with the door to a private home on the right. A Sesame Street swing set was covered with snow. I pulled off my outer mitts, knocked at the door to the house, waited, knocked again. The curtains were drawn, but I could hear people moving around inside. I shifted from foot to foot for ten minutes, knocking occasionally. Finally I walked back to the river to take a photo of the store.

The door to the house flew open.

"What the heck are you doing?" a dark, heavy woman called out. "I don't want any pictures taken of my store. Give me the film."

With a practiced naïveté, I ignored her request and called out that I was looking for the Vanderpools. Was she Mrs. Vanderpool? She said no.

I asked if I could talk to her.

"My kids are sick. I don't want to talk to anybody today," she said, and slammed the door, forgetting about the film.

Bob Vanderpool had been flying, mining, and trapping in the Kuskokwim Mountains since the 1940s. He'd owned a local flying service and had gone out of his way to help people through the years, and they remembered. Everybody in Sleetmute praised his character, even as they did what they could to put him out of business. He'd owned the Mercury Inn since 1967. The Vanderpools lived alone in the mining ghost town of Georgetown; the trading post was being run by their son, Robert, and Robert's wife. That must have been Gail you talked to, said the young woman at the post office, an itinerant special-education teacher who traveled by dogsled between villages on the middle Kuskokwim.

"Gail probably didn't want to talk to any visitors after the accident," she said. "Every time somebody died they closed down the liquor store for a while, but this time they've had it closed most of the winter. This was the worst because it happened right here in Red Devil and people saw it."

In Bethel, one hundred forty miles away, sale of alcohol is illegal, as it is all over the Yukon-Kuskokwim delta. Red Devil is the last liquor store before the Bering Sea. The plane that flew up from Bethel that summer night had four people on board. The pilot woke up the storekeepers and bought four bottles of scotch and four boxes of wine. Investigators said he already had a blood alcohol level more than three times the legal limit for driving a car.

There was a heavy fog by the time the plane took off. Apparently the plane got into the air and made it a little way down the river, turning before it hit the trees. The pilot's daughter was the only one who lived long enough to crawl away from the wreckage, though she'd had one leg torn off. No one heard the crash. The next morning another pilot spotted the wreckage.

There was still plenty of daylight when the mail plane came through to take me down the Kuskokwim.

8. Icons

W here the delta begins, the forest spreads and thins, and the Kuskokwim, one hundred fifty miles from the coast but only thirty feet above sea level, relaxes into wide squiggles and oxbow sloughs that were more apparent on the map than in the snowy landscape I could see from the air. As a site for settlement, the bend of the river below the last hills had always been important, because the Yukon River emerges from the mountains just twenty-five miles north. The two rivers swerve apart and debouch two hundred fifty miles from one another, so the portage here, more across lakes than solid ground, has always been an essential route between. The last hills before the delta are known as the Portage Mountains. Different groups of Natives jostled for position here, and later the Russians used the portage to supply their upriver fort. Today there are two villages beneath the hills, Kalskag and Lower Kalskag, separated by three miles of boreal forest and a schism as old as the one between Rome and Constantinople.

Kalskag was settled near the turn of the century by the residents of Old Kalskag, a settlement just downriver that was laid to waste by a flu epidemic. The people were Russian Orthodox. Soon they were joined by Catholic Eskimos who had crossed from the Yukon, where priests had a mission. Eventually the Russian Orthodox families moved downstream to their summer fish camp and established the lower village. From the air I could see a scattering of old frame houses along the river at the upper village. Farther downriver, small log homes were clustered by the water, and behind them ran a double enfilade of newer government housing.

A large gravel airstrip had been cut out of the woods between the two villages. A dirt road connected the communities—or at least connected each with the airport. It was a long walk in either direction for a visitor who hadn't bothered to make arrangements.

Unfortunately, the truck that arrived to collect the mail had come from the upper village. I watched plane and truck depart, then lifted my pack and crunched down the snowy road in the other direction. The spruce trees were heavy with fresh snow. The temperature was still well below freezing, but it was warmer here than at Red Devil, thanks to a low gray blanket of clouds pulled across the delta. I walked past the new high school, situated by the state in the woods at the road's tactful midpoint. For budgetary purposes, the state was promoting intervillage amity with the school and airport projects. But the nearby shell of another project, a joint community hall that had sat unfinished for years, made the prospects of unity appear dubious.

A pickup truck passed going the wrong way, and the driver waved. Twenty minutes later the pickup truck came by and stopped. The driver was a maintenance man who'd been going to check the school, which was closed for the religious holidays. He dropped me in Lower Kalskag near the St. Seraphim Church.

Father Wassilie Epchook was my one contact in the village. I had spoken with him on the Nushagak River the previous fall, and he'd suggested I visit the Kuskokwim during *slaviq*, the celebration of the Russian Orthodox New Year.

I went to his house and knocked. The door was opened by a thin, red-bearded Viking who told me, in as few words as possible, that Father Epchook wasn't home. He seemed about to close the door when a young Native woman with a child on either leg called me in. This was Irene, Father Epchook's daughter; the taciturn man at the door was her husband, Scott.

Father Epchook had gone to a funeral downriver in Kwethluk. Irene said her father hoped to be home the next day for the New Year's Eve service, but there was talk of a storm. She'd try to reach him on the telephone; meanwhile I could leave my pack at their house.

I went for a walk. The afternoon was growing darker. The blanket of clouds had become a comforter, pillowy with snow. I'd had a headache when I got out of the plane, and it hadn't gone away. I stopped by the village health clinic, hoping to pick up some aspirin, but a handwritten sign on the door said "If you need health aides call them at home or slaviqing."

Irene had said anyone—even people from the upper village—was welcome to go "starring," part of the lingering Christmas celebration. I walked down to a neighborhood of small log homes set in alders, beyond which opened the broad white Kuskokwim. A knot of people shuffled along a snowy path between the houses, led by a young teenage boy carrying a wooden star decorated with plastic flowers and silver tinsel. I followed them through the door of a single-room log cabin.

The crowd nearly filled the room. People pressed close with their coats on. I hung back by the open doorway.

The cabin was dark except for blinking colored lights on a small Christmas tree in the far corner. The peeled log walls behind the tree were papered over with green-and-red Christmas wrapping, and above in the place of honor, the spot known as the "beautiful corner" in the Orthodox church's affectless translation from Russian, was a shrine of several small flat church portraits. The host family, a young couple with two children, stood nearby, welcoming their friends in the Yup'ik language.

The altar boy shed his shiny blue-and-gold Kalskag Grizzlies jacket. Dressed in white shirt and tie, he faced us with his back to the tree.

Someone came forward and lighted a candle at the hub of the star, and when the altar boy began solemnly to spin his wheel, the visitors sang. The music was astringent and sweet. A tiny wheezing woman sang loudest; everyone else seemed to be singing between clenched teeth, as if in deference to the size of the cabin. The singers read from hand-lettered songbooks in which the words had been written out phonetically. The church hymns were in Slavonic, the thousand-year-old liturgical language of the church. Other songs were folk hymns in Ukrainian. Though I couldn't understand a word, it dawned on me that most of the singers probably couldn't translate the songs either. The language was a mysterious medium through which the congregation called to their unfathomable faith.

As they sang, melting snow puddled beneath our boots.

I had already been through a Christmas and New Year's of my own, and this second round of caroling reinforced the impression that time moved more slowly in the bush. The Russian Orthodox church in Alaska has stubbornly remained on the Julian calendar, which went out of fashion in most of Christendom in the sixteenth century. Orthodox churches in the rest of the United States had formally given up the old calendar in the 1980s, but the Alaska church has always been fairly independent from the other Orthodox bodies in America, the former having been brought to the New World by Russian colonialists, the latter by immigrants from Eastern Europe.

Finally there was a song I could understand. "God Grant You Many Years"—they sang those words in a high pitch over and over. At the last note, children ran to blow out the candle in the star. The host passed around a bowl of candies, which the children saved in plastic bags like trick-or-treaters.

I slogged along to several more houses, hanging at the rear, my presence barely acknowledged. In Russian Orthodox villages, the house-to-house feasting, singing, and gift giving of *slaviq* goes on for a week between Christmas and New Year's, as long as people can keep going. A visit to a single house can take six hours at the start of *slaviq*, but it was late in the week now and the singers were into the second full turn around the village. Maybe it was my headache, but the carolers seemed tired and not especially merry. Most elders had dropped out, and multicourse meals had given way to hard candies.

Under cover of darkness, I peeled away and punched postholes through the snow back to the main road.

Irene was at the dinner table when I got back, and invited me to take a plate from the dish rack. She had spoken with her father. I was to spend the night in his room.

On a platter at the center of the table was a small tarry cadaver. "Land otter," Irene said. "It might be kinda tough."

Her husband was examining the piece on his plate, probing with his fork for structural weakness. He had trapped the animal for its skin. The meat, Irene said, was an added bonus.

They had boiled it for hours.

"Is that the traditional way to cook otter?" I asked.

"I don't know," she said. "We never had it before."

I took a bite. The meat had the texture of undercooked Naugahyde. I chewed thoughtfully, listening to the television. "Aviation Weather" was on the state TV channel. When it's snowing in Norton Sound, it may be clear in Anchorage and raining in Ketchikan: Alaska is so big that the weather gets a nightly half hour of its own. On the Yukon-Kuskokwim delta, it looked as if a storm would hit tonight.

Irene poured the meat from her plate back onto the platter. "Give it to the dogs," she told Scott. I took it as a sign I could cease chewing.

Irene spent the evening chasing her two children, who were bouncing off the furniture. Scott stared mutely at the television. I went back to Father Epchook's room and crawled in my sleeping bag to read about the religion known in some parts of Alaska as "the Native church."

Above my head, a priestly black robe hung from Father Epchook's gun rack, alongside a rifle in a camouflage case.

The long journey that brought Christianity to Alaska from the East began in the fourth century with the opening of the "Second Rome" at Constantinople. The Orthodox and Roman Catholic churches evolved separately, argued increasingly, and reached a final schism in 1054 when an emissary of Pope Leo IX and the Patriarch of Constantinople hurled anathemas of excommunication at one another. The Second Rome extended its influence to the Rus tribe near Kiev, and from there into the woods to the north, to Moscow and beyond. The Russian church attained its own autonomy after Constantinople fell in 1453 to the Turkish Sultan Mehmet II. While the Greek Orthodox Church spent four hundred years under the Ottomans, Moscow was proclaiming itself the Third Rome and carrying Christianity across Siberia to the New World. The church maintained its ties even when Alaska was purchased by the United States, but after the Bolshevik revolution, the Russian church was as much a captive as the Greek had been. Alaska was cut off. I pictured Father Epchook's small church in Lower Kalskag as a sort of rocketship hurtling through space long after the planet that had launched it blew up.

A Russian Orthodox missionary first reached the lower Kuskokwim while George Washington was president. The Eskimos made a martyr of Hieromonk Iuvenalii, but it was his murder that marked the church's real beginnings in the region. According to church accounts anyway, a Yup'ik shaman who put on the martyr's pectoral cross was said to have found himself rising into the air. He floated back to earth and declared that the next missionary should be heeded.

Unlike some of the Protestant missions that came later, the Russian church did not try hard to erase the society it found. The first Russian clerics traveled among the Natives and later instructed their missionaries to respect Native marriages and customs. Over the years, certain liturgical rituals of the church melded with Yup'ik ceremonies. *Slaviq* itself developed when starring and caroling traditions, brought by missionaries from the Ukraine, were joined to such Yup'ik celebrations as the *nakaciaq*, the bladder festival observed around the winter solstice. The traditional downriver celebration had consisted of three to five days of singing and gift giving, culminating in the return of seal spirits to the sea. A feast followed this religious act of propitiation and renewal. The songs of supplication known as *agayuliluteng*, "hoping for things to become plentiful," came to be associated with Christian prayer.

In the spring *kelek*, or inviting-in feast, shamans had sought to promote a plentiful harvest by invoking animal spirits with wooden masks, which were manufactured each year, used once, and burned. The nineteenth-century ethnographer Edward Nelson felt that the Yukon-Kuskokwim Eskimos had recognized in the priestly vestments and rituals of the Russians the transforming power of their own mask festivals.

To be sure, the power of the Russians was made manifest soon after the martyrdom of Hieromonk Iuvenalii in other, less miraculous ways, through the introduction of trade goods—iron, copper and beads, and later, foods, such as tea and sugar—and through their firearms, whose distribution to Natives was tightly controlled. Though the Russian priests made some effort to establish schools and improve public health, their opportunities in social matters were constrained. The Russians had come to America for furs. The church's mission, despite the talk of Holy Russia and the Third Rome, was secondary. But then, the Orthodox church had always subjugated social concerns to spiritual ones: that had been the key to its survival under Moslem, Mongol, and czar, and it was a reason cited by social workers today for the church's apparent failure, in some Orthodox villages, to stop the slide into alcohol.

A light snow was falling in the village the next morning, but the sky, calm and infused with yellow light, seemed already on its way to clearing. A plane buzzed low over the house. Fifteen minutes later the archpriest of the Kuskokwim came through the door and stamped snow off his boots.

Father Wassilie Epchook was a short man with a heavy black mustache and wire-rim glasses. The previous fall in New Stuyahok, his voice had rung loudly against smutty videocassettes, but now his trip to Kwethluk had left him hoarse and with a bad cold.

Father Epchook grew up in a church family. His father was a priest from the village of Russian Mission on the Yukon. I'd been told Father Epchook was more fluent in Slavonic than most Native priests, but then he was old enough, in his early sixties, to be part of a generation nearly lost to the church. He could remember learning Slavonic hymns on the lap of a great bear of a priest from Russia. After the Russian revolution, priests and money stopped coming from the metropolitan of Moscow, the seminary in Unalaska had closed, and each village had to reach within to support its own church, often relying on lay church readers and an itinerant priest. Only in the 1970s did a new seminary open, and now young Native priests were again moving to the villages.

Sitting in his living room, Father Epchook said hoarsely he'd come late to the priesthood. As the eldest son in the family, his job had been to support the family, hunting meat and gathering firewood. It wasn't until his father died suddenly, of a heart attack in a steambath, that Father Epchook felt ready to fly to Sitka to study with the bishop.

"People need someone to take care of them, and something wanted me to work for people, not for my career," he croaked. "I was not an educated man. But Christ's disciples were not educated either."

His father had died on January 14. Every year on that day, New Year's Day on the Julian calendar, Father Epchook said, he celebrates a mass in his father's memory. He would mark the day tomorrow.

I asked about the funeral in Kwethluk. His brother's son had died on his way home from Bethel when his snowmachine ran out of gas in a snowstorm. The frozen body had been found several hundred yards from the machine. I mentioned my visit to Sleetmute, and we talked about the church's work with alcoholism. Alcohol, he said, was less ruinous in villages where elders lived by values as an example to young people. Like many Native leaders, he spoke most easily of restricting the supply of alcohol, though I would have thought that as a priest his work would be on the demand side. Later the young village mayor explained a practical reason why nobody thought a dry law would work: "Kalskag would stay wet, and we couldn't build a gate between the two villages. It would be like Berlin."

Father Epchook and I were interrupted by a quick rap on the door. Villagers began filing through the Arctic entry porch into the living room. Father Epchook jumped up from the couch.

"What's this? *Slaviq?*" he exclaimed. "The kids are going to sing?"

It was a choir of children with a few older shepherds. They sang their hymns straight through, even when drowned out by passing snowmachines or interrupted by voices on the CB. The phone rang, and Father Epchook answered in a whisper while the singing continued.

When the starring was over, the *slaviq* choir piled into two pickup trucks, joined by older singers. Father Epchook got in up front, and we drove out the road toward Kalskag. The old people in the back of the truck hunkered down inside fur hats and hoods, but the teenagers wearing light jackets sat up in the cold wind.

I talked with a teenager who, at six feet tall, hovered over the others. He said school was to reopen the next day for basketball practice. Despite having only thirty-three students in the four-year school, Kalskag's boys and girls teams had both won their regional championships, the prize for which was a field trip to Anchorage for the state small-school championship tournament. Because so many villages in the area are Russian Orthodox, the region wraps up its season early, before the *slaviq* break. This presents a conditioning problem for the players, whose tournament opponents are still in the heart of their seasons in January.

Basketball has become the most popular sport in the Alaska bush. Kalskag spends as much as $40,000 a year in state education funds chartering planes for its sports teams and school bands. Part of the appeal, no doubt, is the travel, but adults continue to play after they finish school. The proliferation of high school gyms built with state oil money has given villagers something new for long winter nights. Many of the gyms are tiny and have no room for seating; spectators line the walls, pressing so close that the rules for school games allow players to have one foot in play when they throw the ball in bounds.

The schools play a stampeding, muscular game. Yup'ik players are short and tend to be shorter as one moves west toward the Bering Sea, so the Kalskag Grizzlies often have a height advantage. When Kalskag started playing basketball eight years earlier, before the new school was built, they practiced out of doors in cold that made the balls go dead. On the team's first road trip, one of the players told the coach he couldn't play because he'd forgotten his gloves; he was reassured he wouldn't need gloves indoors.

Nothing has brought the upper and lower villages together like the success of their school teams. This year the Grizzly boys had finally won a trip to Anchorage by beating their archrivals, the Aniak Halfbreeds, who live in the region's mixed-race transportation hub. For the Grizzly girls, this year would be their third trip to Anchorage. The first time they had gone all the way to the small-schools final only to lose to Kiana, an Inupiat village along the Kobuk River in northwest Alaska. Coming home, the girls had been disappointed to find no one to greet them at the airstrip. The population of both villages had been crowded inside the gym, where they surprised the girls with a welcome-home rally.

The two pickup trucks turned off the road just short of the school at a store. The two-story log building, run for years by a white couple named Parent, drew business from both communities. Inside it had the look of an old-time general store, with aisles of groceries set out between the log walls. We trooped up the stairs behind the cash register and crowded into the living room above, where the wood stove felt good after our open-air drive.

Fern Parent greeted us one by one. We had come for a feast in memory of her husband, Joe, who had died of cancer exactly one year earlier. It was a tradition of the Yup'ik community she now called home to hold a memorial feast like this. Fern was from Montana and went to the Catholic church in the upper village, but no Catholic priest lived in Kalskag so she had invited Father Epchook to bless her table.

With a big window admitting the light of falling snow, the *slaviq* choir sang in a living room bare of religious symbols except a porcelain statue of the Virgin Mary. One caroler offered a solo chant, holding a single note until the last syllable:

"Therefore we come forward to meet the owners of this house that they may hear these joyous sounds and live through many ye-ears."

The feast was spread on a round table in the next room. Father Epchook leaned forward to light a candle and utter a brief blessing, then took his seat. The elders in the living room joined him for the first sitting, while others stood and watched. Father Epchook insisted I sit beside him at the table.

The tablecloth was spread with the bounty of wilderness and grocery store both: smoked salmon, baked ham, beans and ribs, yams, pilot bread, sweet blueberry *akutaq*, and peanut butter cookies. Father Epchook filled his plate with the special relish of a priest in a poor village who is supported entirely by his parishioners.

"Tastes better than land otter, doesn't it?" he said.

Early vespers, scheduled for the evening at St. Seraphim Church, were canceled when Father Epchook found nobody had brought firewood to the church. At midnight, though, the bell outside the church began a steady tolling to announce the New Year's Eve mass. The stove in the church was crackling hot.

The sky had cleared and stars glittered like frost. It was five below. In the church entry, the *slaviq* star was hung in a corner above a lawnmower. Father Epchook appeared in a marten fur hat and black robe, waving a heavy flashlight. He opened a double door to the church nave, and I followed him through.

In the year 988 Prince Vladimir of Kiev sent emissaries to explore the world's religions and find the true faith he should adopt for his people. His emissaries worshipped in Islamic mosques and Roman Catholic cathedrals, and then arrived at the center of the Eastern Orthodox religion. There is a famous passage in which they describe the celebration of the liturgy at Hagia Sophia, the Church of the Divine Wisdom, greatest church in Constantinople, a description that brought the Orthodox faith to Russia:

> *We knew not whether we were in heaven or on earth, for surely there is no such splendor or beauty anywhere upon earth. We cannot describe it to you: only this we know, that God dwells there among men, and that their service surpasses the worship of all other places. For we cannot forget that beauty.*

From Constantinople across Russia to Lower Kalskag, where, in its own way, the beauty of St. Seraphim Church overwhelmed. A chandelier of electric bulbs bathed the nave of the church in light. Candles flickered off brass crosses and bells. A miasma of incense mixed with woodsmoke from the barrel stove. Father Epchook stepped to the altar and disappeared through the iconostasis, a wall packed with framed two-dimensional paintings of saints as in a museum that had run out of space. Every arch and frame and light fixture was draped with tinsel and metallic wreaths and artificial bouquets, and further embellished for the season with blinking Christmas lights and doll-faced angels. A plastic Christmas tree stood on a tripod before the altar.

What is an outsider to make of this glittering sorcery? I wondered. It was nearly as far from my experience as the world of the *inua* had been at Cape Prince of Wales. Parishioners filed into the church, pausing to kiss a cross or a painting of a saint. The array of icons did not, in fact, seem all that far removed from the aboriginal world with its multiple divinities, where every bird and tree had shone with its own spiritual light. I knew my notion was possibly blasphemous, but even within the Byzantine world the exact locus of God was not always agreed on. For a century beginning in the year 726, these icons were condemned as graven images. The first Iconoclasts, those who attacked the kissing of icons as idolatry—the raising of "mere matter," of pigment and paint, to the place of God—destroyed many early church paintings, martyred church leaders, and ultimately forced a clarification of Orthodox doctrine, which upheld the veneration of icons not as idols but as representations of the unseen. The flat gilded paintings of Jesus Christ and the Blessed Mother of God are said to be windows on the world beyond. "We do not see the Angels because our sight is weak," one church leader wrote. A saint who died during the struggle with the Iconoclasts said simply: "The icon is a door."

The wall of the iconostasis screened the church nave from the inner sanctuary, where, Father Epchook had explained with baffling matter-of-factness, the holy of holies resides. He came back through a door in the iconostasis, wearing a white silk robe still creased from storage and a flat-topped black hat, a *kamilavka* denoting his seniority in the priesthood. The worn linoleum floor had filled with dozens of parishioners: women wearing bonnets and kerchiefs to my left, men to the right, and an understory of small children moving back and forth.

The core of the choir stood in front of Father Epchook and sang out—in the Orthodox way, without earthly musical accompaniment. They were hoarse, for they had continued starring until the church bell rang at midnight. Father Epchook's voice was even more gravelly as he began to read a long passage in Slavonic.

I wondered again, as I had during starring, if the parishioners crowded into the church understood the words any better than I. I remembered a freshly minted Native priest I'd met at the church gathering on the Nushagak who'd grown up as a candlebearer in a village losing its Native language and had gone off to seminary without every really understanding what the services were about. For him, readings in Yup'ik had been almost as troublesome as in Slavonic. "The first service I attended at seminary was in English and it was like a light bulb," he'd said. "Suddenly I knew what we were saying all these years."

Which turned out fine for him—but for me the language and the glitter left the windows opaque. My sight, too, was weak. I stood against the back wall, grappling with the mean doubts of my own iconoclasm. The congregation was mostly elderly. Was that a sign that in Lower Kalskag the elders were still strong in their values—or did it mean the life of the "Native Church" was draining away, its sad fatalism no match for the traumas of today's rootless young?

At one end of the iconostasis, St. Seraphim looked down from the wall with a gaze steady enough to peer through the centuries of uprootings that had brought the church to these northern woods. I had looked up the saint for whom the church was named: he was one of the *hesychast* saints who withdrew into the wilderness, seeking spiritual knowledge through stillness and detachment. The cheap silver bunting around St. Seraphim did nothing to detract from that quest, but rather, to my eye, seemed to help—a cooler, more sophisticated presentation would have put me on my guard. The dime-store decor was so wholehearted as to be disarming. The beauty of these icons, I decided, was that you really weren't supposed to accept them as divine—they were mere representations, signposts directing your gaze. St. Seraphim had found a door into his own heart and was looking in.

The hour-long service ended with the veneration of the icons. Villagers filed to the front to kiss a painting, then they kissed Father Epchook, and turned and shook hands and kissed each other. The hands of the crowd drew me, shaking and smiling, across the room and out into the night. Doubt and hope, and a fair degree of bafflement—it seemed the appropriate mixture to carry into a new year in an Eskimo village.

As I walked downhill toward the Kuskokwim, people were shouting to each other from snowmachines and launching fireworks. I heard the crack of a rifle shot and flinched.

I had moved my belongings to the village office building for the night. An oil stove had kept the office warm. I spread my sleeping bag on the floor, and the last thing I heard before I shut off the power was a woman's voice on the CB radio, a cry of joy:

"Happy New Year, everybody out there."

In Lower Kalskag, as in many villages, the coming of telephones had not replaced the traditional CB radio that was in every living room. The radio hiss remained at the periphery of conversation, a medium for general announcements and for tracking down individuals—"Switch five," they'd say, and the conversation could be held in relative privacy on another channel.

I was having coffee at the mayor's kitchen table when I heard a voice on the radio say, with no prefatory remark: "Follow the main channel. Take the channel by Akiak, not by Kwethluk."

The mayor said it was the voice of Moses Littlefish, the village police officer, keeping people posted on the latest river conditions.

The people of Lower Kalskag kept their eye on the Kuskokwim at all times. The spring before, an ice jam had backed water up through the sloughs; the water rose three feet in twenty minutes and spilled into some of the low-lying cabins. In summer they waited for barges carrying the year's supplies. People relied on the river for intervillage travel until ice started to run. Then for a while after freeze-up, the ice was unpredictable. People ventured out on snowmachines, but they had to watch for weak ice and overflows. In December a Lower Kalskag trapper coming home after dark had vanished. Search parties checked the open stretches of water downriver but never found a sign of him.

By January, however, the ice was usually more than a foot thick. Each village was responsible for marking and plowing a road down its own section of the river. The mayor said that soon they would have their section connected to Tuluksak, forty-five miles downriver, and then there would be a highway all the way from Kalskag to Bethel. In especially cold winters, they extended the ice road farther upriver to Aniak.

To state transportation planners, the winter road on the Kuskokwim is a nightmare of liability. Official sources will hardly acknowledge it, troopers in Bethel won't give travel advisories. The villages plow the road themselves and watch for trouble spots such as holes in the ice. A traveler going far is well advised to monitor his CB and check in along the way for an update on conditions.

The man responsible for maintaining the river road in Lower Kalskag was a middle-aged white construction worker who had married into the village. He and his wife lived in a modular home near Father Epchook's.

Richard Nash was a hearty fellow full of Jack London tales of survival in the frozen North. He sat back in his easy chair in thick socks the night I dropped by, a plate of fat purple grapes in front of him, while his wife, Malania, made tea. Their small son was doing calisthenics in front of the television.

Nash came from Juneau and had worked in the bush for years. The Kobuk River country in particular had left him stories to tell. One time, traveling cross-country in winter, he had followed the trail of two moose onto the Kobuk, straight into several feet of slushy overflow that swallowed his snowmachine. He waded back to shore, where there was nothing but scrawny willows to feed the fire all night so that his legs wouldn't freeze.

"When I walked barefoot after that it felt like I was walking on two inches of leather," he said.

A clock on the wall chimed a late hour. In the background there was hushed chatter on the CB.

Another time, he said, a bearing on his snowmachine froze up and flipped him over the windshield. Stranded, miles from the nearest village, with a shoulder that felt broken, he followed frozen snowmachine tracks until well past dark, until he came over a ridge and across the river valley could see the lights of Kiana. He had one railroad flare with him. He lighted the red flame and waved it over his head. When it was nearly out, he threw it with his good arm as high as he could. It wasn't long before a friend showed up on a snowmachine to rescue him. The friend had been walking to the village pool hall and happened to look across the valley just as a shooting star flew in the wrong direction.

Another time—but he stopped in midintroduction when we all heard a woman's voice pronounce the word "fire" on the CB.

"That was Fern," Malania said.

We were pulling on our boots and bulky overcoats when a man's voice on the radio said: "Somebody throw water in the stove and close the flue." Apparently it was a stack fire.

Outside, the cold was breathtaking. Every light turned to crystal. We squeezed in the cab of Nash's three-quarter-ton pickup and crunched across the snowy lawn to the road. One January after *slaviq*, Nash said, they had lost a house of their own. Their son had been watching his mother burn trash in a drum out back and imitated her with a fire in the trash basket in the bathroom.

Nash said there was no fire truck in Lower Kalskag. Once a fire got going, there wasn't much they could do except throw snow on it. Several winters ago they'd lost three houses in one cold month. A bucket brigade had saved a fourth.

We sped down the dark road to the Parents' store, occasionally glimpsing the red taillights of a truck on the curves ahead. Behind us, through billowing clouds of snow, came a squadron of snowmachines, their drivers silhouetted in each other's headlights.

The two log stories of the Parents' store were floodlit by headlights. Firefighters were arriving from both directions. A shower of orange sparks flew out the chimney stack, racing up toward a hard moon like shooting stars going in the wrong direction.

Inside the front door, Fern Parent stood at the cash register in her bathrobe, gathering up the receipts. Upstairs, a scrum of men pressed around the woodstove, shooting foam from a fire extinguisher up the stack. In the kitchen, where the memorial feast had been prepared the day before, a plastic bucket filled slowly in the sink. People ran back and forth in the hall.

A trapdoor was open in the ceiling of the hall closet, and crinkled metal shelving marked the path of the firefighters' ascent. On the roof, several men were throwing snow down the chimney.

Later, the stack fire doused with only minor damage, Fern Parent stood tearfully at the store counter, thanking her customers one by one as they departed. People hung on outside, talking awhile before they headed back to their separate villages. We had to wait fifteen minutes for the driveway to clear so we could back out.

"Don't get too many traffic jams in Lower Kalskag," Nash said, enjoying this one.

On the way back to the village, Nash made a sudden turn left. The woods vanished. Darkness closed in where there were no trees to reflect the headlights, but at the same time a new horizon, faint in the moonlight, opened wide. We were on the Kuskokwim.

The river road was a single lane through the snow. Small spruce trees flashed past the headlights: Nash had planted them in the ice to mark the route, and to help him plow when it drifted.

"The first rule is keep to the road," Nash said. "Don't follow snowmachine trails with a vehicle, or ninety percent of the time you will get stuck somewhere—if not in an overflow, then in the drifts that ride up along the edge of the river. Second rule is watch for overflows. Sometimes you can have a crust and it's hard to tell. In a warm spell, the road can get slippery, but when it's zero like this there's good traction."

We were tearing down the river at an astonishing speed.

"Five inches of ice will support a vehicle, but just barely. I check it with a chainsaw. Personally I'll drive when there's twelve inches. I'll start staking the route and hauling loads at sixteen."

I asked about the trapper who'd been lost in December. Nash said he'd been coming downriver on a three-wheeler, following old tracks—"happy going home"—but he came upon a stretch of glare ice with no tracks, guessed wrong in the dark, and hit open water.

"One of the best things you can do is keep on the ice over deep water. Follow the river channel the same way the tugs and barges do. That is the best ice right up until breakup, when the ice finally needles up and rots out."

We fell into silence. There was nothing to look at except the straight-running tracks. We were getting farther and farther from the village. In the warmth of the church, or the excitement of the fire, I had nearly forgotten how big and dark the surrounding country was. Now I started to imagine our trip turning into another of Nash's Jack London survival tales.

I was jolted to attention when the truck swerved suddenly into deep snow. Nash was turning around.

Once home, his relish of cold unslaked, Nash pulled a carton of Neapolitan ice cream from the freezer, peeled the cardboard wrapping as if it were a fruit, and carved thick tricolor slabs with a butcher knife.

Nash said people really got serious about the road after the state's oil affluence put pickup trucks in a number of the river villages. Before that, though, the villages used the river for winter transportation on snowmachines and dog sleds. People still used snowmachines, of course, and you still saw Yup'ik drivers with dog teams on the river, though today, he said, much of the dog driving was for sport.

"The Kusko 300 comes right up the Kuskokwim from Bethel. Kalskag, Whitefish Lake, and back. Three hundred miles in three days. The race is in just a few days. You should be here—it's a big day in the village."

But I continued down the river and caught the race instead in Tuluksak.

9. River People

D id you find a place to build your house yet?"
Anna Phillip liked to tease me about my interest in the
bush. If I was so curious about life out there, why didn't
I go live in a village? Anna was a pretty woman in her late
twenties, with broad cheeks and jet-black hair. We were
walking through the snow to see the river I'd heard so much about.
Anna wore a fur parka made by her mother in the traditional style of
the lower Kuskokwim: pieced-together ground squirrel, with tassels of
wolverine fur. In Anchorage I'd seen her wear the parka proudly over
her Nordstrom outfits.

Anna lived in Bethel now, but when I first met her she was the
battling mayor of Tuluksak, fighting a mining company to protect her
people's river. I'd subsequently gotten into the habit of calling her
when I had questions about politics on the Yukon-Kuskokwim delta.
We visited when she came to Anchorage, and I would pepper her with
questions about the village where she grew up. Her parents were very
traditional, religious, busy people. Anna and her brothers and sisters
learned their lessons by remaining silent and observant. Things were
seldom explained outright—which put them at a disadvantage, she
had said, when they went to school and were expected to ask ques-

tions. Now here I was, learning to keep my mouth shut if I wanted to find out what was going on around me, and I fought to keep from slipping back to my old interrogatory ways in the presence of Anna, who had caught a ride in a truck up the river from Bethel to see her parents, watch the sled-dog race, and show me around Tuluksak.

Maybe I'd come to build a summer home on the Kuskokwim, I teased back. A place to come and be lazy during my vacations. Maybe throw out a subsistence net . . .

We came to the Tuluksak River. A steep bank dropped off at the edge of the village into a channel only fifty yards across and frozen, lined with snowmachine tracks, moribund and anticlimactic.

A wooded island hides the village of Tuluksak from the main channel of the Kuskokwim. Like a midwestern hamlet skirted by an interstate highway, the village sits back and focuses a proprietary interest on a tributary, the Tuluksak, a clear-flowing waterway that comes down from hunting country in the Kilbuck Mountains. The people of Tuluksak travel on the river, fish in it, and pump it for drinking water, so they were quite naturally alarmed when the water turned cloudy in June a few years earlier. The river was so muddy the elders said it was going to flood, but it didn't rise. People got diarrhea and quit drinking from the river. The water turned rusty and orange, and it left a funny stain, so that all summer riverboats from Tuluksak could be recognized along the Kuskokwim by a brown waterline, like the line in a toilet bowl.

Finally the village leaders chartered a plane and flew to the mountains, where they discovered bulldozers tearing up the riverbed to get at gold. To stop them, the village sought help from Calista, the regional Native corporation, but Calista had its own mineral deposits in the Kilbuck Mountains and chose to remain on the sidelines. Anna, who was mayor at the time, led Tuluksak to court. The miners, it turned out, had a legal claim to the river under federal mining laws written in 1872. Indeed, there had been miners on the river since the 1920s. They were just getting more ambitious. Now they planned to dig a new channel and reroute the river so they could scrape gold out of the old riverbed.

The fight had radicalized Tuluksak. The village didn't even have a mayor anymore—a tribal council ran things. They were active partners in the Native sovereignty movement. Anna's father was on the elders council of Yupiit Nation. Anna meanwhile had moved on to Bethel to fight the miners' permits as head of the state/federal coastal zone management program for the Yukon-Kuskokwim delta. In the time I'd known her, she'd been changing, waking to a larger world: she grew more confident and articulate defending the subsistence life-style of the delta, while at the same time flying off to Anchorage for ski weekends and shopping trips. I didn't know how she pieced the two different worlds together, and suspected she was making it up as she went; but she accepted my interest in her parents' world more readily than I did hers in mine.

Anna invited me to come meet her parents that evening. They lived in a new government-financed house already broken in to their own way of life. In the light of a single bulb by the door, the snowy yard was full of split wood and snowmachines and a sled under repair, its runners upside down, everything laid out in an orderly fashion for the chores of hauling water and firewood, hunting and fishing and trapping.

I entered a living room–kitchen of family mementoes and framed pictures and piles of hats and mittens. Anna invited me to sit at the kitchen table. Emma Phillip, gray and matronly, brought me a bowl of moose stew and drew back quietly; she seemed not at all the strong-willed woman I expected. Anna had told me how her mother objected when Anna decided, after high school in Bethel, to go away to bible college in Seattle. Anna went anyway, and at Christmas her mother visited. It was Emma Phillip's first trip outside Alaska. She was to have stayed two weeks, but when it snowed in Seattle she said she was homesick and flew back to the Kuskokwim delta. It made Anna homesick, too. When the year ended, she returned home to Tuluksak to stay.

It must have been a remarkable year in the Lower Forty-eight, though. At spring break she decided to visit a pen pal she'd acquired years earlier in Tuluksak. Anna set out by bus across the country. North Dakota reminded her of the tundra. Her pen pal lived in the South Bronx, in a tiny apartment with her mother and five siblings. The family had to buy a plate and cup for Anna to use. They were proud of their Eskimo visitor from up North but all Anna could think about was that they were so poor, they made the delta villages seem rich. At home, she said, they could go out and get what they needed from the land.

Anna's father was seated at the far end of the living room, absorbed in a state-TV presentation of "Hill Street Blues." I sat with Anna and her younger brother, Willie, who had sled dogs of his own and talked about contenders in the imminent Kusko 300. He said he didn't have a strong enough team to enter a big race like that one yet. Willie used his dogs to haul firewood and work his father's trapline. In summer he traveled on the river in a canoe with a 15-horse kicker. Anna found it amusing that he was so different from their brother Joe, who loved big snowmachines, pickups, and a riverboat with an 85-horse outboard. Willie said it worked out: he helped Joe get food for his family, and when Willie's engines broke down Joe could fix them. Willie fished the deep channels of the Kuskokwim every summer with a drift net. He brought home several thousand salmon every year. He was married, had a small kid, and was responsible for feeding four families, including his parents and in-laws. Being a provider meant more than the work of subsistence, though. He had gone to Kotzebue to learn an electrician's trade, and sometimes he left the village now for union jobs that brought the family cash. In the confused debate over who should qualify for subsistence, politicians sometimes suggested an income cutoff for rural people—subsistence as welfare. Such an idea ignored the reality that the hard-working households with the most income were often the biggest hunting and fishing providers for the village.

Emma Phillip said something to their father in Yup'ik. I heard the word "seven" and asked Anna why I often heard English numbers. She smiled and offered to count to ten in Yup'ik. By five or six I thought she had decided to translate the Gettysburg Address instead.

When the television show ended, Anna's father pulled on a fur hat and boots and went out. A few minutes later he came back stomping off the cold, with an armload of firewood. I wondered if he seemed distant because of the language barrier, or because he associated me with the westernization of his daughter, some unwelcome seducer. But once the stove was loaded he seated himself at the head of the table and, looking squarely at me, spoke in Yup'ik.

"He wants to know if you want to hear some folklore," Anna said.

Joshua Phillip spoke, and Anna and Willie took turns translating. I knew he wasn't just being quaint on my behalf, for I remembered Anna saying her father used to tell stories all the time when they were little. This was a Yup'ik evening's entertainment, pre-television, and their father knew the stories had to be told through countless reruns if they weren't to be forgotten.

Tonight's program, perhaps because of the race tomorrow, was about sled dogs. The people used to travel great distances with dogs, he said. When there were few beaver on the Tuluksak River, they crossed the Kilbuck Mountains to trap around the Nushagak Lakes. I thought of my kayak trip in the upper Nushagak Lakes the previous fall. Crossing the mountains, their father said, some mushers wrapped chains around their sled runners so they wouldn't fly like airplanes going downhill. Those who didn't use chains flew along behind their sleds, holding on, legs straight back. Anna smiled as she translated this, knowing what came next. If they opened their mouths, Anna said, the wind whistled through and made a song.

The night was clear as I walked back to the school later, thinking about other stories I'd heard. A hunter without a compass, lost in a whiteout on the featureless tundra, navigated by watching for "fishbacks," crusty lines of drift hardened by the predominant north wind. When he lost the fishbacks he remembered which way the wind had blown during the first winter storm and dug through the snow to see how the grass was bent. When he spoke of overland travel in the winter, of how the tundra was frozen and you could go anywhere you wanted, Joshua Phillip made winter seem not a shut in and depressed time after all. They would navigate by the night sky and know how long it was until daylight. They would know the next day's weather by watching the high wind, the flicker and pulse of the stars.

R ace day in Tuluksak touched every life in the village.

Mollia Alexie showed up for work lugging her television set and huffing a cloud of steam. Sunlight was just hitting the snow in the treetops, and inside the new log building that housed the health clinic, it was cold. During the night someone had backed into the oil drum outside, crimping the fuel line. Fortunately nothing had frozen. Always ready for the unexpected after sixteen years on the job, Mollia Alexie started race day with a wrench.

Alexie was the village health aide—one of the unsung heroes of the bush. Underpaid, isolated, and on twenty-four-hour call, she provided emergency medical care, tended the sick, advised the pregnant, and challenged the habits of generations with the lessons of modern public health. Public Health Service doctors in Bethel called every day to check in, and sometimes prescribed treatments and medicines over the phone. For them, the village health aides were vital links, and they had described Alexie as one of the best. She was forty-two years old, a big woman who inspired confidence with her sheer presence as well as her deliberate manner, but she was shy talking to a stranger about her work.

The sun had barely reached the snow berms in the road outside when a young mother arrived with two small children wearing bandannas over their faces, like Western outlaws, to ward off the ten-below cold. Alexie used the clinic phone to call the hospital in Bethel, telling them to send more Tylenol on the next mail plane. With the flu going around, she said, it was going to be a busy day.

Out here, the word "flu" conjured grisly images of ghost villages. Part of her job was to keep an eye out for endemic diseases of the delta, such as tuberculosis and hepatitis, but the modern age had put an end to the old-time epidemics—while bringing several new ones. Posters on the office wall encouraged breast feeding and warned against chewing snuff and sniffing gas. She counted herself lucky that she hadn't had to deal with the kind of alcoholic violence some villages faced. She got involved in the controversy over the Tuluksak River, sending water to Bethel for testing after they found fish floating in it. They found some kind of chemical pollutant, she said, and she warned people to quit drinking from the river.

One time a villager accidentally shot himself in the leg, and there were frequent three-wheeler accidents with children. Alexie had quit the job for two years but came back because the village needed her.

"Even if it's not a physical problem they come to me. Sometimes I feel like I'm a priest," she said. "If I didn't really like my job, I'd have quit a long time ago. It's like it's a part of me."

At noon she turned on the television in her examination room and tuned in the public TV station in Bethel. The first racers in the Kusko 300 were starting out. Usually it took about five hours for the lead racers to reach Tuluksak, so the village could expect them just after dark.

When the broadcast ended, she picked up the CB radio microphone and spoke in Yup'ik over the village's open channel. She told me she'd asked people with flu not to walk down to the river to see the race. And if they were going anyway, she'd told them, they should wrap up warmly and not stay out too long. Sixteen years as a village health aide had made Mollia Alexie a practical woman.

Tuluksak's two boyish-looking cops were among the day's patients. Larry George had the flu, and Peter Andrew had skinned his knee playing basketball. They entered the clinic meekly, and Peter Andrew rested his shotgun against a file cabinet. As they left they invited me to come along on patrol.

Most days the two young men patrolled on snowmachines. Today they rode in the cab of the city's bright red fire truck. They had to drive the fire truck periodically, to keep it in tune, because the village had no garage. Having no garage, they couldn't fill the truck's tanks with water, so it could not actually be used for fires, except as transportation.

The state had granted the city council money for a truck but not for a garage (in Kalskag they had a garage but no truck). Tuluksak's village administrator later told me they never had much control over what capital projects came to them from Juneau—"It's like writing to Santa Claus," he said—and they had even less now that the city council had turned local administration over to the village tribal council, an institution of federal Indian law. The state was uneasy about making grants to Indian nations, especially, perhaps, one that was putting whatever state money it could get into a lawsuit against the state agencies that had approved gold mining permits for the Tuluksak River.

In the meantime, the two policemen told me as we drove a circuit of the plowed gravel streets, the most useful thing about the fire engine had been its siren, which they used to announce the nightly curfew for schoolchildren.

Tuluksak was a morally strict village. We drove past a source of that morality, the village's plain Moravian church. In the same parceling of Native Alaska that sent Harrison Thornton to Cape Prince of Wales for the Congregationalists, the Moravians had been assigned the lower Kuskokwim River, where they pushed into territory already Christianized by the Russians but shorn of its Orthodox priests after the sale of Alaska.

In 1884 Moravians established a base at the first trading post of the Alaska Commercial Company on the Kuskokwim and named it for the Bible text for the day they landed: "God said unto Jacob, Arise, go up to

Bethel, and dwell there, and make there an altar unto God that appeared unto thee." The Moravians were committed to learning the Yup'ik language and translated the New Testament, and by working with lay elders eventually turned half a dozen villages their way. But the missionaries' success came at a cost to the traditional culture of the river Eskimos. Unlike the Orthodox missionaries, the Moravians campaigned actively to stamp out the heathen ceremonials, replacing the bladder festivals and feasts for the dead with Thanksgiving and Christmas. They opposed spirit dancing and convinced several villages to do away with dance masks. They worked to break apart the men's communal houses and have husbands and wives live together.

None of the nuclear families was moving around much in the cold yet. In winter villagers were slow to stir.

Flu or no, Larry George said, he would have to be down at the river tonight. A whole fleet of pickup trucks would be headed up the ice road, following the race. In Tuluksak, people always got a little nervous when Bethel crowds showed up.

Tall willows hovered over the small building that served as Peter Waskie's store. The door was padlocked shut. Tacked to the door was a note in a shaky hand, written on a piece of cardboard:
WHEN THIS DOOR IS CLOSED THAT MEANS I AM GOING OUT TO VISIT AND REST. DO NOT LOOK FOR ME AT MY MOTHER'S HOUSE BECAUSE SHE IS OLD. 86 YEAR OLD NOV. 1986.

I was deciding that an outsider would have to marry into a village like this to have a place. I'd met a few white men like that in my travels—Dan Richard in Wales, and others of seemingly more modest ambition. They hunted with the other men and built little houses that were different from the village standard because they didn't qualify for

Indian housing or didn't care for it, maybe instead a California-style double-shed roof with a loft window, where they padded around in sock feet surrounded by little dark-haired kids . . .

A towering yellow grader was rumbling toward the airstrip, and I watched it execute a dinosaur's pirouette and come back through the willows. I stood expectantly by the road, but the grader rolled past. Strangers in the village on race day seemed to attract less curiosity than at other times. I ran ahead and caught up.

Perched on its high throne was a crotchety older white man who said he wanted to make sure the strip was clear before company started showing up.

"You never know what you'll find," he said. "A log will be lying across the middle of the runway, or a snowdrift, or maybe a body."

Fred Hess had lived in the bush for twenty-eight years. He was what I didn't expect to find, a white man on his own. He'd come to Tuluksak seven years ago to help install a power plant and electric lines and had worked here ever since as maintenance man, but his relationship with the village council administration had been stormy. Every once in a while he got fed up and threatened to leave. He'd storm off toward Anchorage, aiming to return to the East Coast, but then he'd cool off and come back. Two years ago, though, he'd had it for good.

"I guess you know what happened then."

He was surprised that I didn't.

"It was on the front page of all the newspapers," he said.

He'd piled his belongings in a riverboat and headed down the Kuskokwim and off the delta. He planned to motor around by the Aleutians to Anchorage and then fly south, but a fall storm blew in, his engine died, and for three weeks he tossed around the Bering Sea. He tied himself to the boat in case he was swept overboard. The coast guard gave up the search and notified his next of kin. His boat wrecked in the surf on Nunivak Island. He was hiking overland toward the village of Mekoryuk when some Eskimos found him.

Discouraged in his escape attempt, he had returned to Tuluksak.

"I was living off the beach, eating seal oil and seaweed. In fact, I was living better than I am now. I've about had it here. Next year I just may go back to Hopwood, Pennsylvania."

At 1:50 P.M. daylight spilled through the dusty window frames of the village corporation store onto half-empty shelves. There was plenty of Pinesol, in family-size jugs, for the honeybuckets in homes without flush toilets. Otherwise, not much—once the ice road opens and customers can make a day-long trip to Bethel's supermarkets, business gets slow.

An elderly man leaned over a counter next to an empty popcorn machine. He was concentrating on a ledger of numbers, muttering softly. Perhaps he was counting in Yup'ik, for it was several minutes before he looked up.

"I heard first team left Kwethluk," he said.

Outside a plywood house a man in a pea army jacket was shoveling frozen salmon out of a drum. He was surrounded by chained dogs, not the first I'd seen in Tuluksak. Dogs in the bush had not been so universally replaced by snowmachines as I'd imagined.

I hung back, watching the dogs wrestle the fish greedily. I was intimidated by their yapping and by the battered-looking face of the man in the old jacket. His jaw was clenched tight on a piece of gauze.

He looked up at me and spit a gob of blood into the snow.

Peter Gregory had been to see the itinerant Public Health Service dentist who had set up a portable hydraulic drill for the day in the elementary school.

He told me he planned to take his dog team trapping up the Tuluksak River. He didn't dare go on a snowmachine.

"There's not much snow now," he said. "No base on the trails. I can go broke buying parts on a snowmachine."

His dogs were bred for strength and endurance, not speed. "That guy there is one-eighth wolf," he said, pointing to a large dog that was studying me closely, as if considering a sudden alternative to his fish diet. "I carried a twenty-two pistol when I was training him."

Gregory paused to take another spit.

"He can lead, he knows gee and haw, but his main aim in life is to piss me off."

Like many villages along the Kuskokwim, Tuluksak was seeing a revival in dogs—and not just for sport, though racing was what gave the whole revival kick. In the Kusko 300, racers from the local villages got to test themselves against the biggest names in the state. There were three teams from Tuluksak in the race this year, and Gregory said it was hard to predict how they'd do.

The year before Joe Demantle, Jr., had been rookie of the year. The family had raised dogs a long time—Joe Sr., a race veteran, was now in charge of the Tuluksak checkpoint. But Joe Jr. hadn't put too many training miles on his dogs this year, Gregory said. John Napoka had been training hard, but his dogs were sick lately and ran like they were drunk. The third racer, Eddie Peter, had a team made up of several teams in the village and was untested.

"It's pretty tough breeding dogs here. We've got a lot of loose dogs running around," Gregory said. "Down in Akiak, they've got a serious loose-dog ordinance. That's a musher's town."

I asked if I'd see him down at the river later. He said he'd be there, "to see who's got the top dogs and see if I can get some." Then as the teams headed upriver, he said, he'd probably be up most of the night, following the leaders' progress over the radio.

"I don't hardly sleep during these three days."

Race headquarters was a comfortable living room that looked out across the mouth of the Tuluksak at the white breadth of the Kuskokwim. Three men in snowmachine suits were settled on the couches with cups of coffee. They had just come upriver from Bethel on their "iron dogs," a sixty-mile trip to set trail for the mushers.

"It's getting windy out there on the river," one of them said. "The drifts from yesterday are already hard."

"They're going to be flying," another said.

As soon as the race officials arrived by plane, the snowmachines would proceed upriver. From the checkpoint the course turned up the Tuluksak River for several miles before winding through frozen sloughs back to the main channel. The next checkpoint would be Kalskag.

In the meantime, the warmth in Joe Demantle Sr.'s living room was lulling. There were houseplants in the window and three teakettles on the oil stove. A wall calendar provided an advertisement for a Seattle "Outlet for Raw Furs."

The Kusko 300 is the first big race of the Alaska season, and Joe Sr. said in some ways it was the toughest race of all. The days are still short and cold in January, and the race is fast—three hundred miles is too short for any serious contender to think about sleeping. It used to be a friendlier race, but then in 1984 Iditarod champ Rick Swenson had bragged he would cut twenty-four hours off the record time of sixty-five and managed to cut twenty. The race had gotten so fast that they'd added a mandatory six-hour layover, more for the dogs than the racers.

Demantle was thin and weather-worn, a former race marshall known all along the river. He'd just lighted the woodstove in his old house, hard by the riverbank where it nearly washed away in a flood the spring after it was built. The mushers would be able to warm up there when they stopped at Tuluksak to feed their teams.

I asked about the duties of a checkpoint official.

"My job is feed 'em. Just like the dogs," he said with a laugh. "Them mushers are my dogs."

The padlock was off Peter Waskie's store the next time I passed by. In my rounds I'd heard that Waskie might be able to tell me something about the old medicine ways. I hesitated at the door, arrested by sudden shyness. How would I manage to raise the subject of shamanism? It seemed far more daunting than approaching a Russian Orthodox priest.

I passed through a porch and entered a small sanctum crowded with boxes and lighted by an overhead bulb. A chicken-wire cage from floor to ceiling enclosed the back of the room. Candy and cigarettes were displayed behind the wire. A gate through the screen was open, but another padlock hung nearby.

Tacked to the wall behind the counter was a handwritten sign: NO CREDIT TO EVERYONE!!! OWNER OF THIS STORE, PETER WASKIE. Next to the sign, the eyes of an owl, clipped from a magazine, held the room under sinister scrutiny.

A man in his sixties emerged from a back room.

"Slow business when they got that race," he said. "People don't walk around a lot. They want to stay by radio and listen."

I could hear a faint voice from a television in back, where a cot was covered in stacks of clothes. Peter Waskie had close-cut gray hair and bright suspenders and a darting energy that propelled him the length of the counter and back as I spoke. He saw my eyes stray up the wall toward the owl.

"They keep stealing those Spams so I put those eyes like that. No stealing no more."

When he realized I'd come to visit and not to shop, he settled on a stool beneath another sign that read I KNOW WHO STEAL FROM THIS STORE WHEN SHE WORKS HERE. P. WASKIE OWNER.

"Them kids is always pilfering from me. They hide under boxes on the porch when I lock door, get in that way when I go to Christmas service. I stay in here every night. I can't leave this room right now."

I picked up a can of Spam. He had written, in Magic Marker, a price of $3.99.

"I bought for two dollars and some cents," he said. "The rest is for tax. I owe I don't know how much tax. It's because I am single. When you are married I think your taxes will be cheaper. After I pay the tax then I will cut everything down."

A box of Lucky Charms cereal was selling for $4.95.

"They could save maybe three dollars at the corporation store," he said.

"How can you charge that much more?" I asked.

He spread his arms, the great shrug of bush economics. "I got to pay for airplane. How can I make money when I pay charter one hundred eighty-six dollars?"

I had no idea how to circle around to the subject of mystical experience. On the freezer was a sign that said CLOSED CHURCH HOURS.

"I thought I was going to make quick grow bigger the store. Money comes in and goes," he said. "Pay tax, phone, everything, eat, too much, eeeee."

"Who do you get for customers?"

"Little kids, most of them. They got to have candy, soda. Parents come too, sometime. If there is no cut green beans in other store, they will come in here."

We both grinned.

"You were closed when I came by earlier. I didn't see your hours posted."

He leaned back on the stool. "When someone knock in the morning early, maybe they're going hunting or trapping, that's when I open. Start up stove. Stay up until time for bed. On Sunday they say, please Peter, open up a little, I got strangers over here and no bread, I need crackers. So I open it for them, little bit."

He'd been running the store eight years. He'd lived in Tuluksak his whole life. I asked if he went to the Moravian church. He said he'd been baptized there, under the name Peter Andrew. A teacher changed his name to Waskie when he was five years old. When he was grown up he asked the state for his old name back.

"They said to pay twenty-five dollars and fill out green form. I told them, oh, that's okay, I will go that way through life. I wanted to keep my twenty-five dollars that time."

The door opened and two small children with bright-red ears walked in. One of them, a little boy, approached the precipice of the counter and peeped, "Ice cream."

Peter Waskie reached in the freezer, removed several frosty salmon, and extracted two Eskimo Pies. "How much money you got?" he asked them, tilting his head suspiciously.

The little boy held out a dime. Peter Waskie gave them the ice cream bars and they left without another word. He dropped the dime in a cigar box.

"Sometimes those pops almost melt when we're without power for day and a half," he said.

"That's not much of a markup on your Eskimo Pies," I said.

"They're my nephew and niece. I know they will help me when I get older and can't walk. It's Eskimo law."

A dusty plastic chicken sat atop a pedestal next to me. Its nesting box said, in bright circus lettering, "The Chicken Machine." If you put in a quarter, a Lucky Egg would come down the chute.

"I got a good deal for that Chicken Machine, but I couldn't get no eggs," Peter Waskie said.

I blew dust off the Chicken Machine. Amid the shelves of macaroni and saltines, this seemed as close as I would get to shamanism.

A young man entered and asked for a six-pack of Coke. "Do you take credit cards?" he asked.

Waskie rattled something in Yup'ik. He handed the young man a six-pack, accepted his credit card, and dropped the card in the cigar box. The customer left.

"When he comes to pay for Cokes he can get credit card," he said.

I looked at my watch and told Peter Waskie I'd see him later by the river.

On the back of my neck I felt the owl eyes follow me out the door.

The small-engine repair class at the high school had calculated that if the race had reached Akiak at 2:45 P.M., the leaders must be traveling 12.5 miles per hour and would therefore reach Tuluksak early, at 4:15 P.M.

The bell rang at 3:30 and the students scrambled. The young white teacher who'd helped make the calculations put on cross-country ski boots and, with two students who'd been taking ski lessons, set off downriver to light a bonfire and watch for the first musher.

A molten sunset poured light up the main river channel. The first dogs, kicking up snow, backlit as they came around the bend, carried their musher along on a crest of golden foam.

Down on the river, several score people stood in the snow, hoods pulled tight against the breathless cold. A dozen pickup trucks sat on the bluff, engines running, their cabs full. Occasionally someone would hop out to scrape ice off the side windows.

The first musher pulled up, spoke to Joe Demantle, Sr., and signed his clipboard, and was gone before anyone could identify him.

But the next racers to arrive set their brakes in the snow and staked out their dogs and pulled out stoves to heat broth. A long-distance race is not like a sprint. A musher must keep in mind the dogs' needs for food and rest. Some dog teams, like some dog drivers, have an athlete's ability to push beyond themselves in a big race. But push too far and a dog team folds pathetically.

Word passed among the crowd that the first racer through had been Sonny Lindner, a tall backwoodsman from around Fairbanks. Probably he was going up the river just a little to feed his dogs away from the crowd. Susan Butcher, whose dogs were winning more respect every year, had staked out her team near the willows as far from spectators as she could, and set about briskly to feed them. Racers could drop dogs along the way but not add them, and a few were pulling dogs— whether sick or uncooperative, they would be left with handlers in

Tuluksak. A local favorite, Myron Angstman, a lawyer in Bethel, was among the leaders.

I asked a race official if Joe Garnie or Libby Riddles was in the race. Neither was. The previous year Joe had been an early leader in the Kusko 300. The bare-ice conditions that year made it hard to follow the trail—several teams ended up swimming in open holes, though no dogs were lost. Joe had been way out front on a record pace when he shocked everyone by dropping out. He said the ice was hurting his dogs' paws. Joe's conservative approach had paid off, as it was only a month later that Libby won the Iditarod with some of the same dogs.

The crowd on the river had grown to nearly a hundred as the light turned gray. The racers, red-faced and breathing heavily when they arrived, wore light jackets among the heavily clad spectators. Village kids crowded around as each racer signed in, carefully avoiding the dogs. Several of the mushers were women, and they drew the little girls. These were the big names in dog racing: it would be like hanging around the dugout at Yankee Stadium.

Eddie Peter was the first Tuluksak racer to arrive, pulled by a long team of fifteen dogs. Several boys helped out by jumping on his runners for the last fifty feet. John Napoka showed up a few minutes later, anchored his sled, and walked home for a meal.

Joe Demantle, Jr., reached Tuluksak well after dark, nearly two hours behind the leaders. His dogs climbed the bank into the family dog yard and lay down. Joe Sr. came over to consult. The dogs were sick. Joe Jr. said if they didn't get better by Kalskag he would scratch.

Each sled and dog team was staked out in shadowy profile beneath the quarter moon. Tiny yellow stove flames were scattered across the flats, like the campfires of an army in bivouac. Under cover of darkness, mushers were slipping away. Most of the villagers had gone home.

Hiking up from the river, I saw Anna's parka waiting in the shadows.

"So did you find a place to build your summer house?" she asked.

I described my day in her hometown and mentioned my visit with Peter Waskie.

"Did you ask him about the gold mining?" she said. "He's really angry about that. You ask him about the mining and he'll yip yap at you."

We had reached her parents' house.

"He wants people to live that old way from the land," she said. "Once you can't rely on the land, everything gets all turned upside down."

"Will he be at the meeting in Akiachak?"

"Sure, lots of people from Tuluksak will be going there."

"Tuluksak seems like a busy place on race day," I said. "I'm not sure how it would be the rest of the winter."

"It's nice," she said—then, more slowly, "It's quiet. I like it better than summertime. *Waa,* my mother made us work all the time in summer. Camping, cutting fish, cleaning, picking berries. We never got to rest. I always used to look forward to wintertime."

"No summer vacations?"

"One time I went on a river trip with some land use planners," Anna said. "It was a wilderness study river. I felt funny. I got nervous the whole time. I couldn't get used to just traveling. Always when I went to the mountains with my family it was to gather food."

I could not tell which was the stronger emotion in her voice, pride or regret. "It was really *amazing* when I found out people took their vacation time in summer," she said. "Sit around in the sun, go swimming—I never even thought about that."

Back by the river, in the light and warmth of Joe Demantle, Sr.'s, old house, the retinue of race followers dined at last. There was beef stew, berry *akutaq,* peanut butter and jelly sandwiches, cookies, Tang and coffee. I recognized several of the party: a radio reporter from

Bethel who turned in hourly updates for KYUK, a writer from the weekly *Tundra Drums*, two race officials from Anchorage.

I thought about how the race would seem to them, following by plane, jumping from place to place. I knew that method of travel well enough. And how different it would be to those who sat here in their village by the Kuskokwim: waiting as the racers approached, rushing to the river as they arrived, and then watching the sleds recede in the night.

"The snow's better than I've ever seen it," one of the officials was saying. "Better than when Swenson set the record."

A pilot who had just flown down from Kalskag entered and collapsed on a chair.

"They're really moving," he said. "I saw the leader's light—might have been Butcher, I couldn't tell. Whoever it was is already better'n halfway to Kalskag."

The two race officials looked at each other with some alarm. They had to be in Kalskag before the mushers. Their pilot stood up. They thanked Demantle for his hospitality and rushed for the airstrip.

I followed them out. The party on the river had about flickered out. Only a couple of teams, out of it already on the first night, were still staked in silhouette on the snow. A dark line of trees marked the far side of the Kuskokwim, and above the trees the stars were fierce, pulsating, engorged with cold. I stood still on the bank, held by something unexpected. The night said, *Here. This is what you wanted.*

A dog team was barking, eager to be off.

The race reached Aniak and then the next day and night rippled back through Lower Kalskag, Tuluksak, Akiak, Akiachak, and Kwethluk. Before the third dawn Myron Angstman had pulled first into Bethel with a new record time for the Kusko 300, and I had caught a ride downriver to the heart of the Yupiit Nation.

10. Yupiit Nation

*T*he Kuskokwim River swerves wider and wider as it moves across the delta. By the time it reaches the village of Akiachak, the interior spruce forest that straggles along the shore finally gives way to dense stands of willow— "little sticks," as they are known locally. People from the coast say they don't like being in the mountains, and even the little sticks seem confining. They prefer the open tundra, and sometimes make jokes about the river villages, saying people from the woods are slow-talking, meaning not so bright; while river people tease back that coastal people smell of seal oil. But they are all Yup'ik, and villages from tundra and forest and little-sticks country all were to be represented at the Yupiit Nation meeting.

High feathers of cloud were drifting up from the coast when I got to Akiachak. A front was approaching and I found myself studying the sky, drawing on its immensity to gauge the tundra that stretched in all directions. Surrounded by little sticks, I saw no tundra, only the frozen Kuskokwim and the houses of Akiachak, piled around in snow.

A road from the airstrip led first to a jumble of older houses strewn like marbles. Half the village's four hundred fifty residents lived here, in houses of log or red plywood, surrounded by snowmachines and oil drums. Skiffs were frozen into snow by the river landing. Farther on was an elementary school complex built by the Bureau of Indian Affairs, the fulcrum of the village. The concrete and lime-green paint evoked a faded era of bush construction by the federal government. A boardwalk around the school gave notice of the bogginess of the land in summer. From the village store a road followed a straight line of a dozen newer homes until you came, at the far end of the village, to the new high school, a steep-roofed, brown-stained wooden structure that evoked the current construction era, in which the Alaska supreme court had ruled every village has the right to a high school if it wishes to keep its young people at home.

Outside a small office building, a chubby-faced man in quilted coveralls was unstrapping a briefcase from the back of a snowmachine. He had thick glasses and a mustache, and black hair hung out from the back of his cap.

He looked up and smiled shyly. "Oh. Hey. You made it."

I pulled off a mitten and we shook hands. His cheeks looked pale.

"I was in Bethel," he said. "Had to get groceries for my family before things get too busy."

I had met Willie Kasayulie several times before, at meetings in Anchorage concerning the consequences of the land claims act. The first time, in a room of big talkers, I almost overlooked him. He stood back against a wall, as unprepossessing as his country of little sticks. But I was intrigued that most of the elders at the meeting seemed to have come from the lower Kuskokwim, from the vicinity of his village. Then I heard that what everyone in the room was talking about, his village had gone ahead and done.

Akiachak was once a second-class city, chartered under state law, but the villagers had voted to dissolve their city council and turn over all municipal assets to the village IRA council, a tribal government chartered under the federal Indian Reorganization Act of 1934. The village corporation intended to follow suit. Working with the fragments of self-government they had inherited in the 1980s, Akiachak's leaders planned to assemble their own small Yup'ik nation. In doing so, they were challenging the state, Congress, and the regional Native corporations formed under the land claims act. It was a fairly remarkable departure from the customary soft-spoken unison that had until then governed statewide Native politics in a simulation of the old consensual manner of village decision making.

I followed Willie Kasayulie into the IRA office, a room filled by a desk stacked with agendas and books on Indian law. For the remainder of the afternoon, as the telephone rang and his lieutenants interrupted, I heard more about Akiachak's revolution from the first chief of the Yupiit Nation.

The historic and economic isolation of the Yukon-Kuskokwim delta was not enough to protect the Yup'ik culture, he said. Change was coming anyway, and the elders were concerned. People were forgetting how to hunt and fish; they were getting wasted on alcohol and drugs, forgetting the words of their ancestors.

Outsiders who came to the delta and visited only Bethel could be expected to assume the worst about the bush. Bethel, the regional center for state and federal government offices, was also the center for bootlegging. It offered escape from village life but nothing else. The breakdown of Yup'ik culture was worst there. If Akiachak was among the first villages to seek self-determination, the reason might be that they were only twenty-three miles from Bethel. People from Bethel came upriver looking for firewood, helping themselves to trees along the Gweek River, from Akiachak's land. Akiachak remembered when Bethel was predominantly a Native town. They'd seen their neighbor grow, and watched the composition of the Bethel city council change until a majority was non-Native.

I couldn't help thinking that Akiachak's activism probably owed as much to the luck of Willie's presence as to geography. Willie had been the first boy in the village to go away to high school at a time when there was no school in the village beyond sixth grade. He had studied at a federal school for Indians in Oregon and then, through a Dartmouth

University program, spent two years in high school in White River Junction, Vermont. He could have remained in the larger world, but instead he returned to the Kuskokwim, worked in the village store for his corporation, and traveled to the Lower Forty-eight for workshops on tribal government.

Willie attributed the village's activism to its elders. They were worried about the threats to Native subsistence, and they were worried about losing their land. The forty-four million acres that went to Native corporations under the 1971 land claims act came with a catch. In 1991 a twenty-year restriction on taxation and sale of Native corporation stock was to be lifted. Unsuccessful corporations stood to lose their land to the banks or the state, prosperous ones to outside takeovers. What's more, the claims act awarded corporate shares only to Natives born by 1971; future generations had a stake in the land only if their parents handed down the stock. The elders were worried that someday in the future, the real people would no longer exist.

The danger was by this time well recognized all over Alaska. The Alaska Federation of Natives had gone to Congress, seeking to amend the original land claims settlement to protect Native corporations against loss of their assets through bankruptcy and takeover. But the AFN amendments did nothing to challenge the structure of the corporations. The AFN represented the views of the biggest regional corporations, Willie said. The business corporation, no less than the city council form of government, was not an institution that could be used to protect Native culture.

To break the patterns imposed by Congress, Akiachak had first created a council of elders. Willie worked as a kind of intermediary between the elders and the outside world. The city council members voted themselves out of business, and the IRA council set up their own police force to handle local problems, with a tribunal of elders to serve as judges. This sort of system was common on reservations in the Lower Forty-eight, he said, but had been pretty much forgotten in Alaska.

Willie Kasayulie described the Native sovereignty movement underway in Alaska in terms of "self-determination." The effort to save
corporation land was giving focus to a larger effort to fight assimilation
and preserve Alaska Native cultures through use of Native institutions.
Yupiit Nation—Yupiit is a plural of Yup'ik—would expand the con-
cept to a regional confederation of villages operating under tribal law.
Already the neighboring villages of Tuluksak and Akiak had joined
Akiachak, and more than a dozen villages were sending delegates to the
meeting. Maybe someday most of the delta would belong to tribal
governments instead of corporations, Willie said.

State officials were less than pleased by attempts to remove Native
lands from their jurisdiction. The state boundary commission threw
up its hands at Akiachak's vote to disband the city council. Commis-
sioners said they had authority to approve creation of new cities in
Alaska, but the only cities they'd ever dissolved were abandoned
mining towns. They decided they lacked statutory authority to say
when a city still in existence was no longer a city. The state government
had withheld thousands of dollars in revenue-sharing funds, waiting for
an application from a city council that survived only on paper. The
Akiachak IRA council refused to compromise and went without the
money.

The Yupiit Nation faced more serious obstacles than perplexed
bureaucrats. The right to declare "Indian country" in Alaska had not
been clearly established by Congress or the federal courts. As in Tetlin,
hunting and fishing groups opposed sovereignty on the delta—more so
because the claims of sovereignty on the delta were more sweeping; less
so because the hunting and fishing resources were more distant from
urban populations. Even the Alaska Federation of Natives was alarmed
by this display of Native self-assertion. As part of the meeting that
week, leaders of the federation were coming to Akiachak to discuss
their differences. It was an uncommon opportunity to witness a
showdown between the two classic strands of Native American politics,
assimilationist and separatist, as they had developed in the Alaska bush.

The part of me that had learned to pull for the Indians in Western movies was looking forward to that part of the week.

Willie introduced an assistant, Jackson Lomack, who had come into the office looking for a Yup'ik-language dictionary. Jackson, the new nation's theoretician, wore glasses and a Lenin goatee. He had on a nylon "Yupiit Nation" cap with gold scroll on the bill. He'd ordered a bagful of caps to sell at the meeting.

Willie explained that Jackson was in charge of drafting a constitution. First he had to find out from the elders what the old rules were, then record the rules in Yup'ik—a complicated procedure, for Yup'ik had been only a spoken language until this century, and there was still disagreement over how to spell most words.

He showed me an agenda for the Yupiit Nation meeting. The agenda was written out in long concatenations of Yup'ik words. The theme, self-determination, was written "Wangkutnek Auluklerkarput."

"There are two kinds of writing," Willie said. "The university has developed a new writing system, which is closer to the sounds. It's easier for non-Natives to read, but the elders can't understand it. They only read the old spelling, which was used to translate the Bible."

"They stole our religion, then they stole our language," Jackson said.

"Which way do you spell, the old or the new?" I asked.

"We don't really spell either way," Willie said. "When we went to school, we were never allowed to speak our own language. We're still learning to write it now."

As more delta people arrived that evening for the meeting, I was disappointed to find myself shunted off among the village's whites. I had dinner with three teachers new to the bush and a fourth held over from the pre–tribal government days. Over canned corn and pork chops, they talked enthusiastically about the bush survival skills courses the school planned to offer. They were all wide-eyed about the changes taking place and a little fearful. They quizzed me about what

I'd learned from Willie Kasayulie, who was, along with his other positions, president of the joint school board recently formed by Akiachak, Akiak, and Tuluksak. For them it was hard to get straight information. They went to the school board meetings, they said, but business was now carried out in Yup'ik.

I spent the night with two teachers who lived in sterile government housing near the old BIA school. We talked about the states where they used to live, and when they went to bed I spread my sleeping bag by the door. On the porch their tiny dachsund, frustrated at not being allowed outside so that he could be devoured by the village huskies, crawled into my pack during the night and shredded my wallet.

The next morning the snowy BIA school playground above the river was packed with snowmachines and pickup trucks. Inside, nearly a hundred people sat on folding chairs in the dim artificial light of the elementary school gym. They faced a table at one end of the room, where Willie Kasayulie was speaking into a microphone in Yup'ik from beneath the banner of "Wangkutnek Auluklerkarput." Several other men, elders, sat alongside Willie in checked wool shirts and quilted jackets, among them Joshua Phillip of Tuluksak, Anna's father, who was listed in my English-language edition of the agenda as the Yupiit Nation treasurer. Anna herself was back in Bethel, but would be coming up to Akiachak to observe the meeting with the AFN.

Speaker followed speaker in Yup'ik. No one stopped to translate, and no one needed to. I had been around enough conventions to recognize welcoming speeches and talk about agendas. Somebody said something with the English number nineteen in it, and then I recognized the names of some villages—Tuluksak, Kipnuk, Kasigluk. I guessed, correctly, they were talking about the turnout.

For a nonspeaker, there was little to do but gaze around the gym at faces. A Native rights lawyer from Anchorage, who likewise did not speak Yup'ik, sat with a legal pad in his lap and stared happily ahead while his clients conducted business in a sort of executive session. Close by, an old man intently sculpted a Styrofoam cup with his dirty green fingernails—an old carver, I imagined. The air in the gym grew hot, breathy, and faintly redolent of fish.

I had heard the theory advanced that the Native sovereignty movement in Alaska really amounted to a power struggle between generations. Two decades ago, according to this theory, militant young leaders of the Native community won a land claims settlement from Congress. Now those same leaders had grown comfortable behind desks in the corporations they'd created, and a new generation, unable to squeeze into the offices, required a new field of battle. A glance around the gym in Akiachak showed it was more complicated than that, because there were two different generations here: those in their twenties and thirties, and elders in their sixties and seventies, patriarchs and matriarchs, solid citizens of the Kuskokwim. The generation between them was the only group underrepresented. Perhaps they would arrive with the AFN delegation.

I realized through a growing tedium that historic though the moment was, this was probably the wrong time to have come to see Akiachak. Daily life had been suspended. The three-day political convention had upset the winter rhythms of Akiachak even more than *slaviq* had disrupted Lower Kalskag.

During the lunch break I appealed to Willie for help. I told him I needed to get out to the wilderness and see something of Yup'ik subsistence in winter if I was to understand the traditions they were fighting for. It was a shameless ploy. Willie agreed to see what he could do, but pointed out that everyone was pretty busy now with the meeting. He was the busiest of all, I knew—as he walked away, I felt guilty for pushing my name onto his list of things to do. In my bush travels I hadn't used my position as a reporter for Alaska's largest newspaper so brazenly before—but then I hadn't been anyplace where the advantages of publicity would have been much of a consideration for the people I met.

After lunch I wandered away from the gym and down the hall of the elementary school. Corkboards were decorated with colorful crayon drawings of rivers and fish and little sticks with arms and legs. I peered into the classroom of the kindergarten and first grade, and one of the teachers from dinner the night before waved me in. A dozen pairs of small dark eyes turned from out of my childhood to look at me, gazing up from tiny desks.

"This is a *boy*," the teacher said, resuming work with her flash cards. It was an English lesson. A round-faced Native woman helped out, explaining certain points in Yup'ik to the children.

When the students switched over to their workbooks, I drew the young Native teacher into the hallway to talk. She introduced herself as Sophie Kasayulie. I asked if she was related to Willie.

She smiled and glanced down demurely. "I'm his wife."

Sophie Kasayulie was a teacher's aide. Her job at the school was to teach English to the youngest students, so they can understand the teachers.

"We've held onto the language more than other villages," she said. She spoke with self-consciousness and delicacy, choosing her words as if she were picking a way across a stream on slippery stones. "When I travel out of town, people think my kids are so cute because they speak in Yup'ik. Everyone makes a big deal out of it."

The local fashion in language instruction has changed through the years, more or less as village feelings about the outside world shifted. When Sophie and Willie were children, the BIA schools were taught in English. A few students, like the Kasayulies, prospered and went away to high school; many never got past the language barrier. There was a swing away from English, and by 1979 the first three grades were being taught predominantly in Yup'ik, but that year parents in the village voted to switch back to English because their children were falling behind in statewide standardized tests.

Sophie's quiet manner belied her activism. She helped lead the fight in 1979, and now she and Willie were working through the local school board to reverse the policy once again.

"One thing we are finding out is if our children learn their first language well, they can have an easier time to learn another language. If they are forced to use a language they don't know, maybe they'll grow up illiterate in both languages."

From the gym down the hall, we could hear the growl and click of an elderly man speaking Yup'ik through a microphone. Here was a village where children could still understand their elders. But between the influence of television and the increasing use of everyday English by young parents, Sophie said, people feared for the language of their ancestors. She was dismayed by the steady absorption into Yup'ik conversation of English hybrids such as "mail plane-aq" and "TV-aq."

Each language had its own strengths, she said. When I asked what she meant, Sophie thought a minute, then mentioned that Yup'ik, with its concern for family relationships, has different words for "cousin," depending on whether the relation is girl-girl or girl-boy. On the other hand, the third-person pronoun is often indeterminate, which explained why I was often surprised to hear a Yup'ik person speak of a woman as "he."

A particular problem confronting Akiachak in its effort to restore Native-language instruction was that only one certified teacher was Yup'ik; in the bush too few villagers who have made the difficult leap to college return to their homes as teachers. In their absence, the burden of preserving language and culture has fallen on teacher's aides like Sophie, a high-school graduate who started a family and never got off to college. She was taking education courses through Kuskokwim Community College, but between work and raising four children it would be years before she managed a teacher's certificate. She offered no complaint about her situation, but it seemed too bad there was no better way to entrust the future generations to the hands of the Sophie Kasayulies.

Sophie gave me the names of several parents, and I dropped in on a father whose mobile home sat behind the IRA offices. He offered me coffee and a chair, though he didn't sit down himself. Pent up by winter, he strode back and forth answering my questions about language as if lecturing.

It was important to have his son speak Yup'ik in school, he said. The family had moved down to Akiachak from a village on the Yukon, where children had already lost the ability to speak the language because all the steamboats and miners passing through at the turn of the century had left too much white culture. His older daughter took Yup'ik like a foreign language in high school and got an F. When he was a kid, he and his classmates had their lunch taken away if they spoke Yup'ik in school, even among themselves.

"It made spies out of all the little kids who didn't like you," he said. He lighted a cigarette and moved over near the flue on his stovepipe so the smoke wouldn't bother me. In the background the radio was broadcasting bilingual announcements from Bethel.

Then he strutted back in the other direction and seemed to take the opposite line. The system wasn't working. It was fine for each village to have a school, but they needed to provide a stronger education in English. Graduating from bush schools were students who couldn't read and write enough to pass a college exam, much less to succeed in the real world.

"But didn't you say you wanted your son to grow up speaking Yup'ik?" I asked.

"I don't want to discuss *technological* things in that language," he said with a wave of his cigarette. "That's the mistake white people make. We need to speak English for those things. But if we can't speak Yup'ik, we can't understand our own value system and the things around us."

Two worlds, two languages. "When I go down to the Kuskokwim with my boy, he has to know how to dig through the ice and put his traps in for blackfish."

He carried a white plastic bucket from the door over to my chair. The bucket sloshed with water, and swimming inside were four fish.

"Those kinds of things we need to talk about in Yup'ik."

Willie Kasayulie had arranged an afternoon audience for me with William Lomack, chief of the Akiachak elders council. To avoid interruptions, I met with the elder chief at the IRA office. William Lomack was seventy, a man with a formidable scowl. We sat across from one another at the council table, and Willie, who came to serve as translator, sat on the end. The interview was stiff and at first the answers were solemnly predictable.

After we spoke of the land claims act and the start of Yupiit Nation, I asked about the old ways. I'd heard that there was always a kind of code, a right way of living Yup'ik people held as a standard; by following these rules, by being Yup'ik, they could achieve a sense of well-being. In the old days how did they know what those rules were?

Willie translated the question.

"He says they learned these things when they were young, in the early 1920s, by observing how the elders were. There was very little disagreement with decisions made back then. Usually there was one individual who did all the talking. They worked by consensus, the same as we are doing now."

I asked how they remembered all the old rules. This question generated an exchange between the two men.

"He says the majority of rules were carried through word of mouth," Willie said after a moment. "There would have been volumes of books if they were writing them."

I asked how they knew which elders to listen to.

"He says that when you get to be fifty, you know the lessons of the past, and when you are older, you become more vocal about your opinions. You are an elder when you are able to voice your opinions and talk about the knowledge you have gained. They prefer elders to be sixty-five or seventy, but it depends on who is in the village."

And what about the young?

"He says we need to teach the children these lessons in the school." William Lomack, a member of the local school board, was organizing a class in traditional skills, such as navigating by the stars. "But they have to go through it for themselves. They can't just learn this in the schools. He wants to see ongoing lessons. He doesn't want students to take one semester and forget about it."

The interview remained formal and awkward. I couldn't tell whether the general nature of the answers owed to the gingerly distance of my questions, to the older man's diplomatic turn of mind, or to Willie's condensing of his replies.

"Tell me, since the elders' council has been created, what kind of decisions have you had to make?"

There was more Yup'ik conversation. Then Willie turned to me.

"The elders said there was to be no more rock-and-roll dancing at the high school."

"But isn't dancing part of the Yup'ik tradition?" I asked.

"The elders were concerned because it is against the church," Willie said. "They felt that at dances the lights are turned down low and certain thoughts flow through people's minds."

I had read that some villages once called the dark month of December—*Cauyarvik*—time for drumming. The only musical instrument in the old Eskimo culture had been the drum. Yup'ik dancing ensured hunting success, marked a person's coming of age or first hunt, stilled the spirits of the dead. But the Moravians, who allowed singing and guitar playing as part of their church services, considered dancing a sin, one that offered unauthorized access to planes of spiritual ecstasy.

"Last year a Yup'ik dance troupe from Chevak came to Akiachak on a state arts council tour," Willie said. "They couldn't persuade any of the elders to get up and join them, the way they do in other villages."

Willie didn't flinch at the irony. And there was a distinction: the old Eskimo dances had a reason, while the new dancing was considered by the elders to be thoughtless, crazy. It was against the true Yup'ik way, it was a thing that would make you unwise.

William Lomack said something more in Yup'ik to Willie.

"He says the elders in Akiachak have always been in the church, from the time the village was moved to this spot. Another name for the village is 'people from the island.' They moved here from up the river to escape the influence of an evil shaman."

B rian Henry, the student council president, lived in a small house by the river. His family said I'd find him at the high school, though it was a Saturday, so I walked the length of Akiachak.

Built by the state for forty-three high school students, the school looked vaguely Californian, with its barnlike dimensions and dark wood exterior. The inside, too, looked as if it had been packaged in California and shipped north. Rules were posted governing such matters as snuff dipping, computer game hours, and "personal stereos in class." I found Brian Henry in a partitioned classroom, using a computer to write a school paper.

"They used to do Eskimo dancing. We do this dancing," Brian said. He was a keen-eyed junior with a boyish mop of hair over his forehead. He warmed quickly to my questions about the dance ban, but I couldn't tell if it was because the edict of the elders still grated or because he liked the idea of being quoted in an Anchorage newspaper.

Brian was active in both worlds: already that day he had hauled drinking water from the river for his family, checked their fishnets under the ice, and cooked food for a team of fourteen dogs. But if some Native villages specialized at turning out spirit dancers and others produced weavers of grass baskets, Akiachak's specialty seemed to be politicians. At seventeen, Brian had mastered the turning of a phrase and an instinct for a political opening, much as a seventeen-year-old from Chevak might develop an early flair for inscribing seals on ivory.

Several times a year, Brian said, students used to hang a mirrored ball from the ceiling of the school gym and string colored lights along the walls. Cassettes provided the rock music, and the whole village was invited. The previous fall a few recent graduates had showed up drunk at a dance and had to be hauled away by the village police. After that Jackson Lomack, who had just been elected to the advisory school board, told them they couldn't hold their Christmas dance. The seniors had planned to raise money through the dance for a class trip to Washington, D.C.

Jackson and Willie had encouraged the students to get involved in the tribal council and the village corporation; they'd said the Yup'ik people had to stand up for their beliefs. Now, Brian complained, they were telling the students they couldn't be themselves.

"At times I hear students say Jackson is trying to make us live in the past," he said.

It had been a sad day for the seniors. Once they lost their faith in *Wangkutnek Auluklerkarput*, something inside of them died.

"They lost something to go for. Like when a flower is coming out, then you take away the sun . . ." Brian spread his palm, then snapped it shut. "It dies."

"But what about the ruling of the elders?" I asked.

"There was the constitution passed back in history that said church and state shouldn't mix," Brian said. "What we do here in the school is our own business."

Jackson Lomack was at the IRA office, gathering up papers for the next day's meeting with the AFN.

"Separate church and state is a white man's philosophy," he said when I told him of my conversation with Brian. "Once the village is working together, religion and government should be working together. As long as we have the Great Spirit watching over us, we will be on the right track."

Jackson was in some ways an odd one to be handing down rulings from the Great Spirit. He liked to race his snowmachine on the Kuskokwim and once dislocated his shoulder going ninety mph. He'd told me sheepishly the accident taught him drinking and driving don't mix. When he was a boarding student at Mount Edgecumbe School in Sitka, he went to plenty of dance parties. Now here he was, the Yupiit Nation's goateed minister of culture—but perhaps he was just the sort to bear the righteousness of the born again.

As we talked, though, Jackson proved less of a dogmatist than I imagined. It turned out the real lessons for the high school students in this first crisis of the Yupiit Nation were in activism and compromise. On the advice of Willie and Jackson, even the elders had been willing to give way.

"Brian and some other students appealed to the advisory school board. The board promised to find other money for the senior trip, but no more dances," Jackson said. "Then Brian came to the board a second time and asked if that meant the prom, too. We talked about it and decided the prom could be an exception."

"Are you sure that's in keeping with the traditions of the ancestors?" I teased.

Jackson smiled. One of the beauties of an oral tradition was that it left room for flexibility. "I told the elders one dance would not hurt their minds, and it would give them a chance to exercise their bodies," Jackson said.

Anna Phillip came for the last day of the meeting and took me to an aunt's house for lunch. A light snow was falling as we walked to the small house in the old end of the village. Anna explained that what seemed a jumble was an arrangement of family clusters. People came and went while we ate, many of them from other villages, too busy for introductions. Anna showed me how to dip strips of dried salmon into a bowl of seal oil. The heady lubricant is much appreciated by the upriver Eskimos, who acquire it from coastal villagers by trading meat and fish.

Then we, too, had to hurry back to the elementary school gym for the meeting with the Alaska Federation of Natives.

In the gym high school students had set up video cameras. I sank into a chair in the back of the gym, recognizing at the head table several AFN leaders from Anchorage.

Janie Leask had been president of the AFN for several years. She had partly Indian heritage, though she had grown up in Anchorage and spoke only English. Cool and preppie, she had helped maintain a friendly and unflappable exterior for the Native community through this time of dissension. But she was always cautious in her pronouncements—one got the impression that her employer, the AFN board, was composed of twelve regional Native corporations that frequently disagreed. She was always careful not to go beyond the agreed-upon consensus.

Next to her at the table was Don Mitchell, a white attorney who had worked for years as a consultant to the AFN. I knew him from various political gatherings in Anchorage where we would take up positions along a rear wall and exchange wisecracks. Though committed to the Native cause, he was always ready to disabuse reporters of sentimental notions about the Alaska Native. His skepticism was no doubt helpful as he attempted to draft legislation to amend the Alaskan Native Claims Settlement Act, which he had helped write, but I wondered if his distrust of easy pieties might make him too quick to dismiss the aspirations of the villages. I decided not to tell him just now about the ban on dancing.

The third member of the AFN delegation was Matt Nicolai, a vice-president of Calista, the regional Native corporation for the Yukon-Kuskokwim delta. Calista's was not one of the prominent and powerful regions whose urban shareholders were eager to play the game of multinational capitalism. Despite its friction with Tuluksak over gold mining, the corporation stayed in relatively close touch with its predominantly rural shareholders. Even so, Nicolai looked distressed as the meeting began, for he knew the Yupiit Nation was not happy with the corporations.

Janie Leask began by describing what Alaska Natives were up against in seeking to change the 1971 settlement. The Reagan administration was "quite happy" with the corporate structure of the original act—in fact, thought it one of the most successful pieces of Indian legislation ever—and administration officials wouldn't agree to any law creating or strengthening racial organizations such as tribal governments. The President himself had said the United States had probably made a mistake indulging traditional Indian life-styles.

She waited while her words were translated to Yup'ik.

The AFN wanted to protect Native lands, she said. It might be possible to win amendments from Congress giving corporations the option to prevent sale of stock and thereby protect corporate assets, but Native shareholders would probably have to be given a chance to cash in their shares if they chose to. Reagan's officials were more interested in the rights of individual shareholders than with the Native people as a whole, so even if AFN's amendments passed, it would be up to the shareholders of each corporation to agree not to sell their shares.

Congress was ready to defer to Alaska's all-Republican congressional delegation, and the delegation was prepared to take AFN's proposed amendments to Congress, but they set one condition: there had to be unanimity from the villages. So the AFN had come to the Kuskokwim seeking the Yupiit Nation's support. If Akiachak and other villages pushed for legislation now to strengthen tribal government at the expense of corporations, they might undermine the whole bill, leaving Native lands subject to loss through taxation and bankruptcy.

When Matt Nicolai had finished translating for Janie Leask, Don Mitchell spoke and underlined the theme. "AFN is not your enemy," he said.

Mitchell added a dose of bitter reality. "You may think tribal government is the answer, but the Interior Department is vehemently opposed. They don't care about Akiachak. They don't care about you."

The audience listened politely, then got its chance to speak. Those who stood were young and old, from such villages as Chefornak, Tuntutuliak, Togiak. They spoke now in Yup'ik, now in English.

They said the Yup'ik tradition was to own the land as a people; an individual could not sell shares if it meant the people would lose their land. How could anyone write a law telling the Native people to behave that way, when the Native people were here first? When the law was first proposed, it never came back to the villages for their approval, certainly never to the tribal councils. Yet the Native Claims Act would terminate the Native people of Alaska; it would do away with their status as an indigenous people.

"You're right," Mitchell responded. "The problem is that the people who did all the terrible things you just described are still running the United States. It would be easy for me to come and tell you all you have to do is sit here and figure out what changes would be good for your community, but there are a lot of people against you. The AFN resolutions try to do as much as they can. If you think AFN is not trying to deal with your troubles as well as it can, you don't understand what the Native people have been through."

This was not something the Yupiit Nation delegates wanted to be told. Now speakers turned on the AFN itself. They said the AFN adopted resolutions supporting tribal government and then ignored them. The AFN conventions were rigged for the corporations that wanted to keep the original structure of the act and protect individual shareholder rights. They were the ones that were pulling everybody apart.

An old man with short gray hair jumped up and rattled in speeding Yup'ik. Elders in the gym nodded in agreement. It took me a minute to recognize the speaker as Peter Waskie, the shopkeeper from Tuluksak. He was shouting; he strode to the front of the room, danced back and forth and waved his arms in pantomime, said something about Russia. He talked about gold mining and pointed at the representative from Calista. He leaned over the table and thrust a finger in Janie Leask's face. Then he stepped back and, switching suddenly to English, pointed at each of them at the table and swept his arms sideways: "One. Two. Three. Push 'em away, little bit."

When the meeting broke apart, I saw Don Mitchell by the door. "How are you feeling, white man?" he asked.

"Glad I wasn't up there with you," I said.

Mitchell headed to the playground to catch his ride in a pickup truck down the Kuskokwim to the Bethel airport. I followed him out to where it was still snowing, the afternoon light fading, and filled in the rejoinder Mitchell was in too much haste to make: "You were." One message of this convention, which would perhaps have been plainer were it being run by someone less genial than Willie Kasayulie, was that I came as a foreigner without a passport. Exciting as it was to find Native people fighting assimilation, the talk of tribalism, separatism, and racial destiny raised dark images as well. It was the price of pluralism: that which preserved Yup'ik culture might well exclude me.

The meeting in Akiachak dispersed with the two sides as far apart as ever. In the year that was to follow, not even the regional Native corporations were able to agree on what changes should be made to the claims act. Many corporation leaders, sympathetic with the general aims of Yukon-Kuskokwim villages, wanted to keep Native lands in Native hands and to issue new, watered-down stock to young Natives. But the management of several of the most successful corporations was too far down the capitalist road to submit to restraints against sale of stock in the name of cultural preservation. They wanted the option of exempting themselves, by a vote of shareholders, from any extension of stock restrictions.

In the end, the only consensus the Alaska Federation of Natives could reach was to endorse a menu of options for the corporations. Amendments incorporating those options passed Congress; each Native corporation was left to find its own route through the year 1991 and beyond.

The amendments were enacted over the objection of a coalition of Alaska villages and American Indian groups. The tribal governments of Yupiit Nation were left to fight for *Wangkutnek Auluklerkarput* in court and on their own.

Overnight the temperature sank to eighteen below. When I got to Daniel George's house the next morning, it was still dark and the air raked my cheeks like a coarse razor. The man of the house was already off doing chores so I sat by the woodstove holding a cup of coffee while Ina George dressed their two small children. The one-room house had a kitchen at one end and bunk beds at the other, with the family's whole life jammed between.

An old Maytag ringer-washer stood by the stove. It was laundry day. Ina pointed to the rime ice built up around the door frame and said it would be too cold to hang the washing out to freeze-dry. She would splurge for driers at the village washeteria.

I heard a snowmachine arrive and boots clomp up the steps. Daniel George entered with a bucket of river water, and Ina started heating water on her electric stove for the Maytag.

Daniel George was a laconic, stocky Eskimo in his late thirties, part of the generation largely missing from the Yupiit Nation meeting (though he'd been at the gym the day before, he said). Here, I hoped, was a working man whose wisdom would be spelled out not in parables or manifestoes but in the everyday routines of life on the land.

He said Willie had told him to expect me. I felt a twinge of guilt over foisting myself on this poor fisherman.

"You didn't ever go ice fishing before?" he asked.

"Once," I said, my desire to appear knowledgeable momentarily getting the better of my instinct to remain silent and have things explained. "But that was with a line and hook," I added. "Never with a net. I can't figure out how you get the net under the ice."

He said something to Ina in Yup'ik and walked out with me behind him. Light was coming up on an overcast day. Daniel climbed in the cab of a pickup truck and fiddled with the key, but he could not kindle life. In front of the houses nearby, neighbors were engaged in morning calisthenics, yanking pullcords on gasping snowmachines and a co-matose three-wheeler.

"I should have plugged it in last night," Daniel said when he got out.

Usually he went by snowmachine to check his net on the Kuskok-wim, but he judged that only a pickup truck would do for his visitor. I tried to talk him into a snowmachine ride, but he shook his head and pulled an extension cord over from the house. "Maybe later it'll warm up."

Instead we took the snowmachine to the camp where he fished in summer. It was close by: across the broad river, through a screen of little sticks, and a short way down a slough. We stopped where a shack, smokehouse, and cache on stilts were tucked in the willows. Even on such a short trip, the wind had burned my cheeks almost white.

"You didn't ever ride a snowmachine before?" he asked.

He pried a nail to open the cache door and piled frozen fish flats on his sled. Some were green with mold; last fall had been unusually rainy and damp, he explained. They were for his dogs, anyway.

Daniel George had started to assemble a dog team three years ago, and the dogs had greatly increased his subsistence effort. He'd never had a fish camp of his own: summertime at his parents' camp had always provided enough salmon for his family. Nor had he bothered fishing under the ice. Now his days, winter and summer, were filled with chores made necessary by his increased need for protein. He used the dogs to help with chores like hauling firewood as well as for racing. Daniel said he preferred mushing to snowmachine travel.

We roared back across the Kuskokwim and entered a brushy area where several teams of dogs were staked. Daniel made a fire and boiled up the fish. From a low of three or four teams in Akiachak, he said, there were now twenty. His needed exercise. He hitched a half-dozen dogs into their harnesses and slid away, silent and unaccompanied, heading for the Gweek River.

By midafternoon Daniel George's pickup truck still wouldn't start, and daylight had begun to fade. I had become deeply embarrassed by the media event I had set up, but there was no stopping it now and I couldn't talk him into going by snowmachine. He walked off toward another house and returned driving his brother's new yellow pickup, one of four new trucks that had come up the river over Christmas. Between the new trucks and the revived dog teams, I was starting to look upon snowmachines as articles of bush nostalgia.

We lurched onto the Kuskokwim in the pickup and followed the road around a distant bend. The river looked quiet and unyielding. Finally he stopped on an empty stretch where two poles were set in the ice about twenty feet apart.

"What are you fishing for here?" I asked.

"Whitefish. You never caught whitefish before?" he said.

Daniel chopped ice several inches thick from a pair of manholes twenty feet apart. He worked without hurry, bent over, silent.

The poles, thrust down through the holes, suspended his gill net like an inverted volleyball net. Daniel said the fishnet had to be hung far enough below the surface that it would not float up and freeze to the bottom of the river ice. Once frozen in, the net would be impossible to pull, and at breakup the broken ice would carry it away.

The system proved to be simple and ingenious. When he'd finished chopping and shoveling out the ice, he switched to dry gloves and pulled out one pole with the net end attached. He untied the pole, tied a rope to the net, then went to the other hole and began pulling up the net. The rope fed down through the first hole.

In a minute he lifted a fish up from under the ice—a whitefish, firm and fat, as big as his forearm. He tossed it in the snow to freeze and leaned into the net for another, like a magician reaching into a hat.

After the long wait, even this successful subsistence effort seemed anticlimactic. Daniel George was too utterly unsurprised at this appearance of life from another realm. I shifted from foot to foot to stay warm, huddled once again in my cloud of down, feeling silly about my faded urgency. The river here was nearly wide enough to feel like a lake. It was like standing on a deserted stretch of highway: in half an hour I counted two pickup trucks, three snowmachines, and one dog team moving along the Kuskokwim. If this was summer, I thought, the river would be busy with boats—and I would be treading water, or be heading "down by the ocean someplace," which is the way Kuskokwim people speak of their nets and other implements lost at breakup.

Daniel pointed downriver. A quarter mile away a red fox was trotting across the snow in the dusk. The fox slowed as it climbed the shore opposite Akiachak and looked back over its shoulder, then vanished into the brush.

When he was finished I pulled the rope up through the first hole and the net spilled back under the ice. He had caught twelve whitefish, now slightly bloody and stiffening, powdered on both sides with snow as if they had been floured for a frying pan.

"In springtime here there's lots of fish," he said. "Too many."

Daniel stacked the fish like cordwood in the back of his brother's new truck, first preparing a bed of snow to keep blood off the truck bed.

"Maybe he'd make us wash it out," he said.

We got back in the cab and he flipped on a blast of heat as we started back for the village. Soon we could see the lights of his home, shining out through frosty windows.

I got out and thanked him for taking me to see his fishnets. He nodded and picked two whitefish out of the truck bed. He started up the steps of his house, his workday in the cold finally over, then stopped and looked back.

"You ever eat any whitefish before?" he asked. He gestured for me to come inside.

The next morning I heard a horn blaring outside the teacherage. My taxi had arrived. Time for a trip down the winter river with Roland Nose, bush entrepreneur.

The morning was bright and calm, pleasantly cold. Roland Nose wore a light windbreaker and sunglasses and was chewing gum. Carrie Nose, his wife, sat beside him in the front of the white Chevy Blazer. She wrote my name in an account book in her lap.

We started past the IRA office and turned into the first yard. I assumed he was going to turn around, but he didn't stop. We continued past the house and crunched across the snowy backyard, past a gray plywood steambath, past a dog team staked in the willows, around two skiffs, and onto the frozen Kuskokwim.

Next stop: Bethel, twenty-three river miles away.

Business opportunities for a forty-three-year-old entrepreneur were few in Akiachak and the Noses had gotten into the tundra taxi line several years ago to come up with cash to support their growing family. At home there were eleven little noses: Robert, Roland Jr., Rita, Rona, Roxanne, Ryan, Ray, Regina, Ronald, Rosanne, and Randy.

This was not a year-round operation, said Roland Sr. Maybe four months in the year, beginning in January, the river is frozen thick enough to support a family man in a three-seat Chevy Blazer.

"When it's dangerous, we don't have to drive down," he said with a reassuring smile. "We don't want to disappear."

Such things happen on the Kuskokwim. The year before a hole swallowed the front end of a nice late-model Ford pickup traveling on the river. By the time help arrived, the truck was frozen immobile. Come breakup, the Ford went out with the ice and was now "down by the ocean someplace."

One year a ski plane crash-landed on the river in front of Akiachak shortly before breakup. The plane seemed destined for a trip to the Bering Sea, but the pilot repaired the skis, hired an Akiachak man to join him as river guide, and taxied down the rotting ice all the way to Bethel.

Some holes on the river stay open all winter, created by currents or warm springs, Roland Nose said. I remembered the trapper from Lower Kalskag, lost in such a hole a few weeks earlier.

I looked around the Blazer. Roland Nose carried no shovel or emergency equipment other than a VHF radio—not on a morning like this one, anyway, with lots of traffic and no wind of the delta to push drifts across the plowed lane.

Where the ice beneath the tires was smooth, he cruised at forty-five mph in four-wheel drive. When a car was coming the other way he slowed, pulled into the snow, and waved.

Halfway to Bethel the ice road veered into Church Slough, a narrow, curving channel through willows that cut off a big bend in the river. The snow on the slough was spotted with brownish-green patches of what appeared to be water. One patch was steaming like a hot bath tub.

"Overflow from the tide in here," Roland explained nonchalantly.

The Bering Sea! I felt my journey down the river coming to its conclusion.

Roland sailed around a curve, spotted overflow in the middle of the lane, and fishtailed to the left around a green pool of slush.

"You thought we was going in a hole," he observed.

The channel opened wide again, and soon the river cab was approaching the long waterfront wall of Bethel. Behind that wall were a hospital, restaurants, a couple of hotels, and jets to Anchorage.

The trip from Akiachak had taken less than forty-five minutes. I pulled two dachsund-shredded five-dollar bills from my wallet while Roland maneuvered around a ski plane parked on the river and climbed a ramp into the neighborhood known as Lousetown. He halted at a stop sign.

No traffic was coming. But he hesitated an extra moment before pulling onto the main street.

"You have to tell me how to get where you're going," he said. "I'm not too used to driving in town."

I gave him directions to Anna's office. Before flying back to Anchorage, I wanted to make arrangements for a return to the Yukon-Kuskokwim delta in spring.

11. The Wake of the Unseen Object

From the hills of Scammon Bay on the far coast of the Yukon-Kuskokwim delta, the great physical bulk of Alaska appears as a low mountain horizon across lake-splattered tundra to the east. Alaska's two longest rivers have poured out of those mountains for centuries, one winding north of the Scammon Bay hills, the other south, silting in a shelf of the Bering Sea as broad and flat as Lake Superior. If the seas that once flooded the Bering land bridge were to rise another ten or twenty feet—if the earth's atmosphere warms—the delta would disappear and the hills of Scammon Bay would be transformed into an island sixty miles offshore. Already the delta is half water, a shimmering insubstantial landscape in spring when the snow melts. For the villagers leaving Scammon Bay in boats to go to fish camp, the prominent hills make a comforting aid to navigation. All summer long the fishing families can look toward home and be assured of a return to firm ground.

Barely a generation ago coastal Eskimo families in this part of Alaska were still scattered across the sloughs and lakes and dry mounds of the tundra. They lived in isolation and gathered at the coast during salmon runs for society as well as for food. Today villages are well established, fewer and larger, and the trip to fish camp has become a trip away from one kind of society and back toward another. The people of Scammon Bay still go to that empty spot on the tundra, forty miles up the coast, where a tent city springs up overnight as soon as the salmon appear. At the mouth of the Black River, fish are cleaned and hung to dry along an eroding sod bank where children find tools carved in stone by their ancestors.

The mail plane to Scammon Bay dropped me at the airstrip at the foot of the hills. The village above was a jumble of old and new houses around a school and a small blue Catholic church. The houses ran crowded up the hillside as in a poor Latin American barrio, with middens of cardboard and plastic trash lying in their midst, freshly exposed by disappearing snow.

By the door of each house was a sign of hand-painted wood giving the occupant's name: Akerelrea, Amukon, Aguchak. These were legal family surnames, used for school enrollment and taxes. In the early census efforts missionaries often assigned an Eskimo man's one-word name to his entire family, adding common English first names. Sometimes, because this struck people as an odd perversion of the personal and private Yup'ik name, which is not a family name, children adopted their father's first name instead: hence one finds families in the villages today with last names like John and Jimmy. The creation of official surnames did not put an end to the traditional Yup'ik names. Such names are still passed on to newborn children from someone recently deceased and may retain their sacred quality as well. Some aspect of the soul was traditionally believed to pass to a namesake. The names are therefore not written on signs and are seldom shared with outsiders or even used to a person's face—nicknames are used instead. Their importance is recognized at birthdays and holidays such as Mother's Day, when a child who has been given the name of someone's deceased mother may receive a gift from the bereaved. People like to look for familiar traits in the behavior of a young namesake. The Yup'ik names, and the network of connections they create, are part of a separate world lying beneath the visible surface of a contemporary Eskimo village.

People moved among the houses with arms full of nets or boxes of food. I had never seen a village so busy. It was early June—*tengmiaret rinitiit*, I had seen one Yup'ik calendar call it, the month when birds are laying eggs. Another source gave the Yup'ik name *kaugun* and the translation "hit king salmon on the head." Life returns all at once in great migrations to this greening breast of the continent. Geese and ducks are everywhere. Subsistence nets had started to pick up salmon. A steady stream of wheelbarrows and three-wheelers moved to the tidal slough at the foot of the village as families loaded skiffs for the journey to fish camp. Small children caught rides up the hill on empty backhauls.

I came to a yellow house and knocked at a door beneath a sign that said "Sundown."

Myron Naneng sat at a crowded table in the dark interior, his mouth full of dried fish. He waved for me to take a seat that had cleared the instant my silhouette appeared in the door.

The house was large and open and had the look of a place where people passed through constantly. Teddy and Mary Sundown were an elderly couple with many grown daughters. Myron was a son-in-law I had met in Bethel. He had read some of my stories, and told me I could come along to fish camp.

Children and grandchildren were gathered around the Sundown table for a lunch of black seal ribs and dried, papery ptarmigan. The adults dipped meat into a plastic bowl of clear seal oil and spoke among themselves in Yup'ik. Like most older people on the coast, the Sundowns spoke only a little English. The family surname had come from a riverboat captain in the gold-rush years, when Teddy Sundown's father had worked on a Yukon River steamboat and could always be found on deck at dusk, watching the sun sink over his native land.

Mary Sundown pushed a jar of peanut butter toward me and nodded encouragingly. Her face was dark tanned and creased by a life spent out of doors, but her throat was white where her parka's hood had shielded her. I gulped out one of my few Yup'ik words to thank her—"*Qiana*"—and gnawed instead on a salty bit of seal, listening like a happy imbecile to the clucks and guttural stops and growls of the delta.

I reached across the table and dipped the meat in seal syrup. All talk stopped. They watched as I raised the black strip to my mouth and took a cautious nibble. I could well believe that homes were once heated with the stuff. Centuries of animal life were condensed in its powerful ripeness. The *yua* of all things sprang to life on the tundra outside the window.

"Good," I exhaled.

"*Assirtuq,*" Myron translated.

They smiled.

Myron Naneng was a good-natured, moon-faced man in his thirties, an up-and-coming political leader on the delta. He came from Hooper Bay, down the coast, and had married a Sundown daughter. He'd attended the University of Alaska in Fairbanks, worked as a bush troubleshooter for the governor's office, and was currently vice-president of the Yup'ik association of fifty-five delta villages. His office was in Bethel, but he came to Scammon Bay every summer. The regional association, struggling to preserve the Yup'ik way of life, was not about to stand in their vice-president's way when he needed a few weeks off for fish camp.

Usually Myron went to Black River with his wife and family, but this year they were back in Bethel and Myron was going mainly for the commercial fishing period at the height of the salmon run. He had a new twenty-five-foot aluminum skiff and a new 40-horse outboard, but he lacked a helper. The man with whom he'd expected to share the work of commercial fishing this season hadn't shown up. Myron smiled reassuringly when I asked if I could be of assistance and went off after lunch to talk to some people around the village.

With Myron gone, I began to feel clumsy and in the way. The pack with my tent and sleeping bag was blocking the flow of traffic in and out of the Sundown home, so I moved it to the porch of a small house next door whose occupants were away. But while I was digging through my pack the door of the small house opened and an Eskimo man stood before me. He was middle-aged, sunburned, and bristle-haired. I explained, embarrassed, why I was on his porch. They told me you were away, I said. He gazed out, quiet and expressionless. I could not tell whether he was annoyed or curious or what. Then he said, "You want tea?"

Francis Charlie and Myron were related through their wives. Theresa, Francis Charlie's wife, was another of the Sundown daughters, a friendly woman with a strong, tired face. She went to put a teakettle on the stove.

Francis did not speak much English. Theresa was more at ease in conversation. She had grown up in Scammon Bay, while Francis had been raised by grandparents on the tundra, in the years before Yup'ik Eskimos abandoned the last inland sites, leaving behind driftwood-and-scrap houses and the graves of tuberculosis victims.

Francis was forty-five and had been going to Black River since he was a boy. His family was among the first to go away to fish camp every year. In fact, they had already been away at Black River—not even Theresa's parents knew they had come back. With six children, Francis and Theresa had left Scammon Bay while snow still covered the tundra and creeks were frozen, when cross-country travel is easiest on the delta. The family rode in sleds behind two snowmachines. Along the way one son took a jump too fast and broke a snowmachine tread, so Francis trained both sleds behind the remaining machine and they continued several hours to their camp, where they set up for the summer and waited for the ice to go out on the river.

They had come back to Scammon Bay that afternoon in a boat for supplies before commercial fishing got underway. Their subsistence net at camp had been filling up, and they brought down a king salmon for the Sundowns—a treat, since kings don't run close to the coast this far south. The trip was made in part out of respect for the old people. The

Sundowns were too frail for the rigors of camp, and would soon be left behind in a nearly deserted village.

That night Mary Sundown and her daughters cut the king salmon into chunks and boiled it on the stove in a wide galvanized pan. Dinner was a bilingual, multigenerational affair staged in shifts at the Sundown table and on the nearby couch. Francis Charlie spoke to his children in Yup'ik; they answered in English. The Sundown elders had to call on their daughters to interpret when they spoke to some of their grandchildren.

The six children of Francis and Theresa ranged in age from six to their early teens. For them, the trip home to Scammon Bay was like shore leave, and after dinner they fanned out across the village.

Myron went off again in search of a fishing partner, and after some halting attempts at conversation with the Sundowns I went off in search of the Charlie kids. I caught up with them at the Royal Igloo, a dusty-blue teen hall with a single pool table and a wall of video games, half of which were out of order. Later we stopped by the new gym, where two men's teams were playing full-court sprint-and-shoot basketball. The gym was in a shiny wooden palace several stories high, the most imposing building in the village. Basketball is such a passion in Scammon Bay, especially in the long dark winter, that construction of a full-size gym had been made the village's top capital priority in the era of Alaska's oil wealth. The village council spent more than $800,000 in state funds on the project. Not everyone was happy about the expenditure; there were those in Scammon Bay who would have preferred to build a washeteria like the one in Chevak. The Chevak washeteria was so popular that people from Hooper Bay had been known to travel twenty miles across the tundra by snowmachine with a load of dirty clothes. When sudden winds across the delta blew down the walls twice during construction of the gym, opponents of the project began to whisper that God did not mean for Scammon Bay to have a full-size gym with a wood-tile floor and a balcony for crowds. But the basketball players, retaining a comfortable majority on the village council, persevered, and now they boasted the largest gym on the delta outside of Bethel.

Francis Charlie's children missed basketball and nights at the Royal Igloo when they went away to fish camp, but after a few hours on the town, Glenn Charlie was getting bored.

Glenn was eleven years old, a slight boy with shaggy black hair who, like his father, preferred the Black River camp to village life. He was less talkative than his brothers—more like his father that way, too. It was understandable that his older brothers would appreciate the night in the village, for they had worked in the commercial fishery and knew about the hard hours ahead. For Glenn, Black River had always meant the carefree life of summer camp: swimming and hunting and playing with his cousins.

He wandered listlessly back across the village late that evening, past smoking steambaths and windows lighted from inside with the colors of the sunset. When he got home he watched television.

It had been weeks since Glenn had slept in his own bunk in the Charlies' small living room. He was sound asleep when his Uncle Myron shook him the next morning and asked if he wanted to go commercial fishing. The invitation came as a surprise. He hadn't been sure if this was to be his summer to join the men fishing. Of course he would go. But even as he muttered a sleepy yes, Glenn said later he had felt a little sadness. Black River would never be the same.

Glenn and I joined the stream of traffic that day, carrying armloads of gear down to the boat landing. An amphibian culture was preparing for travel. Men in their early thirties, some of them Glenn's uncles and cousins, worked fiercely, then stopped for long conversations. They spoke in Yup'ik, switching to English to discuss the performance of Danny Ainge in the recent basketball championships, which they'd seen on satellite television. Ainge was a local favorite because he had the short, powerful physique of an Eskimo ballplayer.

Glenn helped Myron maneuver his new 40-horse out of a trailer. The gleaming engine caught the attention of the other young men, who crowded around for a look. Glenn's lessons had begun. He saw that while the owner of an old mud-caked kicker may have to struggle alone to lift it into his boat, there is never a shortage of volunteers willing to help set a new outboard motor in a stern for the first time.

In tall bent-over grass near the slough, Glenn's grandmother and his aunts were stringing herring to dry. Shoals of herring had moved up the coast the week before, and the slender fish were now stored in piles under grass to keep them cool. One aunt worked with an *uluaq*, the gibbous-moon knife used by Eskimo women, splaying fish along the spine. The knife blade had been shaped and sharpened from the steel of a rotary sawblade, and was set in a hand-carved wooden handle. The knife looked stronger and more serviceable than the souvenir *ulus* I'd seen at airport shops in Anchorage, the ones with Alaska maps etched into the blades.

While her daughter split fish, Mary Sundown sat sprawled on a leaf of cardboard, a scarf over her head. She was one of the accomplished basketmakers of Scammon Bay, whose pieces of tightly woven beach rye had become prized by art collectors, but today her expert fingers were weaving split herring into eight-foot strands of twined grass that would be thrown away in winter as the fish were peeled off and eaten. The strands were hung for drying over venerable-looking driftwood racks, and they stirred as the wind grew stronger.

A storm was moving in and I climbed the hill to watch. Gusts ruffled whitecaps on the sewage lagoon behind the gym. A rush of low clouds trailed rain across the tundra.

Be not afraid of the universe.

I wondered if the people of the tundra coast still saw the Bering Sea weather as a supernatural force. The Inupiat had believed the spirit *Sila* sent storms or clear skies depending on how the people lived, how they respected the animals that gave them food. In the northern reaches of the continent, it must have often seemed that people were weak, or that *Sila* was an angry and vengeful god. The Yup'ik had a similar spirit they called *Ellam Iinga*, the eye of the world. This was the eye that watched over them, that knew if they were living the right way, as Yup'ik people should—if they were being worthy of the place they lived. It was not a presence they necessarily surrendered to Christian missionaries. The Yup'ik elders said that by living the right way in the eye of the world they had been praying to God all along.

The wind nearly knocked me to the ground, then the rain came, and I descended and took refuge in the small village store.

I needed a cap and found one with the initials SBA, which the clerk assured me stood not for the Small Business Administration but for Scammon Bay, Alaska. Mike Akerelrea, the village postmaster, stood behind me in line, buying last-minute groceries for camp. He was a thin, wired man in his thirties who said he wouldn't leave for Black River until the wind died down. He smiled when I said Myron might leave sooner. "The wind's going to blow you out of the boat," he said with a teasing look of concern.

After supper the clouds were shot through with white light and the wind let up. As the evening tide crept into the slough, Myron and Francis Charlie filled their gas tanks from a blue oil drum. Once Francis's boat was floating, Glenn climbed over several other skiffs and handed across Wiggles, the family's white muskrat-size house dog. Francis settled Wiggles in his lap and said to me, "He's my lead dog." His face crinkled with laughter.

Francis pushed off with his son Richard, who was two years older than Glenn. Myron's roomy aluminum skiff boomed beneath my feet as I jumped in. We used oars to pry the boat free from others and poled along the slough's curves until Myron had enough water to drop the new outboard. As we passed the driftwood fish racks, the dried herring swayed and crackled in the breeze, crisp garlands with a thousand eyes.

The slough dumped us in the mouth of a river and we accelerated into the gray evening across a growing chop. I snapped up my down vest and rain jacket.

The Bering Sea coast is so silty and shallow that the trip could only be made at high tide, and even now Myron had to keep the boat far offshore. Tall blue icebergs stood exposed in the shallows where they'd been stranded by the retreating ice pack.

We ran two hours up the featureless shore. The steady hammering of waves precluded conversation. An occasional spray of seawater punctuated the journey. I wrapped my hood tight around my SBA cap and gazed east toward the tundra, where the land was as flat as the sea. Except for the receding hills of Scammon Bay, we seemed to be traveling out of sight of the coast.

Glenn was the first to spot the orange coast guard light blinking at the mouth of Black River. We started into the river, then Myron called out and looped the boat back to show us a beaver he'd seen paddling along the water's edge.

The Black River was several hundred feet wide at its mouth, smooth-running as it left the tundra, silty brown rather than black, though presumably clear inland beyond the tide, which ran stripes up the center of the channel. Steep banks of loam rose several feet on either side, so the surrounding country lay on a separate plane, invisible above our heads. About a mile upstream a line of driftwood fish racks and a few tents appeared along the right shore. Myron pointed the skiff at the first racks and killed the engine.

The boat's anchor was almost as tall as our apprentice seaman. Glenn flung it mightily onto the crumbling black sod, catching himself as he fell forward after it. We climbed the bank and found ourselves on a silent, twilit prairie. The only sound was a faraway rabble of clucking voices. Myron tilted his head.

"Do you hear the swans?" he asked.

For years Francis had camped here in a tent, but now he had built a one-room plywood cabin back from the crumbling bank. The cabin was surrounded by driftwood and sleds and rusting piles of tin cans. Inside, Francis had a small sheetmetal woodstove already pumping out a cozy warmth. There was a window in the rear where two cots were pushed together, and a mess of dirty sleeping bags and old boots covered the floor. In a white plastic bucket, a slab of seal fat was rendering slowly into oil, emitting a faint overripe odor.

We sat on stumps at a low table, snacking on fry bread and strips of smoked sheefish slickened with the seal oil. Myron made smoky tea in a coffeepot over a Coleman stove, adding to the loose-leaf Lipton's sprigs of Labrador tea gathered from high ground outside the cabin. Glenn tilted the sugar bowl so that it avalanched into his teacup.

Myron said it was good to be away from it all. "The thing about getting to fish camp is that you give a sigh of relief and you get a deep breath of fresh air at the same time." He smiled at the phrase he'd just coined. Francis sipped tea as if he hadn't noticed.

It was well after midnight, but in fish camp you went to bed only when you were tired. They decided to fire up the steambath.

Francis sent Glenn's brother Richard to start the woodstove in the steambath while Myron and Glenn set to work stretching and nailing Myron's canvas tent over a nearby frame of two-by-fours. I wandered downriver looking for a dry spot of tundra where I could pitch my tent.

When Richard came by later to tell us the steambath was hot, Myron said he was going to skip it after all.

"I've got *work* to do," he said, exaggerating the swings of the hammer. "You've got to *work* when you're camping, *even if* it's the *mid*dle of the *night*."

Glenn was lifting nails out of the mud and tapping them straight with a hammer for Myron to reuse. He gave his new boss a doleful look, then hardened himself.

"I'm not taking a steam either," Glenn said. "I changed my mind."

On a calm evening a few days later, when the air was cool and the river shone with a pink translucence, Glenn and his brothers and cousins stood along the cutbank watching the water's surface for the sudden appearance of a V.

"*Qavlunaq!*" they cried, and ran to get long-handled dip nets.

Qavlunaq. The wake of the unseen object. *Qavlunaq* was the rippling of a salmon as it swam close to the pearly surface of the river. In Yup'ik, they said the fish was "making eyebrows."

Too young to go out alone in boats, the children waited on shore, their long-handled dip nets suspended in the water. They chattered in English, switching to Yup'ik when some aspect of their surroundings was recognized only by the indigenous language.

Richard cried, "The fish are qavlunaqing!" His insight was rewarded when an invisible king salmon entered his net. A cousin helped lever the twenty-pound fish to shore, where it would proceed to Theresa Charlie's smokehouse.

I tried saying the word, and had to reach deep to pluck the Qs. The sounds were unfamiliar, and Yup'ik vocabulary had not come quickly. Most of what passed at Black River in the old language I was missing. All I caught were a few expressive phrases, but sometimes these came as sudden revelations of what remained unseen. *Qavlunaq.* For the next few days I repeated the word out loud, until people finally stopped laughing at my pronunciation.

Theresa Charlie had arrived in a relative's boat with the rest of the children. Camp was filling up. There had been no announcement from Fish and Game about when commercial fishing would open. The adults were anxious, but Glenn had time to be a kid again.

The tundra was sere and brown in early June and the sun shone steadily. Packs of cousins moved along the worn path beside the river, stopping outside the doors of friendly tents. Small children tagged along behind me singing out "*kass'aq*"—a tag for whites descended from the early Russian traders, the Cossacks. In some villages, in some tones, the word can have the ugly, resentful meaning of "honky," but here everyone smiled like the expression was something cute. They did not get many *kass'aqs* at Black River. The smaller children gathered outside my tent, fascinated by my strangeness, giggling as I clowned with my eyebrows, until Theresa called for them to keep away. I appreciated her thoughtfulness, but it hardly seemed fair, considering how many doorways I had peered into myself.

I joined the older children in their chores. In some ways their society was easier to approach than the world of adults—certainly their rudimentary chores were more appropriate to my level of skill. The children hauled in willows to feed the smokehouse fires, hung salmon on racks for drying, and hiked onto the tundra to gather eggs from nests. If they were old enough they carried .22s, and took skiffs up sloughs beyond the tide, where they filled plastic jugs with drinking water. Later in the summer they would grub through grassy hummocks for little stores of edible cotton grass roots assembled by rodents for winter—mouse food, they called it.

When they had energy to burn, they sought out a relatively dry patch of grass to play a local amalgam of baseball and dodgeball called Lapp game, probably a version of a sport brought to the Bering Sea coast by reindeer herders from Lapland.

One evening the Charlie children brought me out back of their cabin to show me the game. The essential piece of equipment was a spongy pink rubber ball dug out from under the house where its disappearance had brought a previous game to a close. They selected a splintered one-by-four for a bat, narrow enough at one end to get their hands around, and a second plank was set out in the tundra to mark a safe zone.

One of Glenn's sisters was the first pitcher. She stood immediately next to Richard, the first batter. After flipping the ball in the air, she leaped out of the path of the swinging one-by-four. Richard whacked the ball into the tundra and everyone on his team started to run back and forth between home and the safe zone. The fielders chased the ball and threw it at the runners; most often they missed and had to chase the ball again. Wiggles, their father's little white lead dog, barked furiously from a sled.

The tangled roughs and water hazards of the tundra added handicaps for the outfielder. In pursuit of an overthrown ball, I made a show-off broad jump and discovered a narrow slough was wider than I'd estimated.

After about twenty minutes, everyone stopped to watch a flock of a dozen swans rise from a nearby pond, gather noisily in the air, and move away down the delta. Then play resumed until everyone was breathless from running and laughter and the ball was lost in a pile of rusting soda cans.

When the game ended it was time to eat. Though I slept apart in my tent to lighten the burden of my presence, I shared meals with the Charlie family.

Francis sat quietly at the low table as we ate and winced with pain whenever he shifted his weight on his driftwood stool. I had to ask why he was limping. He said he'd been hunting seal two months earlier, riding on a sled behind a snowmachine, and went over a ridge on the pack ice and fell. He'd been too busy to fly to the hospital in Bethel to see if the knee was broken.

"Maybe when commercial fishing is done," he said.

I asked why he spent so much time at Black River. "I like a quiet place," he said. He obliged my questions with short specific answers. When I asked how long it takes to dry a king salmon, he replied, "Until it's dry."

He was not being droll. Nor was it that he lacked the words to say more. Speaking Yup'ik with Myron and other adults, Francis seemed hardly more talkative. Myron was the one who could hold forth on the importance to Yup'ik self-respect of remembering the old ways, on the challenge of living in two cultures. Francis was different, more old-fashioned. He moved quietly, passing on knowledge by gestures, by example, as I imagined his grandparents had to him. During meals I watched and waited.

"Eskimo food," they called the fare: dried whitefish, boiled half-dried salmon, unleavened Pilot Bread crackers. Francis Charlie said if he did not eat Eskimo food he would get sick. Eskimo food was a measure of his well-being. Its consumption was only part of a larger cycle of gathering, and you couldn't have the food without the whole cycle. Each day a Yup'ik father was expected to go out and work, just as my father went off every day on a train to New York City—except that with the Yup'ik provider, the food came directly. If you bought seal ribs with a paycheck, it would not be the same. Myron said boys were still initiated into this role of provider when they caught their first fish or brought home their first seal. One's first kill had to be shared with elders and other families, for that was the proper way to show respect to the animal. Even if other rituals of propitiation were no longer carried out, the importance of sharing was well understood. The idea of "Eskimo food" seemed to open onto all aspects of Yup'ik life. For Francis Charlie, each meal was an act of communion with the land and the past, with the life of the grandparents who raised him and the promise of a future for his children.

I was learning to eat Eskimo food with gusto myself, as if I might ingest understanding along with it. I even got used to dipping my fish in seal oil, though I touched the oil gingerly—hot vapors blew through my nostrils and ears as I chewed, and through another embrasure about twenty minutes later. I shared the oranges and salami I'd brought, glad to have something to add to the table but fearful for the fate of Yup'ik culture when the younger boys neglected the strips of salmon and begged for more sausage.

One evening Francis invited me to join him for a steambath.

The original Yup'ik sweathouse, the *qasgiq* (the word is similar to the Inupiaq *qalgi*), had been home most of the year to the men of a village. It was a place for serious male conversation, and also the ceremonial center of the community. During *qasgiq* ceremonies honoring the dead, when women and children might be invited to take part, pieces of food were thrust through the floorboards—it was a responsibility to one's namesake, whose spirit was thought to rise up beneath the floor. Skins or grass mats kept children from dropping through to the underworld, as the veil between the two worlds during these ceremonies was unusually thin, and the children's souls were newly arrived from the other side.

Today Yup'ik people sometimes call the steambath a *qasgiq*, though Francis Charlie's fishcamp *qasgiq* was certainly a modest structure, built of scrap plywood and only four feet high. We crouched to undress under a shredded plastic tarp and then crawled through a door to the prickling heat.

Thirteen-year-old Richard was already inside. A glass pane behind the stove admitted soft light into the box and Richard pointed to the head of a nail in the wall, which would leave a bright tattoo if I leaned against it. He was paler than others in his family, freckle-faced and more high-strung. Fiendishly he splashed water on the hot rocks. Francis tucked a soft knitted-wool hat over his own ears like a shower cap and held out a hat to me. He murmured something in Yup'ik.

"He says your hair will get thirsty," Richard said.

When Richard had crawled out to cool off, Francis explained that he had been adopted, a nephew joined to the family in the Native fashion as one of their own. They were about to adopt another child, a baby from a relative in Sheldon's Point. Francis mentioned the baby with one of the first big happy smiles I'd seen from him.

Of all his children, Francis was especially close to Glenn, who had been sickly with pneumonia as a boy. At one point they'd considered sending Glenn to Bethel to be raised by relations, but now he was growing strong. On winter weekends, when he was off from school, Glenn liked to go out hunting and trapping with his father. One trip he had watched his father dust snow off blackfish traps; next time out he dusted them himself without having to be told.

"He likes work," Francis said.

By now we were both running with sweat. I shifted my legs and felt my blood pound. Francis's carefully measured words were coming just slowly enough for me to take them in. There was little serious male conversation during our twenty minutes in the steambath, and we undertook no sacred ceremonies, but the rite was having its effect: I began to feel less a visitor, more a grunting participant in a life that had gone on long before my world knew it existed. Francis ladled water on the rocks and blinked at the steam.

He said that Glenn's Yup'ik name, the name handed down when its possessor had passed on, was *Ayagina'ar*. It had been the name of Francis's own mother. Sometimes, Francis said, he called his son *Aanaq*, the Yup'ik slang for Mom.

Yup'ik elders sometimes refer to the past of the *qasgiqs* as "the time of wars." It was no Golden Age. The last of the great conflicts on the delta, remembered as the Bow and Arrow wars, had continued for generations. Villages from the lower Yukon fought villages farther south on the coast. Whole settlements were massacred, sometimes in sneak attacks when the *qasgiq* would be sealed shut and the men inside killed by arrows shot through the smoke hole above. Boys were slain, too, so they would never grow old enough to seek revenge.

Hostilities ended in the early nineteenth century when Russian fur traders created an economic incentive for peaceful travel and exchange between regions. At the same time smallpox arrived. The survivors dispersed, and the strict rules of marriage that once united villages in times of war or famine broke down.

Some ancient family associations have endured. People return to rivers and lakes where their ancestors fished before the populations were mixed up like berry *akutaq* in the mission villages. But the map of the Yukon-Kuskokwim region is overlaid with modern boundaries as well. At Black River, for instance, the land is now private—and it belongs to Native corporations not from Scammon Bay but from Yukon River villages. Despite its history of use, Scammon Bay had been too many miles distant to qualify for land around Black River.

The expectation of the claims act, that villages would be able to generate income from Native corporation land to help offset an eventual decline in subsistence skills and resources, seemed particularly fatuous as I looked out at the tundra around camp. There were no minerals or trees or tourists. Someday, maybe, the fishermen from Scammon Bay would be asked to pay rent to the Yukon River Eskimos, their enemies in the Bow and Arrow Wars.

Nor was the surrounding landscape any longer immemorial. Since 1980 the outlying tundra lay within the Yukon Delta National Wildlife Refuge. Even on this outermost coast, land use was subject to policing by the federal government; the harvest of fish and game was regulated by the state and policed by a division of the state troopers.

In the calm daze of camp life, however, it was easy to forget the clouded prospects of Yup'ik survival, even to forget the new trouble that had come to Black River the previous winter.

I was struck by the quiet along the river, by the absence of three-wheelers. People moved by boat. Fishermen had their gill nets spread on the grass, mending the damage from winter. Walking along the crumbling bank, I could hear a steady squawking and hooting of waterfowl out on the tundra and occasionally the tinny voice of an AM radio inside a tent.

The breeze off the Bering Sea was just enough to keep the mosquitoes inland. The year before, when the wind blew the other way, had been one of the worst anyone could remember for mosquitoes. Dogs staked along the river had to have their faces smeared with Crisco or motor oil to keep off the bugs, and still a few had swelled up from the bites and died. This wind from the west kept the mosquitoes off and it was good for fishing, too, because it blew the salmon in against the coast.

People were still picking up king salmon in subsistence nets. Kings were *qavlunaqing* in the river. The commercial fishermen grew edgy— they wanted to be working, because processors paid six times for kings what they paid for the chum salmon that came later. Everyone was afraid Fish and Game would let the kings get past, and then the Yukon River fishermen would get them all.

Commercial fishing had brought another overlay of complications to life at Black River, though such fishing itself was nothing new. After the 1867 transfer of Alaska to the United States, when fur traders, gold miners, and military personnel started traveling through the delta on dog teams, Yup'ik fishermen began catching and drying extra fish to sell for dogfood. A floating cannery arrived at the mouth of the Yukon in 1918, and when airplanes replaced dog teams for bush transport and the local dried-fish market closed, the demand from canneries had expanded to replace it.

The commercial catch on the Yukon delta had always been of "surplus" salmon, according to a study I'd seen by the state's Department of Fish and Game. Fishing for cash had never supplanted the subsistence effort. "The economic system is 'mixed' in the sense that food production for subsistence use is combined with commercial fishing, commercial trapping, and wage employment," said the study, which looked at lower Yukon villages and seemed to apply to Scammon Bay as well. "The local economy incorporates both subsistence and commercial activities, neither of which is sufficient to support the population alone. The economy is 'subsistence-based' because resource extraction for local use is the most reliable base of the economy from year to year."

For a hundred years delta fishermen have managed to adapt the work of hunter-gatherers to the modern need for cash, but here, too, the future is uncertain. Each year the fight for allocation of the commercial salmon catch has grown more intense. Fishermen from the lower Yukon villages complain that Black River boats are intercepting fish returning to the Yukon. They feel the salmon are rightfully theirs. The Black River was rumored to connect with the Yukon somewhere in the delta's watery maze, but nobody seemed sure where. State biologists say there really isn't much of a spawning run in the Black, but the fishery there has gone on too long for the state to cut it off.

Meanwhile the Indians who fish with current-borne wheels far up the Yukon complain about the Eskimo nets of the lower Yukon villages. The Canadians argue that because most of the salmon spawn in tributaries far up in the Yukon Territory, Alaskans should let more fish reach the border. At Black River fishermen are unhappy because the seine boats of False Pass intercept the runs at sea where they funnel through passages in the Aleutians. And everyone was angry about high-seas fishing by factory ships from Taiwan, Japan, and other nations, which catch millions of Alaska salmon under the guise of fishing for squid.

This year the fishermen from Scammon Bay had received an unhappy surprise when they reached their camps at Black River. Someone had come by during the winter and broken into the storage caches. The intruders had gone at the nets with knives, slashing cork lines off the gear. Nearly every net left in camp had been cut that way.

I heard a lot of talk about how the vandals must have come from the Yukon, though there wasn't great bitterness. People figured this was the act of a crazy person, not a resurgence of the Bow and Arrow wars. Nobody had bothered reporting the incident to the state troopers. What were the troopers going to do about it—patrol the tundra coast in the middle of winter? The only time the troopers cared about this place, one fisherman grumbled, was when they wanted to catch Eskimos breaking the fishing laws.

Francis Charlie worked alone at his end of camp, calmly threading his net back together. He had cousins on the Yukon and was reluctant to fix blame.

"Maybe it was mice," he said.

"They don't like that you've been taking mouse food," I said. Francis grinned.

State troopers were on Myron's mind that afternoon when he took Glenn and me in his skiff to the Amukon store. In a state-sanctioned rite of passage, Glenn had to buy his first official crewmember's license.

The store was one of the farthest sites upriver. We approached a plywood house surrounded by wooden-slat barrels, old outboard motors, stacks of nets, drift logs for firewood, fish racks set atop oil drums, a child's swing, and the hoses and tubs of the salting operation that helped launch the Black River fishery.

A fierce little woman in the yard wore a dirty flower-print *qaspeq* dress over pants and salt-crusted rubber boots. Angelina Amukon was angry because the Black River fishermen were no longer going to sell them kings, just because cannery tenders paid more money. "My husband gave them boats, gave them their nets," she said.

The Amukons still packed king salmon fillets in barrels of salt for specialty export to Japan, but now they counted on relatives to catch the kings. Other fishermen said the Amukons had been tough bargainers, hard people to get receipts from. They relied on the Amukons mostly for their little store. From a wall of shelves in the front room of their cabin the Amukons sold breakfast cereal, work gloves, rubber fishing boots.

Angelina sat at a table and was filling out a state license for Glenn when a floatplane roared low overhead, buzzed the camp, and landed on the river. It was the first plane I'd heard land at Black River all week. The population had grown steadily, strictly from boat traffic.

Angelina Amukon was loading the arms of a young customer with soda pop when two large white men stooped through the door and straightened up.

I sank into a shadowy corner. They came from my world, but I had been at Black River long enough to feel the strangeness of their presence.

The state Fish and Wildlife Protection officers were tall, big-shouldered men, suntanned and sandy-haired, wearing brown uniforms and hip boots and guns strapped to their sides. They towered over the Eskimos seated around the low table. Angelina shooed a boy away from a chair, and the bigger of the two wardens took a seat. Elderly John Amukon rose from a bed in the back room and shuffled out in his slippers.

The big warden got right to the point. There would be a commercial opening tomorrow, he said. Twelve hours, chum gear only. He'd appreciate it if they would pass the word.

He looked from John Amukon to Angelina. This was bad news for the saltry, bad news for the fishermen of Black River. The kings, being so much larger than chums, wouldn't be trapped by the smaller mesh of the chum gear. They'd swim on by and head up the Yukon.

"I don't know anything about a king opening," the warden said preemptorily.

Several boys along the wall gazed up at the belt buckle of the second warden, who stood with his arms folded, blocking out the light from the door.

"Maybe I put one king net in," Angelina said, peering over her glasses at the seated warden.

"Better not do that," he said.

"I only teasing you," she said. She broke into a big grin.

Everybody smiled, and then the game wardens started out the door.

"Thank you for coming," Angelina called after them.

That evening during supper Francis was back and forth to the CB radio, talking in Yup'ik with a cousin about where they should go for the next day's opening. Some fishermen planned to stay and fish off the mouth of Black River; others thought more salmon would have gathered farther north, nearer the mouth of the Yukon.

The AM radio was on as well, crackling with oldies drifting across Norton Sound from Nome. Then the local news: a distant report from Congress, something about offshore oil development in Norton Sound. I came to with the jolt of science-fiction travel and looked about at my gracious hosts tearing at strips of dried whitefish with their teeth, then went back to work on my own dryfish. I was getting to quite like the dense oily taste and stringy texture, though if I dipped the meat I carried the fumes of seal oil in my beard for hours after.

The door of the cabin stood open, the river outside, the tundra beyond. During the day Richard had pointed out three small figures, a mother and two children, holding hands as they walked far from camp. I'd imagined them to be engaged in some timeless gathering activity. Perhaps they were looking for eggs. The larger birds' nests were off limits now—part of a cooperative agreement with federal authorities to protect declining goose populations—but smaller eggs were still part of the fish camp diet.

"What are they looking for?" I asked Richard.

"Shoes."

Shoes?

"One of their dogs took some."

I realized that I had yet to leave camp on the riverbank and see the tundra myself, so after supper I pulled on my rubber boots. The golden evening hours were beginning. I picked a winding course along the edge of ponds and clear streams, doubling back off dead-end peninsulas. Black earth bubbled beneath my boots. It was a country without wood or stone. The grass was short and chaffy, still brown from winter, but fresh blushes of green followed the water courses, where small swimming birds skittered and splashed away from my advance.

A circus clatter of birdlife was all around. Five geese flew low to the ground in a V, making eyebrows for the coast and intent on getting there in the next few seconds. I was heading vaguely east, toward the mountains.

Far ahead two sandhill cranes danced noisily on stilt legs, lunging, broad wings outspread. I picked them as a destination.

After a while I stopped and looked back. With the river dropped out of sight, the camp looked like a prairie boomtown in a movie western: a line of wall tents out in the treeless open, with a few wood-frame buildings adding a tentative permanence. I counted thirty tents and half a dozen plywood shacks. Usually the Black River camp is seen from the water. This was an unusual perspective, perhaps known only to gatherers of eggs and shoes.

I spotted Glenn in the distance, following my trail. The family's golden dog chased in excited circles beside him. Myron had said if they decided to leave tonight they'd send Glenn for me.

I started back. By the time I drew near to their messenger, he was wading thigh-deep across a pond, exploring in the shallow muck and in no apparent hurry to catch up. Glenn was studying the sucking sensation produced by a pair of hip waders his mother brought from the store in Scammon Bay, a present for his first commercial fishing trip. A shrewd investment, since every night Glenn returned to camp wet and muddy to his knees.

"Dogs are better than people, you know why?" Glenn said as he splashed out of the pond and caught his breath. "Dogs find more little birds' eggs than we do."

He held out his hand. In his palm were three small eggs the size of macadamia nuts, outfitted in a camouflage pattern of green and brown.

"Did you see any nests?" Glenn asked. "Did you see any birds flying funny?"

I took the eggs and we started for the river. The eggs felt warm. Was it the warmth of his hand, or had they been warm like this in the grass where he found them? I felt I was walking home with something tugging at my fist—the heart of the tundra, a living thing. *Qavlunaq.*

"Watch for whales!" Glenn cried out as we left the mouth of Black River and turned north along the coast. "I hope we see a seal!"

I looked around the skiff. There were no guns. It was not the cry of a young Eskimo hunter whipping himself into a survivalist frenzy, but rather an eleven-year-old's cheer of delight at the abundance of life and home—the excitement of setting out to sea under a richly colored sky, across a little riffling chop, nets piled ready in the bow, skimming just above the water as lighthearted and fast as an Emperor goose.

Francis and Myron had decided, after several CB calls and an assessment of recent subsistence catches, to fish the opening at the southernmost of the Yukon's many channels to the sea. That meant a trip north of about an hour in two boats. We left at midnight, though the twelve-hour fishing period didn't begin for another six hours. No one had brought a sleeping bag except me. I was wondering how the Yup'ik fishermen of the Bering Sea spent the night when they went out to fish.

Along the black beach, piles of driftwood glowed in the creamy evening light. Myron stood in his life jacket with his hand on the outboard, scanning the water ahead for drift. The year before had been a big one for floating logs, after heavy spring floods on the Yukon. A bad year for fishermen, with drift logs tangling and ripping their nets. On the other hand, the people of this treeless country seldom lacked for firewood, thanks to the two-thousand-mile river.

The outboard sputtered, the boat lurched, and then we moved on smoothly again. Myron's 40-horse kicker was plenty strong for this work, but it was still new and untested. Engine trouble was a worrisome possibility on this wild coast, even with Francis and Richard following in a second skiff. Perhaps we had simply run over a sandbar. I looked back, but no cloud of mud was spreading in our wake.

"Fish," Myron said.

I knew he was kidding me, but then we lunged forward again.

"Another fish," he said.

The salmon ran so thick in the silty water that we were grinding them up. I could feel the prop slicing meat and bone into salmon puree.

The water got a little choppier. Myron said it was the river's current. We were still at sea as far as I could tell, but we had entered a channel of the Yukon, a path cut across the offshore shallows. At low tide, Myron said, you could scoop up water here that was almost fresh enough to drink.

After ten minutes a low sandy island to our left marked the mouth of a more visible channel. The two skiffs aimed for a promontory on the mainland where a fish rack and plywood tent frame stood at a ghostly fish camp. There was no beach to nose onto, just a six-foot wall of turf slipping into the water. Behind the old camp the coast guard had erected a billboard of green-and-white diamonds as a navigation aid for freight barges headed into the river.

Myron lashed together a tripod of driftwood poles from the fish racks, working by the last red glow of the setting sun, then pulled a dirty canvas tarp out of his skiff and flung it over the skeleton, anchoring the bottom of his improvised tipi with logs.

Dusk was rising, cotton-gray, out of the tundra. I might see darkness tonight, I thought—maybe even the moon. Would the moon be full? I'd lost track. You could go all summer in these wide northern spaces without seeing the moon. Sometimes you felt it was because you were on it.

Glenn heard swans calling from not too far away, and we walked inland to find them. I was excited and did not want to stop exploring, but Francis called out sternly to his son and Glenn headed back to rest.

It was somehow brighter underneath the white canvas, as if the dusk had been trapped inside. We spread our life vests and dry rain gear on the dirt and made ourselves comfortable, fitting our legs like puzzle pieces. Francis, wearing a small-beaked fishing cap that made him look like a Japanese army captain from a World War II movie, flinched as he shifted his injured knee and then smiled again. Myron made tea on the Coleman stove. I was struck again by how easily they shifted between the roles of commercial and subsistence fishermen as they brought out the usual dryfish, along with rolls smeared in Crisco—"Eskimo butter," Francis called it.

The tarp flapped in a wind off the sea. Inside the canvas, the light grew dim. Glenn and Richard sat talking until Francis looked over and spoke sharply in Yup'ik. I didn't know the words, but it was clear Francis wasn't speaking just then to his "Mom." Boots off, coats and wool hats on, they curled into a mat of men and boys.

The temperature was dropping, but I was too self-conscious to pull out my sleeping bag. Still stuffed in its sack, I set the bag where Francis and I could share it as a pillow. Then I went to work fussing with my sock feet, tucking them under the canvas and wrapping them neatly in a nest of oilskin rain gear. I squirmed around, trying to make myself as comfortable as possible. Francis finally looked over at me with a little smile.

"You are going to lay eggs?" he asked.

Glenn lay hidden under his coat, paying no attention as the others pulled on their rubber boots. His father poked him once more and finally he sat up, rubbing his eyes. He was surely wondering, as I was, where the thrill of this first fishing adventure had gone. "I'm never going to get up this early again," he muttered.

We had slept two and a half hours. The sun was already well up, and as Myron made coffee inside the tent, we heard skiffs roaring past on their way to the fishing grounds. The two men seemed wide awake, the boys dragged, and I—I wanted to be as alert as the men, attentive to every detail, but it was all I could do to pull myself along to the boat.

Half an hour later, precisely at six, Glenn was in rain gear and hip boots, hanging over the bow of Myron's aluminum skiff, trying to grab a bright-red buoy as it sloshed up and down. They had left the buoy anchored a quarter mile off from camp to get a quick start. Myron did not offer a lot of instruction; like Francis, he seemed to expect Glenn to learn by trying things and watching his example.

With the outboard idling, Myron stepped forward, grabbed the buoy, and tied on one end of the net. He sent Glenn back to the stern. "Reverse," he said. As the boat backed off, Myron fed the net over the side. The fish hit right away, splashing where they found themselves snared. The water beside the red buoy was soon boiling with life.

They tied off the other end of the net to a buoy and threw out a second anchor. The gill net hung in the water like a curtain. Judging by the froth along the cork line, it was directly across a salmon freeway at rush hour. Myron had guessed exactly right.

In half an hour they were already picking the gear. With the engine killed, Glenn and his uncle stood in the bow pulling the net over the side. The boat tossed in a sudden morning breeze. Six or seven chum salmon dropped into the boat on every pull, bright silver and bouncy.

I sat back sleepily in the stern and looked around at the brightening sea.

The two fishermen worked hard, licking from their lips the spray kicked up by new fish that hit as soon as the net went back over the side.

"This is what I call fishing," Myron yelled. "Had enough?"

"No," Glenn said with a pant.

"Hee-hee!"

A few skiffs roared by in a hurry, headed upriver in the direction of Alakanuk and Emmonak. Myron and Glenn had the broad entrance here to themselves.

Each tangled salmon was a puzzle to be solved as fast as their brains and fingers could work. Myron pulled out several fish for every one of Glenn's. Then the ratio reached four to one. Glenn was still sleepy, and after nearly an hour he paused to stare wistfully at the net passing back into the water. The boat was swaying . . .

"Pull the net!" Myron cried. They leaned over the side and scooped the net under a fifteen-pound king salmon. Its gills were barely snagged in the webbing.

"Put your gloves on," Myron said. "Your hands will get red."

"I told you. The net pulled one of my gloves into the water. You said okay."

"I did?"

Myron bent over and showed Glenn how to grab several strands of webbing and pinch a salmon's cheeks to pull it through.

"Dumb fish," Glenn mumbled at his feet.

I took a turn with the net while Glenn rested. The twine pressed sharply into the flesh of my palms. I was happy to be working. It took more than two hours to pick through seventy-five feet of net. When we had finished, bloody salmon filled the skiff above the knees of Glenn's waders.

Myron left the net where it would continue to fish and ran twenty minutes to a big gray fishing boat with a wheelhouse anchored by the island of sand. Two non-Native deckhands lowered a steel bin from a crane, and Myron and Glenn started tossing in fish.

The young white skipper of the tender stood to one side, counting fish with a clicker. Each salmon jerked the arrow on the scale another five pounds or so. "A couple years ago they gutted one fish and found a bunch of outboard parts inside it," the captain said, addressing me, perhaps thinking that I represented the Small Business Administration.

Myron flung a chum by the tail that slapped Glenn in the cheek and made him stagger.

"Did I hit you?"

"No."

Tires had been hung over the side of the gray boat as fenders, but the loaded skiff was so low and the empty tender so light that the tires dangled uselessly above Glenn's head. Only when the last bin had been loaded did the skiff begin bouncing off rubber instead of the boat's gray beam.

Myron climbed to the tender and removed the embossed plastic limited-entry card hanging from a string around his neck. The tender crew recorded his delivery, to be credited against the money he'd borrowed from the processor for the skiff. The morning's catch so far: 330 dogs and 14 kings, worth around $1,600. They gave Myron and me coffee and handed down a Styrofoam cup of fruit punch to Glenn. He leaned against the big boat, tossing up and down in the waves. The rough gray paint was warm in the sunshine. He was sleepy. The boat was swaying . . .

They returned to the net and started picking fish again. The boat filled more slowly this time; the tide was starting to turn, and the movement of fish up the channel had tapered off. After half an hour they pulled Glenn's missing red cotton glove over the side, still twisted in the webbing where he'd lost it. There were whitecaps on the waves now. Glenn was slowing down. He stopped to watch Myron work. Eight more hours . . .

Glenn closed his eyes and toppled backward, sinking peacefully into the slimy pile of salmon.

In early afternoon Myron ran the skiff back to the canvas tent and dropped off Glenn. About the same time Francis showed up with Richard. Francis and Myron decided to go out together to pick their nets one more time. Sheepishly I climbed out of the skiff and joined the boys. I felt guilty invoking my status as a guest, but was too tired to care. The boys and I lay down in the tent, out of the sun and wind, and plunged like anchors into sleep.

I had tea ready that evening when the two men returned from their final delivery. The twelve-hour period had closed, and Francis and Myron brought soda pop from the last tender for the boys. Their fishing instinct had been good: they had made some of the biggest deliveries of the day. Myron had just about finished paying off the loan for his boat; Glenn's crew share would go to his parents for school clothes. Richard was speaking groggily of the fishing as "yesterday." It was time to head home.

The aluminum boat banged emptily as we got in. The sides were smeared with gurry and drying fish scales, and as we roared off, the scales flew up around us—a triumphant launch in a shower of silver confetti. The rays of evening were again long and rich, and we skittered home through rainbows in the sea spray.

We were alone in the wide horizon, alone in the eye of the world. Surely the eye smiled on us—its weather was a benediction. It had always been the way with Yup'ik families that one became a part of the community not by reaching a certain age but by learning to contribute, by learning to be a provider. Today the route to manhood was no longer so clearly marked: fish camp life was about cannery loans and commercial openings as well as Eskimo food. But hard work and knowledge of the sea and learning to live right were all lessons that would help carry the world from this generation to the next. I found myself thinking that while change from afar might kill Yup'ik culture, some kind of metamorphosis like this might save it.

Salmon were jumping clear out of the water as the skiffs turned into the mouth of Black River near midnight.

Three of Glenn's young cousins ran to the riverbank to meet the returning fishermen. We unloaded gear. Francis stopped suddenly and watched, a dignified figure despite an oversize rain slicker, as his son climbed onto the bank and started proudly toward the family cabin. The boy walked stiffly, still tied up in his life jacket, as if not quite comfortable with his new role in the grown-up world of Black River.

His brothers and sister joined the cousins, besieging him with questions. "Did you catch anything?" "Did you fall in?"

Glenn told how he lost a red glove and it reappeared.

His mother was sewing on the bed at the rear of the cabin when he walked in.

"There he is!" She jumped up. "How's my baby?"

I slept soundly in my tent that night and woke refreshed from a dream about my cabin. At least it had seemed to be my cabin— friends had come from all over, and we were preparing a meal, though the layout of piney, rough-sawn rooms was unfamiliar, and the woods outside were not like the spruce where I'd built my cabin, but were filled with the trembling green light of a deciduous forest, more the shimmer of the eastern forests of my youth. I lay in my sleeping bag awhile, basking in that green light, wondering what had been going on in my life back home, a life I'd hardly thought about all this time. On the river I could hear thumping in boats. It was time to leave.

The family network that had looked out for me all week had scouted up a skiff headed back to Scammon Bay, but I'd slept too long and they didn't disturb me. The boat had already departed by the time I emerged.

So that evening I walked the length of camp to see Mike Akerelrea, the young Scammon Bay postmaster, about a ride down the coast.

Mike Akerelrea was a bush entrepreneur who sold candy and drink mixes at his fish camp cabin, and back in Scammon Bay, in addition to his post office duties, he was active in the village Native corporation. He believed the corporation should be strictly a money-making enterprise and had little patience with anyone who would take such a tool and try to preserve Yup'ik culture with it. Akerelrea had left the post office in the charge of his wife during fishing season. He'd done well in the chum opening, but now he was pacing the riverbank, fretting about whether there'd be a king opening and plotting a commute home to Scammon Bay to wait.

Mike's brother James, visiting for a week to help fish, waited patiently for a decision. He had taken a bigger step into the business world, moving away to Anchorage to work for Calista, the regional Native corporation. James admitted, with a broad, ingratiating smile, that while he sometimes got homesick in Anchorage he had been gone so long from Scammon Bay he felt a little out of place when he was back. He said he found himself picking up trash around the village.

While I stood on the riverbank with the Akerelrea brothers, an old man with scratchy whiskers floated by below, his skiff full of fat kings. Subsistence fish for his smoker. Mike looked down at the fish and ground his teeth.

The whiskered man gazed up as contentedly as if he were surrounded by grandchildren. He spoke to the brothers in Yup'ik.

Mike turned to his brother with a sudden sly smile. "Maybe we could go out that way, huh?"

The old man had seen whales spouting off the river's mouth. It took me a minute to penetrate the conversation's vagueness, which reminded me of the *endji* of Chief Titus back in Tetlin, who'd told me it was bad luck to boast about coming success on a hunt. James turned down the invitation from his brother, in any event—whether from a new urban fastidiousness or the memory of unhappy boating experiences with Mike I couldn't guess. I volunteered to go in his place. For all the time I'd spent among Native hunters in the bush, I had yet to go on a hunt.

"Can we borrow your harpoon?" Mike asked the old man. A handmade wooden shaft was handed up from the floorboards. At the tip was a sharp point of polished brass.

As we gathered equipment I barely had time to think that I might regret this. Killing a whale was not high on my list of lifetime goals. Whales had always seemed noble, graceful creatures, possibly intelligent, certainly mysterious—symbols of Nature owing as much in my personal mythology to Melville as to the tracts of Greenpeace. It was a blessing of Alaska to have them all around; the sight of their immense life rising out of the sea never failed to thrill me. But the whale had a further meaning in Alaska. There was no more widely acknowledged symbol of the enduring importance of aboriginal subsistence. When the Eskimo said he was going to "catch" a whale, he chose the verb not as a euphemism to mislead animal protectionists, but as a translation of the customary belief that an animal's spirit passes on after giving its body to man. Even with an endangered species as quarry, and even with hunters who spent part of the year working on oil rigs or listening to Walkmans, most conservation groups were willing to allow Eskimo hunting of the bowhead whale—regulated and observed by an international body—to continue.

These were not bowheads gathered off Black River, however. Compared to the elaborate preparations surrounding the pursuit of the bowhead farther north, this hunting trip seemed weirdly impulsive. Doubt snagged me, but the very casualness with which young Yup'ik men would launch a whale hunt, as if grabbing their sneakers for a late-evening game of basketball, was enough to restore my energy and curiosity.

We climbed in a big aluminum skiff with Mike's friend Sebastian. In addition to the harpoon they brought two rifles: a seal-hunting rifle and a lighter .22. We stopped at the Charlie camp on the way out the river and I ran up to the cabin to borrow a life jacket.

"First time I saw you, I never thought you would eat Eskimo food," Theresa Charlie had said after I'd been with her family almost a week. I'd surprised her—though I never quite got over being brave. Now she was thrilled to hear I was going hunting. She followed me out to the riverbank and said something in Yup'ik to Mike and Sebastian, who had waited in the boat. Then she smiled and waved as if I were one of her children.

"Bring us back some food to eat," she called as the current carried me away.

Mike Akerelrea was smiling as he steered out the river mouth. The sub-Arctic sky was full of gold an hour before midnight. He couldn't catch the salmon but he could catch the fish-eating whale that followed them to the Black River. All worry about regulations and commercial openings was left behind. He was an Eskimo again.

We raced across the wind-dappled water under the thrust of a 65-horse Evinrude. The boat was a hot rod. I sat in front of Mike on an aluminum thwart and in the bow stood Sebastian, a big grizzled marksman in his thirties, seal gun already in hand. Sebastian's cigarette was broken at the filter and fluttered in the wind. He turned and parted his lips and the cigarette flew away like an insect.

We were off in pursuit of a white whale.

I knew that belugas are small whales and that they travel in herds throughout the Arctic. Overhunted by commercial boats in the North Atlantic, belugas are still commonly seen in schools of one hundred or more in the Bering Sea. They are a traditional part of the Eskimo diet, providing meat as well as a thick fatty skin called *mangtak* rich in vitamin C and protein. The beluga whales follow salmon in summer along the coast, swarming in river mouths and sometimes even chasing fish to fresh water. They are blue-gray in their first few years, but as they grow to full size, as much as eighteen feet long and three thousand pounds, the skin of an adult turns chalky white.

Almost immediately Sebastian spied the spouts, no higher than splashes in a swimming pool, far out on the sparkling water. Both hunters let out a triumphant whoop, as if racing across an open field to a touchdown.

Another thing I had heard about belugas is that they are noisy creatures: sometimes their squeaks and clicks are audible even above water. Early mariners called them "sea canaries." We heard nothing, of course, but the scream of the outboard. Mike throttled down. There was no more sign of the whales. Sebastian looked around. He pointed. We sped back toward the river, stopped, idled.

Sebastian stood in the bow and drew a bead with the .22-.250. He saw something I didn't.

The white back of a beluga appeared with a steamy puff twenty feet off the bow and folded quickly back into the waves. Sebastian fired, hitting the water just in front of the target. The bullet seemed to skip on harmlessly across the surface. The whale disappeared. The hunters looked around.

"That it over there?"

"Yeah, maybe."

Mike threw the kicker into forward and swung the boat in a new direction. Sebastian drew another bead. This time nothing appeared.

"They keep sitting on the ground," Mike said. He continued circling.

Several gallons of gasoline later, Mike opened the throttle suddenly. Sebastian lifted the high-velocity seal gun and squeezed off several shots.

"Don't get too close," Sebastian yelled back in frustration. Mike smiled. Sebastian was usually such a cool dude; it was fun for Mike to see him rattled.

Sebastian thrust an oar over the side. This will scare the whale toward shallower water, he said.

He pulled back the oar and banged it on the metal bottom. As if in answer, the whale surfaced ten feet away. It was gone before Sebastian could grab the rifle.

We began to chase. Somehow they followed the whale's trajectory. I asked Mike what they watched for. He said there was a way of seeing where the submerged whale was swimming. When the water was shallow enough you could see its wake on the surface.

"Qavlunaq," I said. "Making eyebrows."

Mike's own eyebrows lifted with surprise, and he started laughing. "That's right," he said. "The whale is making eyebrows. Are you an Eskimo in disguise?"

Sebastian was watching ahead. "It's getting smart," he said with a smile. He pulled off his heavy coat, sweating.

The whale came up beside the boat, almost close enough to touch. A white leather sofa. Sebastian fired. The smell of gunpowder. Mike hollered something in Yup'ik. It looked like a hit.

Mike made a sharp turn and the whale came up even closer, but we were rocking on our own wake and Sebastian's next shot missed.

Another flash of white. This time a red spot the size of a coin was visible on the crest of the whale's back. Then it was gone.

We sat there, rocking, waiting, gazing out at the inscrutable sea.

They felt what any good hunter would feel, that it would be bad to wound the animal and not bring it home. We motored slowly, in widening circles.

For twenty minutes we circled, watching.

There were two other skiffs out on the water, far off. Occasionally the sound of a shot rolled past. I wondered what direction the other hunters were aiming.

Belugas aren't the only whales that come here, Mike said. Sometimes the tall black fins of killer whales appear off the coast. Killer whales are the main natural predator of belugas, able to swim three times as fast as their smaller prey. Eskimos never hunt killer whales, he said—they're taboo. His parents had told him a story about people who hunted killer whales. He didn't remember the story, except that it turned out the hunters weren't at the top of the food chain after all. "They get revenge," he said of the whales.

Approaching midnight, the sun low across the water, the water growing flat, there was still no sign of the missing whale. We came upon more splashing belugas. "Here we go again," Sebastian said, lifting the rifle.

Mike managed to cut one out of the pod. He made sure to stay between the whale and deep water, trying to run it toward shore. He kept the sun to our backs.

Sebastian held his aim on the water ahead, telling Mike to go left, go right, slow down.

As we sprinted alongside, the beluga rose every thirty seconds or so. The *yua* of this whale was not prepared to give itself up easily to its Eskimo pursuers. Mike was often the first to see the whale: "Right there! Go on! What you doing?" Sebastian kept shooting until he ran out of shells. He picked up his .22.

"No more heavy artillery," he said.

Mike yelled to Sebastian, "Hey, man, that's a gray. A small one."

Their reaction at learning they had managed to separate a juvenile from its mother was not one of remorse. A tender baby beluga would be easier to butcher and a more reasonable haul of meat for camp.

I found it hard not to feel sympathy for the whale as it tried to find a way to safety. With its darting intelligence, the beluga was beginning to seem more like a forest animal, less like a fish. I confess, however, that I stood to improve my view, holding on as we bounced forward. I shouted if I saw the beast surface at an unexpected tangent. There was a wild headlong excitement to the pursuit. At any moment the terrorized whale might vanish into a plane where we could not pursue, but it had lungs like our own that would bring it back.

After each shot with the .22, a shell casing plinked into the boat.

There was a sudden swimmer's gasp in the water beside us. We looked down and saw blood on gray leather. Sebastian grabbed the harpoon.

A coil of clothesline tied the brass harpoon point to a wooden shaft whittled to fit a palm. A collar of orange Styrofoam would keep the shaft afloat.

Sebastian balanced, pointed at the wake, and heaved. The harpoon struck the water eight feet off the bow. There must have been a moment when the whale hesitated. "Try to get in close," Sebastian yelled. He leaned over and grabbed the shaft and pulled it free. The point stayed buried, and as the whale fled the unfurling line made the orange float spin.

"Now we can shoot it," Sebastian said calmly.

The bay was too shallow for the young whale to dive. Wherever it went, the orange float followed in humiliating fashion. We probably wouldn't lose this one.

The whale made a run for deep water. Mike tried to keep pace, staying just ahead of the float to drive it back to the shallows. If they could get it into a few feet of water, they'd have an easy shot. The orange float stopped dead in the water, then moved back in the opposite direction, cutting behind the boat, the line running straight at the outboard shaft. Mike yanked up the heavy motor and the prop squealed in the air, spraying water. The float thumped beneath the boat.

The whale seemed to be trying to figure a way out of its predicament. Mike sped beyond it, and the float zagged again. Sebastian had a shot as the whale surfaced behind the boat, but he didn't even raise the rifle since it would have meant shooting between Mike and me.

"He'll get tired," Sebastian said.

Our skiff was the last one on the water. The rich yellow light was gone. Several miles offshore, we danced back and forth with our unseen partner. Three times the float cut back behind the boat toward the deep. Finally the float hesitated and turned back toward land. Sebastian took another shot.

"Hit the blowhole, man," Mike said.

The whale was not going so fast now.

Sebastian was down to his last two .22 bullets. He made a big loop with the anchor line, scooped the float off the water, and tied off the harpoon line to the bow of the boat. Mike killed the outboard.

Suddenly the speedboat evening turned very quiet.

The whale turned to the deep one last time. Silently our boat pivoted on the water and began to move toward the horizon. I had always dreamed of catching a fish so big it would pull me out to sea. I did not want the moment to end. The only sound was the boat tapping through the ripples. The tug of life was steady. Sebastian stood with the rifle sighted, watching for a little boil in the water.

The whale arched just ahead of the boat and gasped. Instead of blowing water, this time it issued a geyser of blood.

Sebastian fired.

The line went slack. We were drifting.

We pulled on the line until the whale was beside the boat. The beluga had a small head, somewhat like a porpoise, set off by a crease at the back of its neck. Its big brow nodded very slowly. The tail moved just as slowly, back and forth, barely treading water. Mike held the line tight. Sebastian pointed the .22 with one hand, execution-style at the blowhole in back of the head, and pulled the trigger.

They used a gaff hook to turn its bulk in the water. No one spoke. They tied the stiff, rubbery tail fluke to an anchor line strong enough for towing. The whale floated in the ashen water, and Sebastian started the engine. We moved slowly into the mouth of the Black River, the outboard churning powerfully, throwing up a rooster tail of water higher than Sebastian's head.

"It's what we have to do," Mike said softly.

I told him I didn't like the part where the whale spouted blood.

"That kind of got to me too," he said with a grimace.

I looked away toward the dark tundra and felt grateful to Mike for saying what he did. I felt in that moment I could understand perfectly how he could go out to hunt again.

The rooster tail must have been a proud sight as we paraded past the wall tents in the twilight. A reassuring sight, after the ruthless hunt. The Yup'ik people were still there, still trying to live the right way, trying—not always with success—to be worthy of the place where they lived. And the whale had sent itself back.

By the time we reached a grassy bank near the far end of camp, a dozen men had gathered. The other boats on the bay that evening had come home empty. Everyone took hold of the tow rope, and together we pulled the slender whale from the water. The body of the young beluga lay in the grass, eight feet long. The hunters were congratulated.

Mike asked his brother Thomas to take charge of butchering. With a heavy knife Thomas slit the gray hide, cut out a handhold, and peeled off a strip of *mangtak* three inches thick: gray skin, white fat. Others joined in the fading light, ripping back strips of fat from the steaming black meat.

Lungs, heart, kidney, and liver were set aside on cardboard. Mike and Sebastian took first pick. A teenage boy held up a hot loop of intestines, wondering what to do with it.

"Assirtuq," someone said. It's good.

The butchering was over quickly. Eskimo food was shared all around. Men took their meat and *mangtak* and called out thanks as they got in skiffs to return to their tents. Thomas Akerelrea made up a special selection for me to take to Francis and Theresa: ribs, lungs, blubber. Mike Akerelrea clapped me on the shoulder. I picked up the box of meat and when I looked back I saw nothing on the grass but a bloody sheet of cardboard.

Sebastian poled the last of us across a black slough. I squatted on the far shore to wash the slime off my hands. The water felt warm. When I stood up, I was alone.

I started back the length of the camp along the cool riverbank, following the footpath toward the sea. Bands of color to the north poured down in trails through the dark and filled the river with the deep red of a blood orange. The whale on my shoulder was heavy. I was deeply tired. The chill in the air felt heavy, too, and old, like the subterranean air of a root cellar.

I stopped to rest, balancing the cardboard box on someone's fish-cleaning table. There was a quick snore from inside a tent, and the hiss of surging water. Low fog covered the tundra, out where Glenn found the eggs—good weather tomorrow, the meat cutters had said when they noticed. Rising above the fog were driftwood racks of fish, ink silhouettes against the trace of a new day.

Qavlunaq.

I set the box inside the sleeping Charlie cabin, where dogs would not get into it, and walked on to my tent. The next morning, as I was packing to leave, Theresa came by. She told me how she woke and found the whale beside the door.

"I was so proud of you," she said.

Acknowledgments

The travels in this book were undertaken originally for a series of stories that appeared in the *Anchorage Daily News* under the title "Northcountry Journal." When I first set off to write about the bush, my editors at the newspaper told me if I came across a good news story to turn and walk in the other direction. For such shrewd encouragement and confidence I am indebted to Howard Weaver and Pat Dougherty. I am grateful too that they allowed me to revisit those first and second drafts that ran on a three-day-a-week deadline, some of them scribbled in a tent on legal pads or dispatched over satellite phones from a battery-powered laptop computer, and to retell the stories of those two years here, in the context of my own unfinished journey.

The people I met in the bush, Native and non-Native, were generous with their time and hospitality. Such generosity was more than helpful—it became one of the subjects of my book. In addition to those whose assistance and forebearance is described in these chapters, I would like especially to thank the following people, who at different points and in different fashions helped to send me on my way: Anna Phillip, Rick Caulfield, Jim Magdanz, Jerry Liboff, Elsie Mather, Gene Peltola, Nancy Lord, Eric Smith, Mary Kancewick, Michael Penn, Joe Senungetuk, Chip Brown, Steve Williams, and Nancy Gordon. Many colleagues at the *Anchorage Daily News* also helped me to think about what I was doing, and I am indebted to them as well.

My agent, Alice Martell, and my book editor, Bill Strachan, sustained me with their belief in this project. Sally Kabisch offered support, read drafts, and married me as I wrote these chapters, for all of which I thank her.

Of the many books and publications that contributed to my understanding of the places I visited, I should mention in particular the following:

Regarding the general situation of Alaska Natives: "People in Peril," a 1987 series published in the *Anchorage Daily News*; numerous studies and papers of the Subsistence Division of the Alaska Department of Fish and Game; *Alaska Natives and American Laws*, by David S. Case (Fairbanks: 1984); *Village Journey*, by Thomas R. Berger (New York: 1985).

For the Seward Peninsula: *The Alaskan Eskimos as described in the posthumous notes of Knud Rasmussen*, edited by H. Ostermann (Copenhagen: 1952); *Among the Eskimos of Wales, Alaska*, by Harrison Thornton (Baltimore: 1931); the unpublished letters of Ellen Lopp (Alaska Collection at the University of Alaska Anchorage); *Whales, Ice, & Men*, by John R. Bockstoce (Seattle: 1986); *The Eskimo about Bering Strait*, by E. W. Nelson (Washington, D.C.: 1983); numerous books and articles by Dorothy Jean Ray, including *Artists of the Tundra and the Sea* (Seattle: 1961); *People of Kauwerak*, by William A. Oquilluk (Anchorage: 1981).

For Athabaskan people and the Interior: *Report of an Expedition to the Copper, Tanana and Koyukuk Rivers*, by Henry T. Allen (Washington, D.C.: 1887); *Exploration of Alaska 1865–1900*, by Morgan Sherwood (New Haven: 1965); *People of Tetlin, Why Are You Singing?* by Marie-Françoise Guedon (Ottawa: 1974).

For the Yup'ik country: the reports on the Central Yup'ik in *Inuit Studies*, edited by Ernest S. Burch, Jr. (Quebec: 1984), particularly those by Lydia Black, Ann Fienup-Riordan, Phyllis Morrow, and Robert J. Wolfe; *Doors of Perception*, by John Baggley (New York: 1988); *Bethel, The First 100 Years*, by Mary Lenz and James H. Barker (Bethel, Alaska: 1985); various works by Fienup-Riordan, James VanStone, and Wendell H. Oswalt. A book by Wendell H. Oswalt published as this book went to press, *Bashful No More* (Norman, Okla: 1990), summarizes decades of work along the Kuskokwim River and contains a wealth of ethnographic and historical material about changes in the region.